Praise for

Career Bliss

"It's not only people in offbeat jobs who are enamored of their work, [Joanne Gordon] has found. People who are skilled and are challenged by what they do, who are proud of the product of their work and who like—or at least respect—the people they work with, are most likely to love their jobs."   —*The New York Times*

"Don't remain trapped in the awful cycle of hating your job. Joanne Gordon's sound advice and the inspiring stories make *Career Bliss* an important book for any woman who wants to do good—for herself, her family, and her employer."

—TORY JOHNSON, CEO, Women for Hire and co-author of
Women for Hire: The Ultimate Guide to Getting a Job

"A recent Catalyst report found that women are just as ambitious as men, and this book is a wonderful illustration of that fact. These 100 women have more in common than just career happiness—each has worked hard to achieve success on her own terms."

—ILENE H. LANG, president, Catalyst

"What is significant—and absolutely inspiring—are the enthusiastic voices and the seven lessons to be learned from them, from knowing what you want to exuding confidence. Eminently personal and approachable."   —American Library Association

"Joanne Gordon, the author of *Career Bliss,* insists that women can craft their own happiness at work. Through the stories and voices of 100 women, the message is clear: Take an honest look at your life and then take care of yourself. After all, you make the choices."

—*Kansas City Star*

Career Bliss

Career Bliss

Secrets from 100 Women
Who Love Their Work

Joanne Gordon

Originally published as *Be Happy at Work*

Ballantine Books   New York

2006 Ballantine Books Trade Paperback Edition

Copyright © 2005 by Joanne Gordon

Published in the United States by Ballantine Books, an imprint of The Random
House Publishing Group, a division of Random House, Inc., New York.

BALLANTINE and colophon are registered trademarks of Random House, Inc.

Originally published in hardcover in the United States as *Be Happy at Work*
by Ballantine Books, an imprint of The Random House Publishing Group,
a division of Random House, Inc., in 2005.

Grateful acknowledgment is made to the Hal Leonard Corporation for permission to reprint an
excerpt from "Our Deliverance," words and music by Emily Saliers, copyright © 2002 EMI
Virgin Songs, Inc. and Godhap Music, and an excerpt from "Hammer and a Nail," words and
music by Emily Saliers, copyright © 1990 EMI Virgin Songs, Inc. and Godhap Music. All rights
controlled and administered by EMI Virgin Songs, Inc. All rights reserved. International
copyright secured. Used by permission.

Library of Congress Cataloging-in-Publication Data
Gordon, Joanne.
    Career bliss: secrets from 100 women who love their work / Joanne Gordon.—1st ed.
        p.   cm.
    ISBN 0-345-46856-2
    1. Women employees—Job satisfaction.   2. Women employees—Interviews.   I. Title.
    HD6053.G63 2005
    650.1'082—dc22

                                                                    2004057387

Printed in the United States of America

www.ballantinebooks.com

9 8 7 6 5 4 3 2 1

Text design by Laurie Jewell

For Dorothy, Virginia, Susan, Alex,

David, Matthew, and Theo

Foreword

S tories are powerful motivators. They engage, educate, and can empower us to move our lives in more fulfilling directions.

In my twenty-one years working in program development and guest bookings at CNN, I realized the most touching news stories were not about celebrities, government leaders, or CEOs, but about everyday people to whom viewers could relate. A space shuttle landing or a presidential speech may have led newscasts, but features about rescue dogs or interviews with airplane crash survivors always received the most positive response. After all, while most people will never become astronauts or high-ranking public officials, almost everyone has pets and travels on planes. We relate best to ordinary beings leading their lives in extraordinary ways.

That's why personal stories are so powerful when it comes to career advice. I always try to fill my books and speeches with anecdotes from my own life and from women I have met over the years, and I was thrilled to see *Career Bliss* tackle with a journalistic eye the topic of women and work, letting women's own tales of career success unfold with color and honesty.

In this compelling book, Joanne Gordon artfully captures 100 women's distinct voices and inspiring stories. The single mother of three who after her husband's murder must support her family gives us hope in the face of our own life tragedies. The Wisconsin wife too scared to apply for a job as a flight attendant until she is in her forties gives us the courage to pursue our own dream job sooner rather than later. The entrepreneur who climbs her way out of bankruptcy shows us how to make a fresh start, and a hospital administrator suffering from cancer reminds us how resilient women can be. In the pages of *Career Bliss,* divorcees reinvent their lives, twentysomethings break away to big cities and make names for themselves, and grandmothers discover the rewards of work.

Through these stories and Joanne's astute observations, *Career Bliss* delivers on its promise to help women find work they will love. That's important, because happiness and success go hand in hand. Loving work is empowering. It makes us feel good about our potential, and the happier we are in the present, the harder we try, the more we want to achieve, and the farther we are likely to go in the future. At its heart, *Career Bliss* is a book for women, by women. And when we are happy, we win in the workplace.

GAIL EVANS
Author, *She Wins, You Win* and
Play Like a Man, Win Like a Woman

Contents

Preface

I haven't met that many happy people in my life.
How do they act?

—The Big Chill (1983)

Pain is easy to write. In pain we're all drably individual.
But what can one write about happiness?

—The End of the Affair (1999)

What better way to find happiness than to see it in action and watch it unfold. Want to get rich? Read about Warren Buffett, the second-wealthiest man in the world. Want to be a great cook? Watch chefs prepare meals from scratch on the Food Network. Want to learn how to love your job? Meet The Happy 100, women who already do.

The Happy 100 are real women, not career experts, whose stories are about life itself, with all its inherent twists and tears. They are single and married; some are mothers, others are childless. They are black, white, Asian, and Latina and range in age from twenty-one years old to eighty-two. They hail from twenty-five states; some work for themselves, others for large corporations. Their salaries vary from $25,000 to more than $1 million a year. Some never went to college, and others hold Ph.D.s. For many, it's often impossible to discuss present happiness without tapping past sadness. Death and divorce. Depression and disease. Discrimination and debt. Out of Enron's corruption, a secretary finds her calling. Recovering from breast cancer, a mother discovers new life as a librarian. A judge recalls growing up in poverty, while a once-bankrupt entrepreneur starts all over again.

Even The Happy 100 women whose roads are not unusually dramatic have lessons for anyone trying to untangle herself from an undesirable work situation. Some of the women left stifling positions for more empowering ones. Others broke into unfamiliar industries with no connections. Still others forged new careers after being fired or let go. They pursued untraditional channels when friends and family said they were nuts. They networked, saved money, and went back to school. They turned naysayers into fans and dead ends into choices. Again and again, The Happy 100 saw opportunity where others saw zilch, and they took chances despite feeling scared to death.

Although all are fulfilled and satisfied by their work, The Happy 100 are not some perky lot hardwired for happiness. These women have their difficulties, and are not cheerful or even content every minute of every day. They are serious and sincere, and more often than not their on-the-job joy has been hard won. So rather than sneer with jealousy, you're likely to cheer them on like newfound friends. I did after hearing their tales.

As the author of *Career Bliss,* my role is analytic observer rather than participant. Still, I'm admittedly passionate about the topic, as seeds of this book have been with me a long time. For years I wondered—both as a worker looking inward at myself and as a journalist looking outward at others—why so many people labor at jobs that support them fiscally but not emotionally. Given that we spend more than half our lives on the job, it's tragic that about one-third of employees in North America feel intensely negative about their work.

The first time I thought about happiness as it relates to work was at the impressionable age of thirteen, when I naively picked up a copy of Studs Terkel's book *Working* (Pantheon Books, 1972). I spent hours reading its profiles of exhausted waitresses, uninspired lawyers, beaten-down stockbrokers, and disheartened executives. *Working* captured my imagination because, at its core, it was heartbreaking. Terkel's workers were trapped and lost in dull routines. They were, as he aptly wrote, experiencing "a Monday through Friday sort of dying." Work was not something to enjoy; it was something to tolerate.

Terkel's world was not that far from my own in suburban Chicago. Each morning, neighborhood fathers donned beige raincoats and stoic expressions and, briefcases in hand, trekked silently to the train, which transported them downtown. I was fascinated with this daily march of men (at the time, most women were stay-at-home mothers) who promptly returned at dusk to rejoin their families. I was troubled by what I perceived as the routine of it all: the predictable schedules, the neutral suit-and-tie ensembles, and the mandatory five-day-a-week office appearances. Where was the fun? Did it exist? My own father, a career marketing executive, shared few details with his two daughters about his daily life, although the details we did glean about his various jobs always made us proud. At the dinner table each evening, Dad preferred to hear about our lives, and I always thought he would have made a terrific counselor or professor. I suspect he thought so as well, but changing careers with a family to support was not an option.

When I was in college deciding between a career as a writer and a more practical route in marketing, my father and I had some tense discussions about whether loving one's work was a luxury or a necessity. As for my mother, she became a psychotherapist when I was in elementary school, and the job fit her inquisitive, listening nature like a glove. It still does. But that is not the case for most people. Why, I worried, and what can anyone do about it?

I pondered the issue during six years working in marketing communications, and later, after attending graduate school for journalism, as a reporter and writer at *Forbes* magazine, where I spent five years. One year in particular the topic was on my mind. I was part of a team researching the country's wealthiest individuals for the annual Forbes 400, that iconic list of rich Americans. In speaking with dozens of real estate moguls and entrepreneurs, and the occasional insurance industry billionaire, the question I really wanted to ask was not how much money they were worth, but whether they were happy. That is what I truly cared about and, I imagined, what some readers also wanted to know. After all, is not happiness supposed to be the point of such wealth? It was simply assumed that being worth $625 million—the minimum "value" a person needed to make it onto the list that year—would make one ecstatic. But did it, really?

In researching this book, I spent more than a year identifying women— a population whose working lives are usually discussed only in the context of work/family balance and gender discrimination—who could honestly say they loved their work. Once I found them, I asked why. The discussions that followed were poignant and intimate. The lessons, invaluable.

The ultimate goal of *Career Bliss* is to help other women craft happy working lives by profiling those who already have.

Help comes in the form of practical advice and heartfelt inspiration. Some of the jobs described in *Career Bliss* are undeniably unique—few of us will ever be a circus performer or a national broadcast journalist—but on the whole, the jobs The Happy 100 hold are attainable, not outlandish, options. Some are occupations you may not realize exist—herb buyer for a tea company, hospital clown, sound engineer—while others you may think you know about are, in reality, nothing like you imagined. Even if a particular job does not interest you, the tactics the woman used to attain it, and the happiness it brings her, may. To that end, I tried to not gloss over the nuances of career paths in each woman's profile, but to show the steps—whether serendipitous or calculated, mistake or lucky break—that led her to where she is today, so you can see and learn from her journey.

Most important, the reasons why women love their work can help you rethink your own career, your own job, and your own definition of success. My conclusions are not meant to be scientific, hard-and-fast prescriptions for happiness. Still, several key themes came up, and by focusing on them, *Career Bliss* is designed to give you a new vocabulary and fresh angles from which to consider your own relationship with work. In conversations with happy working women, I looked beyond the conventional answers—flexibility, variety, ongoing learning—and found deeper motives for why each woman was so satisfied and fulfilled.

One of the most important messages of The Happy 100 struck home for me three weeks before this book was due to my publisher: I had a miscarriage two months into my first pregnancy. Despite my grief and healing body, I still had much editing to do to meet my deadline, and it was during this time that my thoughts wandered to many of The Happy 100 women who have suffered personal tragedy. At least sixteen have had a major disease, such as cancer. Sixty have experienced periods of depression and low self-esteem, while almost seventy have been sexually or racially harassed or discriminated against in the workplace. What's more, some dozen Happy 100 women have been through divorce, while others have forever lost loved ones.

To realize that misfortune can coexist with, or precede, a happy state of mind inspired me on a level I had not yet fully experienced, and in the weeks following my miscarriage I looked to my work as an emotional and intellectual salvation. I dove into my job, more appreciative than ever that I already loved it.

Perhaps as you read this you are on a bus or train commuting to a tiresome office environment. Maybe you are on a business trip dealing with clients or colleagues you don't respect, or at home in bed trying to unwind after an exhausting, purposeless day at work. Or, you are standing in a bookstore, debating whether *Career Bliss* is the right resource to help you jump-start a new working life. Whoever you are, wherever you are, I urge you to open your heart and mind to the women in the following pages. Their stories are extraordinary and ordinary, hopeful and helpful. They prove that loving work is not a luxury reserved for the healthy or the wealthy, the brilliant or the beautiful, the married or the well connected.

Loving what you do is an option available to all of us, and a choice you can make, starting right now.

Joanne Gordon
New York City
September 2004

Career Bliss

Introduction

As a path to happiness, work is not highly prized by men.
They do not strive after it as they do after other possibilities
of satisfaction. The great majority of people only work under
the stress of necessity, and this natural human aversion to
work raises most difficult social problems.

—Sigmund Freud, *Civilization and Its Discontents**

To love what you do and feel that it matters—
how could anything be more fun?

—Katharine Graham

There are no happy jobs. There are only happy workers. And at first blush, women who love their work could not be more dissimilar from one another:

A massage therapist and a chief executive
A singer and a scientist
A mechanic and a sales manager
A park ranger and a banker
A chef at the South Pole, a nude model on the ocean,
    a synchronized swimmer in the desert

But look close and you'll notice common themes. It is the argument of this book that these themes can help women everywhere craft their own happiness at work.

*W. W. Norton & Company, 1961, p. 27.

First and foremost, a happy working woman takes great pleasure from the day-to-day activities her job requires, whether that means selling, managing, writing, designing, driving a truck, building a team, analyzing data, or running a company. In other words, she is skilled at and challenged by the *processes* her work entails.

Second, a happy working woman invariably feels good about the reasons why she performs her labor. The reasons need not be altruistic, just in synch with her values. Whether a woman is fund-raising for cancer research, investing money on Wall Street, writing press releases to promote products, entertaining, training animals, or manufacturing screwdrivers, she believes her labors lead to a worthwhile outcome—that is to say, she takes pride in her job's *purpose*.

Third, a happy working woman likes and, at the very least, respects the individuals she works with. In addition to colleagues and supervisors who show her respect, her company's management style and corporate culture foster her talents and further her education. It means her colleagues are mentors, can make her laugh, and offer her support and flexibility when she needs it. It means she feels appreciated by and identifies with customers and coworkers. In short, a woman who loves her work admires the *people* with and for whom she works.

Process. Purpose. People. These three surprisingly simple concepts can mean all the difference between loving and disliking your job.

The "three Ps," as I refer to them, comprise a simple framework for evaluating a woman's relationship to her work. Not happy with your job? Unpack how you feel about each of these issues and you'll quickly understand what's missing in your career. Love what you do? Then you probably have satisfied each of the three Ps. I spent the last year and a half searching for and interviewing self-described happy working women so that their struggles and stories might help other women understand their own relationship to work and inspire them to seek out happier working lives. One hundred of these women—The Happy 100—are the basis for *Career Bliss*.

Happiness Does Not Just Happen: Making the Most of The Happy 100

You do not have to like each member of The Happy 100 to learn from her experience, nor must you recognize yourself in every story—or even want the particular job a woman holds—to learn from her. By simply approaching the profiles with an open mind, you're bound to benefit. Whether you read the chapters in sequence or jump to specific women, the profiles are designed to help you achieve one or more of the following goals:

Redefine your definition of career success and happiness. Today's workforce tends to measure job-related satisfaction against stereotypical notions of success, such as fame and fortune, and thus many people pursue the wrong goals. By contrast, most women in The Happy 100 love their jobs for reasons that have nothing to do with conventional notions of accomplishment, but for reasons within almost anyone's reach.

Learn about jobs you never knew existed but that match your skills and values. Most Happy 100 profiles show not only why a woman loves her job, but what that job entails in concrete terms, to give you a better understanding of its daily activities and required skills. In the end, you may discover new jobs in unexpected industries that fit your values and abilities.

Reenergize your job search with creative, practical tactics. Most Happy 100 profiles show, in detail, how each woman got the job she has today by tracking her career path and highlighting the tactics that landed her various positions along the way. Think of each of these stories as the anatomy of a career, meant to demystify the job search process. Happiness does not just happen. You'll see where each woman began her career and how her experiences, insight, unexpected opportunities, and planning led to her current profession and state of mind, and they may, in turn, help you untangle yourself from an unhappy work situation.

Unfulfilled? Dissatisfied? You're Not Alone.

The turn of the twenty-first century is an ideal time to consider the meaning of happiness at work. Not only does the job marketplace continue to shift, but American workers are not nearly as fulfilled as they should or could be. All the signs point to a workforce that feels overwhelmed, bored, unchallenged, and underappreciated. Consider that one-third of employees feel "intensely negative" about their work, according to a 2003 study by human resources consulting firm Towers Perrin, and only 17 percent felt "highly engaged" when it came to their jobs. The majority, 64 percent, described themselves as only "moderately engaged."

Other studies confirm these findings: A Gallup Poll conducted in August 2003 found that 41 percent of adults were only "somewhat satisfied" with their jobs. And in September 2003, The Conference Board, a not-for-profit business research organization, reported that Americans continue to grow unhappier with their work. Indeed, less than half said they felt satisfied. Finally, in an informal poll on Forbes.com, which accompanied an article I wrote in January 2003, 60 percent of more than 6,000 respondents said they were not happy at work.

The cynics cry, "Who cares? That's why they call it work!" and simply lament their own lot or roll their eyes at dejected colleagues instead of trying to improve circumstances. It's tragic, really, considering the average American spends 1,976 hours a year on the job—about one-third of her waking hours. An unhappy working life does not have to be everyone's fate.

Why Women? The Opt-In Generation

Although both male and female workers are disenchanted, *Career Bliss* focuses on women because their work experiences are, innately and historically, distinctive from men's. And, quite honestly, working women deserve some positive attention after years of discrimination, unfair treatment, and exclusion from the workforce. Given the unique challenges women face, it's understandable why the national dialogue about working women focuses on negatives such as gender inequality, lack of work/family balance, and the dueling roles of motherhood and career. More recently the public debate has addressed why women leave the workforce rather than why they stay in it.

By contrast, *Career Bliss* looks at what women have rather than what they lack, giving America's 61 million working women an opportunity to discuss, debate, and celebrate the goodness of work itself: the duties women perform, the decisions they make, the problems they solve, the organizations they build, the money they earn, the knowledge they share, the products they create, the people they help, and the sensitivity they bring to the workplace. *Career Bliss* strives to get women rethinking the wonders of labor, not just the difficulties. And at its highest level, it attempts to elevate the notion of loving one's work from pure luxury to absolute necessity. Women deserve to feel good about *how* they earn a living—not just that they *can* earn a living. Expecting to garner joy—not merely wages—from her job should become as entrenched in a woman's psyche as expecting fair pay, health care benefits, or a family-friendly schedule.

That is not to say that inequality and lack of work/life balance have disappeared from the working woman's experience. Far from it. Both remain hurdles for women at all economic levels. For starters, there is still a very real salary gap in this country: Women make about seventy-seven cents for every male-earned dollar, according to the U.S. Census Bureau. As for leveling the so-called playing field, women are still underrepresented in the upper echelons of business. In 2003, only 13.6 percent of board-of-director seats at the country's 500 largest publicly held companies were held by women, according to research firm Catalyst, and only 8 public companies were run by women, less than 2 percent.

What's more, too many women still suffer discrimination. In fiscal 2003, female workers filed 11,572 cases of sexual harassment with the Equal Employment Opportunity Commission and state and local agencies; another 24,362 cases of sexual discrimination were also filed, the majority by women. And a *USA Today* poll found that 36 percent of women believed their ideas would get more attention if they were male.

These are serious problems that must be solved, and many books are dedicated to just that. *Career Bliss* takes the next step by asking women to reflect on the nature of work itself, in an intellectual and emotional sense, not just as a scheduling problem or an income concern. While the latter two issues are important factors in *liking* one's work, in and of themselves they do not cause one to *love* it.

So although I researched and wrote *Career Bliss* with the knowledge that balance and inequality are still very painful problems working women face, the book does not dwell on them unless central to a particular woman's story. Perhaps surprisingly, many Happy 100 women do not have sky-high salaries or ideal work/life balance and still struggle to achieve them. In short, happy work is not perfect work. A job can have deficits and still satisfy, gratify, and engage.

So what makes work *work* for The Happy 100?

Happiness, Defined

Whenever I told men I was profiling 100 women who loved their jobs, they invariably had two distinct reactions. First, they could not believe I found 100 women who loved what they did for a living. Second, men always asked, in a skeptical, challenging tone, just how I planned to quantify happiness, and how I knew that women who claimed to love their jobs weren't lying. (Curiously, women never raised these concerns.) I won't hypothesize about what the men's rejoinder implies about gender differences, but I will answer the second question because it's a fair one.

The Happy 100 is not a scientific research project, and I did not try to measure each woman's happiness level or rate her on some made-up or scientific scale. Personally, I believe that emotions are honest and that feelings don't lie. If you feel happy, you probably are. So if a woman told me she loved her work, I gave her the benefit of the doubt and interviewed her to decipher why. If, in the course of our conversation, I sensed she was not truly comfortable in her job or thrilled with her work, I simply did not include her on the list, and that happened only a handful of times.

Many women volunteered reasons why they were happy. The most common explanations included variety, ongoing learning, opportunities for advancement, and because they "love the people they work with." While all were valid, I detected deeper, perhaps subconscious reasons, and those reasons became the basis for how I organized members of The Happy 100.

Defining happiness is not easy, as University of Toronto philosophy professor Mark Kingwell explains in *In Pursuit of Happiness: Better Living from Plato to Prozac* (Crown, 1998, p. 6): ". . . trying to provide a one-sentence definition of [happiness] is always a mug's game . . . there are many more questions than answers in this particular quarter of the philosophical field." Rather than present a tour de force summary of the history of happiness (I'll leave that to Professor Kingwell), I'll focus on two modern theories that correspond well with two of *Career Bliss*'s own themes: process and purpose.

The first theory comes from the work of Mihaly Csikszentmihalyi, who while at the University of Chicago conducted research in which thousands of people around the world were interviewed about happiness. Csikszentmihalyi wrote a number of books, including *Flow: The Psychology of Optimal Experience*. He believes the essence of happiness lies in how we evaluate experience rather than in our factual circumstances, such as salary or job title. In his view, controlling what happens in our mind is the key to so-called happiness. More to the point, it's the key to achieving the desirable state of mind Csikszentmihalyi calls "flow." People are in "flow" when they are engaged in a self-contained activity—running a marathon, doing a crossword puzzle, writing a book—that is done not with the expectation of some future benefit, but because the activity itself is the reward. The notion of flow evokes one of the Ps shared by all of The Happy 100 women: process. With all the woman I interviewed, I invariably discovered that each one was thoroughly engaged in her job's required activities.

Dr. Martin E. P. Seligman proposes a second theory that also ties in to another of The Happy 100's three Ps: purpose. In *Authentic Happiness: Using the New Positive Psychology to Realize Your Potential for Lasting Fulfillment*, Seligman writes about three types of happy lives. The first, which he calls the pleasant life, is a kind of giddy existence of smiles, ebullience, and good cheer. In leading the pleasant life, people actively pursue and experience positive emotions. The second type of happy life, the good life, is filled not so much with good feeling but with absorption, immersion, and, not coincidentally, a version of flow. To experience the good life, people must know their "signature strengths" and then craft jobs, relationships, and leisure time around them. Seligman's third type of happy existence is the meaningful life, which consists of using one's signature strengths in the service of something greater than oneself. Most members of The Happy 100 lead versions of the meaningful life because they labor for a *purpose* in which they believe.

In other words, and this is very important, work processes have the potential to engage women intellectually, while the purpose behind those activities can engage them emotionally. And as long as women also work among people they like, or at least respect, they are well on their way to leading happy working lives. *In the context of work, I define happiness as being engaged in activities whose outcomes you are proud of and with people you respect.*

Beyond the Three Ps: From Lovers to Hurdlers

To restate, women of The Happy 100 love their work for three primary reasons:

- Process: They take joy in and excel at the variety of tasks they do each day.
- Purpose: They feel good about why they do those tasks.
- People: They like and, at the very least, respect their bosses, coworkers, and customers.

The three Ps do not always exist in equilibrium. Some women are more purpose than process oriented; others, the reverse. And there are, of course, other differences. One Happy 100 woman focuses on achieving a long-term goal; another focuses on what's directly in front of her. There are those who thrive as readers and writers, while others create tangible products by hand. Some dislike sitting at a desk all day, while some spend hours in secluded offices at a computer.

As stories poured out of these women, I tried to spot commonalities among their varied preferences and experiences. Eventually, ten "types" of Happy 100 women emerged, and I divided the 100 women—and the book—into ten categories that broadly define a group's predominant traits and values. You may see aspects of yourself in each type, but only one, two, or three will likely apply to you. The types are not absolutes, but rather a novel way to reevaluate your own personality, strengths, and preferences, as well as consider how to transfer them to your work. Summaries of the ten types follow, and each chapter addresses one type in greater detail.

Process-based Happy 100 Women

The Builders. Women who love to build communities, relationships, and things—from high-rise buildings to corporate cultures—from scratch. These happy workers find joy in the process of creation.

The Surviving Artists. Women who make a living at what otherwise would be considered a purely artistic endeavor, such as painting, performing, or writing. Rather than living the impoverished life of a so-called "struggling artist," hoping to one day be discovered and paid for their efforts, these women channel their artistic talents into self-supporting or lucrative activities, without compromising their values.

The Thinkers. Women who love their jobs mainly because their daily activities put them in a mental state of flow. They glean pleasure from either problem solving or synthesizing disparate pieces of information to achieve a specific business goal. The processes they enjoy range from analyzing and calculating to managing and writing.

The Counselors. Women who are adept listeners. Compared to the more analytical Thinkers, these women solve on-the-job problems with a psychological component. They engage in processes such as mentoring and managing, teaching and advising. Counselors use communication skills to further someone else's success in business and in life.

Purpose-based Happy 100 Women

The Lovers. Women who have an innate enthusiasm and interest in some *thing* (animals, music, jewelry) and have fashioned working lives around promoting, discussing, and just being associated with whatever they adore. Essentially, Lovers work for the purpose of championing their passions.

The Determinators. The über-achievers of The Happy 100, these are women for whom being in control and influencing business decisions is particularly gratifying. These women find tremendous purpose in mastery of a skill set or body of knowledge, as well as constantly excelling in their careers.

The Heroines, Healers, and Sisters. Women who are, first and foremost, helpers and caregivers. Heroines are the activists, seeking to enact large-scale change. Healers prefer helping others via more one-on-one interaction and personal relationships. Sisters are specifically devoted to helping other women overcome obstacles. This trio is intensely humanitarian.

The Faithful. These women feel a strong connection between their work and religion, spirituality, or some intangible sense of faith. While not necessarily religious, their companies' values and mission are somehow tied to a greater power, however each woman chooses to define it.

The final three chapters of *Career Bliss* focus on women who, in addition to falling into one of the above categories, have atypical career paths that warrant separate discussion.

The Loyalists are women who have worked for the same company for fifteen years or longer. Despite more than a decade or two (or three) with the same employer, these women are still happy, or happier than ever. They show that it's possible to build a fulfilling career at a single organization.

The After-Achievers are *not* women who are done achieving great things, but rather those who reached significant goals—be it the top rung of the corporate ladder or what others typically define as success—and then moved on to another happy job or career. After-Achievers' stories suggest that a woman's work, and work happiness, need not end when she reaches a certain age, retires, or masters a profession. These women illustrate what job happiness can look like when the spotlight fades and after goals have been met.

The Hurdlers. The book concludes with some of The Happy 100's most inspiring stories. Hurdlers are women whose lives and career paths include unusual tragedy, loss, or hardship, further proving that on-the-job happiness is not limited to the lucky and the healthy, the rich and the strong.

The Cast of Characters: A Snapshot of the Group

The Happy 100 shows us that women in all types of jobs and at all levels of business can love what they do for a living. As already established, it is not an exclusive group of senior executives or well-known women, but a diverse collection of women that encompasses a variety of industries, backgrounds, ages, and locales.

So, what do Happy 100 women have in common in addition to the three Ps?

First, there are several things I did *not* observe as critical reasons why they loved their work, mainly high pay, power, fame, even work/family balance. This is not to say that money, prestige, and balance were neither important nor valued, but in and of themselves they did not yield on-the-job joy. One well-known and wealthy businesswoman whom I asked to interview for the book politely declined, saying she had been happy once, but no more. Apparently, the daily grind overshadowed the biweekly paycheck, and I could almost hear the melancholy in her e-mail. One Happy 100 member spent more than ten years pursuing high-powered, impressive job titles only to finally find happiness working at a little-known, small-town newspaper. As for balance, any woman allowed to leave her office in time to get home to her children but who distrusts her boss and bickers with colleagues certainly would not say she loves her work. She may tolerate it, accept it, she may even be grateful for the income and flexible hours, but she is not happy in her working life.

On the flip side, many women who thoroughly enjoy work actually lack balance or high salaries. About 35 percent of The Happy 100 say they have yet to achieve an acceptable level of balance in their lives, and 41 percent make less than $75,000 a year; 27 percent make less than $50,000; 12 percent less than $30,000. Of course, these women all want to make more—who wouldn't—but the message is that money and pay do not necessarily correlate with a happy work experience.

Most women of The Happy 100 are also not stereotypically successful. Yes, powerful businesswomen and celebrities are members of the group, but the majority of women hold more familiar, ordinary, accessible jobs and are not famous or in charge of large companies; yet their stories are no less interesting than those of their more renowned cohorts. In fact, 81 percent of all Happy 100 women consider themselves "very successful." Not one—not the truck driver, the doorperson, or the stay-at-home mom—said she was not.

The overall nature of The Happy 100 also dashes conventional assumptions about what constitutes happiness in the workplace—for example, that happy workers don't *have* to work, that they must be self-employed, that they don't work long hours, are thrilled with any job they can get, or that they are simply hardwired for happiness and never question their career paths. I hope the following statistics* will put these assumptions to rest.

Assumption:

Women who love their jobs are innately happy and have never really been unhappy.

Reality Check:

- 46 percent of The Happy 100 held a job they did not like at some point in their career.
- 14 percent have been fired at some point in the career; 21 percent have been laid off.
- 44 percent quit a job without having another one lined up.
- 55 percent have taken a personality test; 36 percent have taken a skills assessment test; 16 percent have seen a career counselor; 19 percent a life coach (proof that even happy working women need outside aids to help them better understand themselves and see potential career paths).
- 77 percent of Happy 100 women have cried in the workplace.
- 86 percent have felt frustrated in their current job.
- 61 percent have seen a therapist at some point in their lives.

Assumption:

Happy working women don't have to work for money because they are already wealthy or have spouses who support them.

Reality Check:

- 70 percent say they *must* work to make money, not solely for pleasure or as a hobby.
- 38 percent are not married.
- 56 percent are the primary breadwinners in their family.
- 42 percent have one or more children between one month and nineteen years old whom they help or solely support.
- 15 percent of married Happy 100 members have significant others with income between $50,000 and $75,000; 14 percent of Happy 100 spouses make less than $50,000.

*Percentages are based on 95 of The Happy 100 women who completed a survey.

Assumption:

Happy working women are popular, outgoing people who don't require a lot of help in their careers.

Reality Check:

- 48 percent belong to formal networking groups.
- 76 percent had a mentor.
- 70 percent asked for a raise (rather than wait to be given one); of those who asked, 91 percent got one.
- 72 percent admit some coworkers probably do not like them.

Assumption:

Women who love their jobs don't work long hours or report to someone else.

Reality Check:

- 88 percent work full-time.
- Only 25 percent are self-employed.
- 54 percent eat lunch at their desk.

One other common trait among the women of this book is that most Happy 100 women can trace the origins of their current job back to childhood. For example, 61 percent had mothers who worked while they raised a family, which likely established an expectation in their daughters that they, too, would hold down jobs. Some got the bug early. Avon's national sales manager actually sold makeup door-to-door at age fifteen. Other women say childhood activities were precursors for present-day careers: An ATA Airlines mechanic built model planes growing up; a day camp director attended overnight camp for more than twelve years; and songwriter Diane Warren would sit in the back of her college classrooms and make up songs instead of taking notes. The engineer built dollhouses; the movie producer hung out around Hollywood film sets; and a judge raised in poverty vowed to rise above it.

The sights, sounds, hobbies, dreams, and even fears of youth manifest themselves in adult life. What does that mean for you and others in search of work to love? Childhood is a critical place to look for and identify your own innate interests and motivations. Put another way: What did you want to be when you grew up?

How I Found The Happy 100

Finding happiness for oneself is tough. Identifying hundreds of women who have succeeded at it is an even trickier business. After all, sadness and dissatisfaction are easier to spot. Unhappy people cry, complain, look depressed, mope, pine, reach for a Kleenex, write in journals, go to therapy, or talk about problems with friends. Happiness, however, is more elusive. We don't express positive emotions to the degree that we express negative ones. Happiness is experienced much more quietly.

I realized I could not assume a woman loved her work simply because she was famous and attractive, laughed a lot, had her face on magazine covers, held a powerful position, or worked for a cool company. And because finding happy workers was equivalent to finding needles in a haystack, I had to let them find me.

First, I created a Web site, www.thehappy100.com, which featured a brief application that women could fill out online. To get women to the site, I used several tactics. I contacted large companies' public relations representatives and invited them to submit employees for consideration. Estée Lauder, Unisys, Avon, GE, AstraZeneca, and JPMorgan Chase are among the corporations that responded. Milwaukee-based Midwest Airlines actually held a contest for its flight attendants, inviting those who loved their job to explain why in 100 words or less. The winners were sent my way. I also asked industry associations to tell their members about The Happy 100 project. Judge Maxine Aldridge White came to me through the National Association of Women Judges, nurse Jan Pickett via the American Nurses Association, and Mary Ann Eiff from Women in Aviation International. Several Happy 100 members also belong to the Society of Women Engineers. Slowly, word started to spread. A friend of a friend suggested she apply, or a woman's daughter e-mailed her the Web site address with an encouraging note, "Mom, you must do this!" Sometimes serendipity took hold: After I told a friend about The Happy 100 over lunch at a tiny, crowded diner, a man sitting next to me handed me a scrap of paper with Andrea Varga's name and number on it. "I couldn't help but overhear," he apologized, "but my friend is a costume designer who loves her job. You have to call her!" I did, and he was right. Two women I interviewed suggested their siblings for the project, and

Nancy and Susan Holson, as well as sisters Betty Jagoda Murphy and Lori Lowell, are all members of The Happy 100.

I always kept my eyes and ears open. When a reader wrote to *The New York Times* about doorperson Katherina Kunhardt, I tracked Katherina down, just as I did with Enron secretary Debbie Perrotta, who appeared in the magazine *Fast Company*. I found tour guide Mary Kocher when my husband and I visited Hearst Castle in California, and I caught up with synchronized swimmer Ana Cukic after seeing Cirque du Soleil's extravagant show in Las Vegas. Occasionally I approached women if I heard them declare, unprompted, that they loved their jobs. Executive chef Sally Ayotte announced her love of the job on CNN; mechanic and auto shop owner Catherine Simpson said just as much on the *Today* show in a segment about women in trade professions; and at a live panel discussion in Manhattan, broadcast journalist Lesley Stahl told an auditorium full of people that she loved her career. As for the singers the Indigo Girls and *West Wing* actress Stockard Channing, all three are women I perceived loved their work, and when I told them about The Happy 100, each agreed to be interviewed. Our meetings confirmed my suspicions.

I tapped my personal and professional network: My sister Susan Newman recommended Chicagoland dog lover and publisher Janice Brown, as well as boutique owners Kari Kupcinet Kriser and Cheryl Sloane. My aunt, Judy Wharton, met boutique owner MaryLouise van der Wilden at a dinner party, and my father's college friend put me in touch with female park ranger Jennifer Stowe. When I asked friends if they knew anyone I should interview, rarely did more than one or two names come to mind. Kim Birbrower introduced me to her Shoah Visual History Foundation coworker Kim Simon; Stacey Steeg to her camp friend and current camp director Joanie Henson (whom I also knew from my years at camp); and *Forbes*'s Kasia Moreno suggested I call her in-law, cancer fund-raiser Julie Ratner. Marc Cenedella directed me to his fellow business school alum Marla Malcolm Beck, and New York artist Lori Greenberg recommended muralist Tracy Lee Stum. While I maintained a rule to not interview friends or family, I did reach out to a former roommate, Lara Mitchel, who is now a full-time mother of four boys.

Other people who led me to happy working women include publicists Jamie Moss, Hope Kaplan, Jeff Sanderson, Gregg Rosenberg, Pete Judice, Peter Himler, Scott Lyons, and Judy Kalvin. I also wish to thank marketing maven Paige Arnof-Fenn, career counselor Carole Hyatt, serial entrepreneur Jim Milligan, Nike's irrepressible enthusiast Kevin Carroll, and my former journalism school professor Craig LaMay, whose wife happens to be a very happy librarian. The chief executive of Roadway Express, James Staley, e-mailed me the name of a company truck driver, and Boston radio talk show hostess Gay Vernon pointed me to hospital clown Jeannie Lindheim, who in turn told physical therapist Nancy Roberge to apply to The Happy 100, which she did.

It's important to note that some women I asked to interview declined. Whether it was because they were not happy with their work, were too busy, or were not interested in the book, I do not know. Also, at least three women on the list changed jobs between the time I interviewed them and the date the book went to press. Broadcast business journalist Jan Hopkins left her longtime anchor spot at CNN to work for Citigroup's private banking division; consumer retail executive Ivy Ross left toy maker Mattel to work for the Gap's Old Navy stores; and technology powerhouse Patricia Sueltz bid adieu to her job at Sun Microsystems—where she was one of the multibillion-dollar company's top twelve executives—to work for newcomer salesforce.com. After Jan, Ivy, and Pat each served several months at their respective new workplaces, I followed up to see if they were still happy. They all were, mainly because each essentially engaged in the same activities her previous job required and believed in the mission of her new employer.

Finally, only three women I planned to include in The Happy 100 voluntarily opted out: One took a "once in a lifetime" job after almost twenty years with the same company, another explained that her work environment had become toxic after new owners took over, and another admitted she never really loved her job—but couldn't bring herself to tell her boss (proof that employers can erroneously assume workers are happy even when they're not). It's likely that some women will have moved on to new jobs before *Career Bliss* is published, but I expect that. Sometimes, to continue to love what we do, we must leave where we are.

I learned quickly never to assume up front why any one woman loves her work. If I did, she usually proved me wrong. For each conversation I had questions handy, but more often than not the dialogues meandered according to each woman's own story. Sometimes she spoke in detail about her career path, other times we discussed her current duties.

I met as many women as possible face-to-face, many in their places of employment. I chatted with the Indigo Girls backstage before a concert and met Stockard Channing in *The West Wing*'s cluster of production bungalows at Warner Bros. Studios in Los Angeles. Chief executive officer Betsy McLaughlin took me on a tour of Hot Topic's headquarters; the retailer's office—with its flaming sconces, red velvet furniture, and multiple TV screens—resembles a Gothic nightclub. In Midtown Manhattan, Grace Vandecruze has a breathtaking view of the city, while Estée Lauder's Annie Carullo has an office that majestically overlooks Central Park. Margaret Sullivan's spacious office has room for a graffiti-spotted park bench and looks out over Lake Michigan's lush shoreline, and Kim Simon works in a cramped trailer converted to office space. When Judge Maxine Aldridge White is not in her wood-paneled, high-ceilinged courtroom, she works out of her peaceful judge's chambers, replete with scented candles and a tabletop waterfall. At the foothills of the Wasatch Mountains in Utah, I watched animal trainer Lynne Seus and her husband cuddle with Kodiak bears, and in a building at the corner of Hollywood and Vine I peered inside songwriter Diane Warren's dark, cluttered office—aptly nicknamed The Cave because it hasn't been cleaned in nearly twenty years.

I wish I could have visited everyone, but even when I did not, the phone interviews and e-mail exchanges were remarkably insightful. When I read each woman's profile to her to check for accuracy, most agreed that I had captured not only her work, but her being.

In the end I encountered more than just 100 happy working women—all told I heard from almost 400 and interviewed about 150 in depth. But because the final group had to be diverse in terms of age, background, experience, geography, job type, and industry, many women I spoke to or who applied do not appear in *Career Bliss*. To them I extend my heartfelt thanks for their interest and participation. You already have the best reward of all: You love what you do. For me, it was nothing short of an honor to meet each and every Happy 100 member. I laughed out loud, I sat quietly while women cried, and I learned so very much about the American workforce as well as myself.

As for me, I satisfied my own three Ps long ago: The process of writing challenges and engages my mind, and the purpose of informing and empowering readers fills my heart with pride. As for the people with whom I work, the women I met in the course of my research were gracious, instructive, and ultimately touched me in a way I never could have imagined. Those who know me personally had everything to do with this project becoming reality: My amazing husband, Matthew, proved once again that he is a gifted editor and an unwavering supporter. I am truly blessed to have him in my life. My parents, David and Virginia Gordon, volunteered their expertise and their ears, and, as always, their love. Author and Downtown Women's Club doyenne, Diane Danielson, offered innumerable insightful suggestions, and reporter Allison Fass helped me fact-check with the diligence only a first-rate journalist could bring to the task. I am also grateful for the publicity efforts of Kim Hovey, Cindy Murray, Heather Smith, and Jamie Moss—an author's dream team. This book would not exist without two very special women: my editor at Ballantine, Allison Dickens, helped shape my original idea and championed the book from proposal to completion; and my prescient agent, Lisa Bankoff at ICM, also helped me refine the original concept, always seeing potential where others did not. As usual, she was right and I am grateful for her support. Not only do I respect the people I worked with to complete this book, I consider many to be dear friends.

That said, while I did not include myself among The Happy 100, please consider me 101.

Chapter One

The Lovers

Movie music supervisor, tour guide and nude model, librarian, airplane mechanic, day camp director, ergonomist, pet magazine founder and editor, animal trainer, boutique owner, songwriter, and NASCAR travel coordinator.

The most common career advice, "follow your passion," is dramatically overused and often misapplied. What if you don't know what your passion is? And if you do, not all passions translate obviously into jobs, which is one reason many women relegate their passion—their joy, their interest, their love—to the status of a hobby. This first group of Happy 100 women, the Lovers, can help you answer those two questions for yourself because each woman has identified her own passion and built a working life around it.

Specifically, Lovers are women who love some *thing*—airplanes, art, animals, music—and who have found a way to channel that love into a paying venture. Rarely are Lovers' jobs the most obvious manifestation of that passion. The lover of airplanes, for example, is not a pilot. The lover of animals is not a veterinarian. Two lovers of music are not musicians. As for the lover of art, she's not an artist. In fact, her job may shock you.

As you will see, each Lover fashioned a happy working life in one of two ways. Some identified an existing company or industry associated with her interest and then found a specific job in an organization or field that matched her skills. Other Lovers struck off on their own, creating a product or company from scratch and, in turn, inventing their own role. Because Lovers champion some *thing*, they tend to be motivated more by purpose than process, yet each is still highly skilled at whatever activities she is called upon to perform: negotiate, teach, sell, write, or lead.

While you probably won't follow the exact path of any one Lover or adopt her specific career as your own, you may glean ideas about how to spin your own passion into a happy working life.

Which song does she wake up humming?

Many women love music—whether singing or listening to it—but rarely can they transform that love into a career. This was not the case for self-described "rocker" Lia Vollack, president of worldwide music for Sony's Columbia Pictures. Lia oversees big-budget film sound tracks—the music at the beginning of a movie; the background melody that sets a mood during a scene; and the songs that play as the final credits roll. Her films include *The Usual Suspects* (1995), *Charlie's Angels* (2000), *Spider-Man* (2002), *Adaptation* (2002), and *Big Fish* (2003). Among the musicians Lia has worked with: Jennifer Lopez, Aerosmith, Destiny's Child, Sean "P. Diddy" Combs, and Dave Matthews.

Lia must come up with music that not only frames and helps promote a film but will also top the music charts. On one particularly hectic Thursday morning during the spring of 2004, Lia was in the mad throes of choosing the single for the upcoming movie *Spider-Man 2*, and she talked about the unique challenges of crafting songs for film. Articulating to musicians the idea and feelings a song should convey is only half her battle. Knowing a hit when she hears one is the other.

Right now I have several different bands writing potential songs for Spider-Man 2, *including some big, multi-platinum artists. It's not exactly a bake-off, though, because I must put together an entire album, so if a particular song doesn't end up being the movie's single, it can still be included in the film. I'm really looking for a rock artist rather than a pop or hip-hop singer, someone who can sing an anthem, but not in a Queen,*

"We will rock you," sort of way. Just someone who can have emotional lift and soar.

Not all songs are one-listen hits. Some songs must be heard several times before you wake up and hear it play in your head. That's the process I'm going through right now: "Which song did I wake up humming? Which one did I sing in the shower?" Sometimes a slight musical change can improve it, so I might suggest that an artist lengthen the bridge or add a pre-chorus before the chorus to give it the right kind of build and flow.

Lyrics are very important, and I have a lot more purview to discuss lyrical content with songwriters, especially if it's a movie's title song and one the studio will use for advertising. Often it's just a matter of saying to a band, "I love this, but can we get something into the lyrics about how he feels about her, not just how she feels about him?" If a musician can't see the movie before she writes a song, I tell her about the story, the emotional touch points, and universal themes.

Right now there are some potential Spider-Man songs that I feel are magical, and others I know are magical, but I have to convince the bands to do it because they're so busy. Dealing with bands is what makes doing music for film uniquely challenging because musicians see movies as a side thing to do, unlike actors and directors, for whom movies are their primary business. It's also hard for a lot of artists to make that leap from writing a song that comes entirely from within themselves to something that is specific to another person's art. A lot of times someone writes a song that is so on the nose, it almost makes you cringe because it too blatantly tells a story, like, "She walks across the room, she really loves him . . ." Or, on the flip side, a song can be so oblique that it doesn't have the proper relationship to the movie or fails to tell the film's story.

The most stressful part of this job is having so much at stake, especially with a huge franchise movie like Spider-Man. But I'm comfortable with ultimate responsibility. A lifetime of experiences brought me to this current place. This job is who I am.

Or rather, it's who Lia has become.

Her story begins in Colorado, where Lia played piano and saxophone in high school and developed a penchant for musicians. But Lia was no groupie. "Hanging out with bands was not about the fame, but being with a group of people like me," she says. (Plus, boys in the band were cute.) At the end of the day, Lia simply wanted to make music. She graduated from high school two years early and spent several months studying music in college before realizing that becoming a musician was not practical. "I knew that if I chose to be a musician, I'd be an unsuccessful one," she laughs.

Lia's story shows that passion can rarely be forged into a career without a dose of practicality, and the place Lovers end up is often not where they expected.

After music school, Lia went on the road with punk bands, operating soundboards backstage at concerts and in recording studios. The technically savvy music lover was finding her niche. "Doing sound engineering was a way to be part of the musician lifestyle," says Lia. "Creative people need structured people around them, and I'm sort of a blend." She began a theatrical design degree at the University of Colorado but, anxious to get on with her career, left school to move to New York City, where she would hone her craft in the real world. Again she toured with bands, from the Ramones to the Rolling Stones, and occasionally Lia made extra money working not-so-glamorous venues, such as corporate events. During the early eighties, Lia was also one of the few women "mixing music" and, over the course of six years, was a sound designer for 150 shows. Recalls Lia, "I was the first woman to design sound for Broadway, which is actually what I'm most proud of in my career."

As often happens with Lovers, Lia's career transitioned unexpectedly when a director she knew asked her to supervise music selection for a film called *Longtime Companion* (1990). Lia accepted, and when the movie was done, the director asked her to work on another film, *Prelude to a Kiss* (1992), starring Meg Ryan and Alec Baldwin.

The head of music at Twentieth Century Fox didn't want me to do Prelude to a Kiss *because he didn't want to hire "a girl who had only done one movie." My technical and theater background didn't count in Hollywood, but eventually the movie's director just forced them to hire me. That was my first studio feature, and when I realized I loved working in film. So I moved to L.A.*

It was very difficult to get work here, and I went from being at the top of my game on the East Coast to being someone no one had ever heard of on the West Coast. I didn't know many people in L.A., and I definitely didn't know a lot about supervising music for movies. One person told me I might as well forget it. But I didn't. Instead, I shifted my focus. You know how your mother tells you to have something to fall back on if "the creative thing" doesn't work out? Well, there was a time I didn't want to follow her advice because I thought it would keep me from pursuing my dream. But my mother was right, and once I got to Hollywood I fell back on my technical proficiency. Instead of being a music supervisor right away, I became a music editor, the person who synchronizes all of the songs and the score into the film.

I couldn't have made a better decision. Editing taught me about film production and gave me the training I needed to be a supervisor and do the job I have today. Much of my current job involves translating what a director wants. When a director says, "I need the music to be more yellow," my hands-on, technical background helps me know what he means. Making a film is a collaborative art. You just can't create for yourself. There are a lot of people I have to please, from the filmmakers and the studio to the record company and the marketing department. I'm able to see how all the pieces fit together.

Just because I'm passionate about my job doesn't mean there aren't days when my head hurts and my body aches and nights when I can't sleep. You have to have a thick skin in this business. Plus, Hollywood is very competitive, and working in entertainment is not a nine-to-five job. We're in meetings or on the phone all day, and at night I go to dinner meetings and movie screenings. This job is my life—it's both brutal and amazing.

Most people don't even know a job such as Lia's exists, yet in every field there are hundreds of such nuanced, behind-the-scenes positions that require uniquely skilled individuals. For Lia, the technical expertise her job requires is at the core of why she loves her job—not the glamor of making Hollywood movies or the "adrenaline rush" she gets from being in charge. This music Lover says one of her favorite on-the-job tasks is attending to a song's technical details, like working with an artist in a studio or sitting in on a scoring session with a composer. Such hands-on activities take Lia back to her sound-engineering roots—and help soothe those occasional aches and pains.

She got goose bumps.

Perched on the hills above California's Pacific Coast Highway is the fabled Hearst Castle at San Simeon—a 165-bedroom mansion built in the 1920s by newspaper magnate William Randolph Hearst. For many visitors, one of the most memorable aspects of touring the mansion is not the gilded Roman pool or the picturesque views of the sea, but a very animated tour guide named Mary Kocher. Mary, her red hair tucked into a safari-style hat, does not just spew facts and answer visitor questions. Instead, Mary tells stories. Every anecdote—be it about Hearst's lavish parties or a 2,000-year-old vase in his art collection—unfolds as if Mary is sharing it for the first time among friends.

What's so surprising, though, is just how long Mary's been a "historical interpreter" at the castle: For eleven years she's conducted some 5,000 tours. Talk about monotony. You have to wonder how anyone can repeat the same information, day after day, and stave off boredom, let alone love her job. But here's Mary's secret: She loves art and art history. Mary loves to be surrounded by it and to talk about it. What's more, she's constantly updating her knowledge.

Mary's appreciation for artistic beauty sparked at age six, but it took almost forty years—and countless nonartistic, uninspiring, and low-paying jobs—before she indulged it as a career.

I remember standing in front of a painting when I was six, and my mother leaning down to say, "That's a real El Greco, Mary." I got goose bumps! In grade school, if I was not talking to my neighbor, I was drawing, and in high school I decided I wanted to be a Renaissance woman and know a little bit about everything, from ancient Greece to the Middle Ages to the present day. I didn't want to be a teacher—that seemed too structured—so I didn't know what I'd do with all the knowledge.

Two and a half years into college, at eighteen, I got pregnant, got married, and left school. I had my second child by the time I was twenty-

four, and my husband and I lived in remote towns in Washington State and California to escape society. We were in survival mode and had no choice but to take whatever jobs we could get. I held a bunch of minimum-wage jobs: I was a sheriff's dispatcher, a mail carrier, a secretary, a ballet store clerk, a personal trainer, an aerobics instructor at a gym . . . anything just to pay the bills while I raised my kids.

Twice a year I would drag out a canvas and paint.

Finally, at forty-one, after I was divorced, I woke up and realized I couldn't keep doing dinky jobs I didn't enjoy. I'd always loved art, and I decided I wanted to work around beautiful things, even if it only paid minimum wage. I happened to live near Hearst Castle, and when I applied to be a tour guide all I knew was that the man who built the mansion was really rich. I wasn't qualified for the job—a lot of tour guides had master's degrees—and I had to convince the State of California, which operates the Castle, to count my aerobics instruction toward the mandatory number of speaking hours required of Castle guides. Once I started the job, I received about 120 hours of basic training, but I did my own independent study about history, art, and the famous people who were Hearst's guests, like Winston Churchill. That way I could say something interesting about Churchill instead of just name-dropping. A good tour guide can't just give facts. We have to get people interested by putting Hearst's life and home into a larger context. If I want to talk about Hearst's upbringing, I tell people he was thirteen when Custer was defeated in the Battle of Little Bighorn. Instead of just pointing out a beautifully carved piece of furniture, I talk about what was happening in the world when the chair was made.

Every tour group is different, and I start reading groups the moment they step off the tour bus. Older people know all the old movie stars, but younger people aren't the least bit impressed that Cary Grant visited the mansion forty times. Some visitors want to know how Hearst made his money, others are curious about the scandals swirling around Hearst's wife and his famous mistress, and still others want to know about the antiques. My goal is to get each group asking questions, and I base every tour off their questions. When I find myself getting bored, I just read a new book. When I learn a new fact, I place it between facts I already know. My *memory has improved so much since I started working at the Castle. Even if I didn't work here, I'd still learn all this stuff. I'd just have nobody to share it with.*

But wait. There's more. Mary has a second job that also indulges her love of art: She is a model who poses nude for artists and art students. Apparently, Mary first wanted to be an artist's model when her grandmother took her to a sculpture class. "The live model was one of the most beautiful things I'd ever seen, and just so comfortable with her body," recalls Mary, who was brought up to feel comfortable with her own nudity. Unfortunately, her first husband refused to let Mary model in the buff, and it wasn't until after her divorce that Mary finally started posing. Now her lithe, statuesque body is in high demand.

I've been told I sit well. A lot of models can't hold a pose, and that is a must because modeling classes last about three hours. I'll usually warm up with two-minute poses, then ten minutes, then twenty-five. It can be very painful to sit the same way for a while, fighting gravity, but I swear I get into the deepest, most meditative state. I try to conceptualize what I look like from the different angles the artists are viewing me. I'm a gangly five feet, nine inches tall and weigh about 135 pounds, but it doesn't matter what shape you're in—you could be 300 pounds and be an artist's model—as long as you understand that it's an artistic endeavor. I've studied so many art books that a lot of times I strike a famous pose, and it takes a while, but one of the artists eventually exclaims, "Hey, you're Michelangelo's David," or "You're one of Degas's little dancers!" It was a struggle to learn how to model for artists, but it was worth it. Being involved in art—being the object of beauty—is the whole purpose.

Whether object, student, or teacher, Mary has finally surrounded herself with art and escaped the career doldrums of her twenties and thirties. Her salaries also beat working for minimum wage: Hearst pays about eighteen dollars an hour, and Mary charges up to fifteen dollars an hour to model. Her advice to other women stuck in unfulfilling minimum-wage jobs: "Find an area you're interested in and get an entry-level job where you can work your way up. Even when you're not making much, at least it's in a field you like."

In her own words

Karrie Fisher-LaMay, 43
School Librarian, Roycemore School
Evanston, Illinois

While recovering from cancer, Karrie had an epiphany that led her to pursue a master's degree in library science. Today, the mother of two is the librarian and media center director at a private preparatory school outside Chicago. While it appears as if Karrie stumbled across her profession serendipitously, it was, as you shall see, in the cards.

This is not a boring bun-in-the-hair profession, and my colleagues are not the stodgy "shushers" people assume they are. We're wild when we're outside the library. We play poker at night and have been known to dance on tables. And library science is an especially great profession for younger people, because soon a slew of older librarians will be retiring.

I first got interested in this profession when I was doing transcription work. I had started a transcription service while I was going through chemotherapy for cancer because it was a way to make money and work out of the house. I'd simply listen to tapes and type out the content, word for word. One day I was transcribing a speech that a librarian gave at Columbia University, and the way she described her job—to be able to help people find information on a day-to-day basis—just knocked my socks off! In the middle of transcribing her talk I came down from my office to the living room and blurted to my husband, "I have to go back to grad school and become a librarian." He jumped on it—and even signed me up for the GRE.

My first step was to contact the librarian I heard speak on tape and ask her about the profession. She steered me toward Rutgers University's program in library and information science. My first misstep occurred on the first day of grad school, when I had to choose a track: Did I want to be a generalist or a children's librarian? Since I wanted to work with kids but had no library experience, I assumed I should be a generalist. Bad move. I soon learned that children's librarianship requires specific educational training, and once I started I was not allowed to switch tracks. In retrospect I should have asked the department chairman to help me make my decision, but I was always a little intimidated by professors and never approached them. So I was stuck being a generalist.

After grad school I worked in the young adult section of a public library from 8:30 A.M. to 5:30 P.M., but of course kids never came into the library during my hours. If I wanted to work in a public school library I had to get a teaching certificate. I was not able to leave work early for night classes, so I began looking for another job that gave me the flexibility to attend school. A coworker told me a local private day school needed a new librarian, which was perfect because private schools don't always require teaching certificates. I actually got offers from two private schools, but I chose the less cushy of the two, Roycemore, located in a hundred-year-old building which had a lot of character.

When I arrived at Roycemore five years ago the library had been neglected and had become a huge lounge for students; the collection was also outdated, and the card catalog was maybe 40 percent accurate. I took the job because the place really needed me, and I felt I could make a difference. The library would be my little kingdom. I would bring it into the twenty-first century and make it a place that could influence every student and teacher.

It wasn't easy. One of the biggest challenges was getting the students to change their behavior and stop treating the library like a noisy lounge. They ignored me for the first semester, and it came down to a battle of wills. Eventually I called a meeting with all the problem kids and made them sign a contract. They had to follow my new rules if they wanted to be in the library. They balked at first, but it worked, and from then on they at least attempted to be quiet. I even have a nice relationship with many of them.

As for the library itself, I had to weed out about 2,500 books (one book hadn't been checked out since 1938). The school's library budget was tiny, and so I applied for an $18,000 grant to help pay for a new book-tracking system. I had an electronic library-card system installed and created collection and policy-development programs. It really is my little kingdom. And now that the library is in better shape, I can branch out and focus on my true love: helping kids develop lifelong reading habits and skills. Last year I challenged the kids to read a total of 1,000 books. They read 1,067! We celebrated with pizza.

Although my budget is still too small and I still get into battles with kids, what keeps me going is the knowledge that I make a difference in their lives. The most satisfying part of the job is helping a student find a piece of information, helping her make some kind of connection. I appreciate little things, like when I can e-mail a student the database archive she's looking for, or when she learns a new way to conduct research on the Internet. Not all kids grasp basic stuff. That's why I truly love being a librarian: I can open their eyes and help prepare them for college. If I didn't, most of them would flip out when they got to their university library. Even if all I teach them is how to find books electronically, or that it's okay to ask someone for help, then they'll go further. (It's ironic, of course, considering how I failed to ask a teacher for help when I returned to school.)

Here's the crazy part of my story: Several years ago I was helping my mother move and clearing out my childhood possessions when I found a box filled with my old Nancy Drew books. As I leafed through the pages, I noticed that as a kid I'd pasted paper pockets and mock checkout cards on the inside front covers. As I sat there in my mother's house, a chill went down my back. Amazing. I'd completely forgotten that when I was young, I pretended to work in a library. Apparently, a part of me never forgot.

I do think there's some sort of destiny for all of us. We may go about finding it in a roundabout way, but if we really listen to our inner selves, we end up where we're supposed to be.

She never wanted to fly.

Like latent librarian Karrie Fisher-LaMay, many women's working passions are born in childhood. The trick is how—indeed, whether—we nurture them as adults. For Mary Ann Eiff, a lover of airplanes, the solution was leapfrogging from one aviation-related job to the next. Her current position has made her the happiest yet.

Mary Ann grew up in the midwestern farmlands, where she spent weekends building and flying model airplanes with friends. A tomboy, Mary Ann was the only girl among a gaggle of male playmates. One day, while they were romping through the fields flying their rickety, homemade models, Mary Ann stumbled across a man restoring *real* airplanes in a large garage. Fascinated, she asked to assist him. The little girl was hooked, and, for the next seven years, Mary Ann and her buddies spent almost every Saturday helping the mechanic restore old planes. "It's funny," says Mary Ann today. "I never really wanted to fly the planes, I just loved restoring them." It turns out Mary Ann was also prone to airsickness.

Her career path seemed obvious: This lover of airplanes—how they functioned and flew—should build a career in aviation maintenance. But it wasn't that easy in the 1960s, a time when young Midwestern women were far from encouraged to study engineering. Rather than fight the status quo, Mary Ann took another path and, instead, majored in Bible studies and mathematics, graduating with a degree in Christian education.

Apparently, God didn't want me to be a director of Christian education. After college I had trouble getting a job because employers always asked if I planned on having a family. "Not for a while," I always said, but doors still slammed in my face. [Laughs.] Meanwhile, my husband and I took some of our savings and bought our own little plane, a 1946 Taylorcraft.

Mary Ann and her husband eventually had two children. Since she still had to work to help support her family, she flocked to a variety of aviation-related jobs. She was a mechanic's apprentice. She kept books for an aviation company. For five years she even managed inventory at a small recording studio that produced background music for public venues, including airports! To an outsider, the jobs were completely random, but Mary Ann was circling the industry, looking for her landing.

Meanwhile, at night, Mary Ann and her husband toiled away in an aviation electronics shop they opened in 1972. The company, Central Illinois Avionics, specialized in electrical wiring and repair for aircraft. The business thrived until, one winter, thirty-foot-high snowdrifts blocked the shop door, preventing planes—and customers—from moving in or out of the shop. Compounding the problem, the 1970s oil embargo forced many small planes to stay grounded. With no planes to fix, Central Illinois Avionics was forced out of business, and Mary Ann and her husband had to find higher-paying day jobs. Landing jobs that corresponded with her passion was not easy, and Mary Ann faced nonstop turbulence.

Our shop wasn't making money, so we closed it. My husband found a job teaching aviation electronics at Southern Illinois University. As for me, I decided to finally get my airplane mechanics license, which despite years of fixing planes I still did not have. In 1981, I finally got it, and for six months I worked for Air Illinois, a local commuter airline that flew small planes around the state. It was a really bad experience because the industry was less regulated back then, and I was forced to sign off on questionable planes. Finally I said, "I can't do this! I want to go to bed and not worry at night!" So I told Air Illinois to take their job and shove it. The airline closed down about a year later.

I thought I would teach at the university where my husband worked, but the school wouldn't hire me because I didn't have a master's in education. They wouldn't even let me fix the planes the school used to teach students flying until I had a certain number of "points," so I had to work for five years as a university secretary to earn all the points required to be a mechanic. Finally, in 1986, I got a job as a mechanic and inspector for the university's training planes. But by that time, years of using screwdrivers and other tools had completely destroyed my wrists. I had carpal tunnel syndrome and could not do much maintenance work.

Although devastated that her hands had given out, Mary Ann did not give up her passion. Teaching, she decided, was another option. So she set out to earn a teaching degree, only to face a discriminatory job market upon graduation. There were not many female maintenance instructors in the 1980s. But Mary Ann persevered and went out of her way to attend university job fairs, which is how she eventually got a teaching position at Purdue University in Indiana.

I taught college for seven years, but teaching mommas' babies how to fix airplanes became a big problem. They were good kids, just frustrating. A student would have a 2,000-degree welding torch in his hands and be swinging it around the shop floor because he was hung over from partying the night before! After I had a seventy-year-old man in my class, I realized that I needed to teach adults, not seventeen-year-olds. I thought, Why not teach in a maintenance environment where people are working on airplanes, where they know what they need to learn and appreciate education a lot more? *So that's what I do now.*

At age fifty-nine, I'm an aircraft maintenance instructor at ATA Airlines in Indianapolis. I teach ATA's thousand mechanics (only about fifty are women) required courses, like how to fill out a logbook; airline policies and procedures; how to enter critical data into our computers, or pull up an airplane's history and figure out who we bought certain parts from. There are classes on safety, management, wiring, and how to troubleshoot. What do I like best? Seeing people I teach go out and do a good job and apply what they learned. If they don't follow the rules they could not only lose their mechanic's license and their livelihood, but someone else could lose a life. ATA has never—knock wood—had a major accident in thirty years. There's no room for error in an airline mechanic's work. We're a different breed, all dedicated to safety or else we'd go off and be car mechanics. Unlike cars, planes just can't pull off the road when their engines break down, so airline mechanics must go the extra mile. Take a look in an airplane mechanic's toolbox sometime. The mechanic knows where every single tool is, and each tool is always in the same place to make sure not a single one is left in an airplane. Have you ever seen a car mechanic's toolbox? It's just a jumble of tools.

Forty years after airplanes captured a young Mary Ann's imagination, she was still determined to keep aviation in her working life. Some jobs along her career path were more enjoyable than others, but all kept her close to what she loved. And at critical junctures, Mary Ann fine-tuned whatever was broken: When unethical business practices disturbed her, she quit. When she needed more education to become a teacher, she went back to school. And when teaching college students became unre-

warding, she switched to training adults. Like an effective mechanic—
and creative job jumper—Mary Ann consistently isolated the problem,
fixed it, and moved forward, never completely abandoning her craft.

A camper for the rest of her life

Most women don't find a job they love overnight. Indeed, finding work
that makes you happy often requires embracing one not-so-perfect job at
a time. Job by job, layer by layer, you discover who you are and gain skills
and experience.

In Chicago, Joanie Henson is a woman who knows exactly what job
she wants but has yet to attain it. That does not mean, however, that
Joanie is not happy. In fact, her story is proof that a woman can be happy
with a job even when it's not her final destination.

Quite simply, Joanie wants to own and run her own overnight camp.
The thirty-three-year-old has been a camp fan from the first summer she
spent eight weeks at Camp Birch Trail in the remote woods of Wisconsin. Everything about camp life enthralled her. Swimming and singing.
Cabin life and campfires. Organized activities and kitchen raids. She
also loved that "success" at camp was not about grades or building a résumé, but about being a true friend, being silly, being positive, and being
creative. At age nine, Joanie won a camper contest to be the camp's director for a day, and as a teenager she returned to Birch Trail as a counselor and later as a program director. Joanie was drawn not necessarily by
the prospect of playing with kids every day, but by the opportunity to
help create and manage the camp experience *for* kids. (Bonus: Joanie
also met her husband at Camp Birch Trail; he was a member of the staff
when she was a counselor.)

After college, Joanie's professional camping aspirations faded. That
life was impractical, or so she believed. Recalls Joanie: "I remember
graduating and telling a career counselor I just wanted to be a camper
for the rest of my life. He told me it was not realistic and that I'd have to
find something else, so after I took a career test he said I should be working with people. Or that I should be a florist."

In pursuit of a more acceptable profession (but one that did not include flower arranging), Joanie went to graduate school for social work but disliked it intensely. "I couldn't believe someone was teaching me how to talk to people," she'd fume. But Joanie stuck with school because Birch Trail's camp director and her first mentor, Richard, told her she would need the training if she ever wanted to run her own overnight camp. "Richard said parents would always ask, 'What makes you qualified to work with my child?' and I should be able to tell them I have a master's degree in social work." Following graduation, Joanie looked for any job in and around Chicago that even remotely "smelled" like camp. Anything that brought her closer to her goal.

The local Jewish Community Center, the JCC, had just opened a new, beautiful building, and I was hired to plan enrichment programs for kindergarteners through fifth graders, which meant teaching cooking and taking 150 kids bowling. Mind you, I really wanted to work at an older kids' camp, but I thought, Okay, it's not camp, but it's like camp. I worked diligently, on weekends and holidays, but always felt like I was watching the clock. I just didn't love the job, plus I didn't really have the support I needed. I still can't believe I didn't quit. Eventually I was made the director of a new, small camp for little kids; again, it was not the camp I dreamed of, but it was a step closer. The camp had nine kids in its first year and only fifteen the next. I tried to give my supervisor ideas, but she never listened to anything I said. Finally, the woman in charge of the JCC's most successful camp—her name was Gayle, and everyone called her the Queen of Camping—took me to lunch to discuss my career. At first I didn't say much, but Gayle prodded until I told her that I'd been going to camp all my life and knew how to run a successful program. All I needed was the chance.

Long story short, Gayle made me feel as if someone was finally listening to me. She saw my enthusiasm and appointed herself my new boss, putting me in charge of seven different day camps, including a creativity camp, a sports camp, and a golf camp.

After a year, the JCC decided to cancel all its smaller camps and create one big eight-week summer program called "Z" Frank Apache Village for four-, five-, and six-year-old kids. Gayle asked Joanie to be Apache Village's director, saying, "This is your camp, I give you the power." As a silly token of her confidence, Gayle handed Joanie a prize from inside a Cracker Jack box. Joanie took the prize, which she did not unwrap, and accepted the job. In its first summer, Apache Village signed up 250 children. The next year it had a waiting list, and by year five, Joanie welcomed 300 campers and managed a staff of seventy-five.

This is my camp. I run it and I love it. I work full-time during the summer and three days a week during off-seasons (which lets me spend valuable time with my own three children). During the off-season, I plan camp activities and special events, hire the staff, prepare paperwork, and purchase materials like art supplies, snacks, lots of Band-Aids. I also talk on the phone to hundreds and hundreds of parents! During the eight-week camp season I'm like a firefighter from the moment each day begins. Parents call me because their kids were crying when they got dropped off. The drama teacher doesn't show up and I have to ask a counselor to pretend to be a drama specialist for the day. One child pees in her pants. Another is allergic to peanut butter. Someone else has an asthma attack. Throughout it all, my job is to delegate and make decisions, and before I know it, the day is over.

The administration, the behind-the-scenes work, is what I find the most rewarding, and success is a chain reaction. When I'm excited about my job, the assistant director is excited, and so are the unit heads. Then the counselors work hard but have fun, which makes the children grow, learn, and smile and become confident in themselves and their new skills. That, in turn, makes their parents proud and happy, which makes them sign up again for camp and spread the word to other parents. When we start registration in the fall, we fill up in a matter of weeks.

Although Joanie truly loves her job as a day camp director, she and her husband still intend to operate their own overnight camp. Her career tale is a wake-up call: Sometimes, before you land that perfect job, you must hold others that, while not ideal, can still yield joy and valuable experience, as well as introduce you to lifelong mentors. When Joanie is ready to leave Apache Village, she plans to finally unwrap that symbolic Cracker Jack prize and mail it back to Gayle. That's how the Queen of Camping will know her protégée is ready to move on to her ultimate dream job.

In her own words

Mindy Smith, 28
Occupational Ergonomist
Raleigh, North Carolina

An ergonomist designs work and office spaces to ensure worker health and safety. Is a chair the right height in relation to the desk? Are repetitive motions risking injury? These are the questions ergonomists like Mindy ask. Mindy works out of her home and is currently on contract with the U.S. Navy. Over the years she has helped redesign and repair offices, mailrooms, laundry facilities, kitchens, aircraft, and ships, all for maximum worker-comfort.

The whole goal of ergonomics is to fit the workplace to the worker, not the other way around. The desk, the chair, a computer, even a conveyor belt must all be set to accommodate workers' geometries or people will contort their bodies.

When I tell people in my field that I knew I wanted to be an ergonomist at age sixteen, they don't believe me. I was in a Florida magnet high school program for math, science, and engineering, but I took psychology classes whenever I could. A family friend finally noticed my dual interests and suggested I study psychology engineering, similar to the field of ergonomics. Not many colleges offered that as an undergraduate degree, so I studied the broader field of industrial engineering at North Carolina State and then got a government grant to pay for a master's in ergonomics at the University of Michigan. In school I studied safety, injury prevention, industrial hygiene, and biomechanics, which looks at the body as a system of levers, pulleys, and forces. The best class was about car design because designing car interiors to fit drivers is so similar to designing work spaces to fit workers.

These days, a lot of people have something at work or as part of a hobby that causes them a degree of pain. Many people, especially politicians, say ergonomics is bunk science, but all you have to do is look at injury rates. The military is made up of thousands of people working behind desks and building and repairing equipment to support the few people going on ships. We see a lot of carpal tunnel syndrome, nerve disorder, back injuries, and tendinitis.

I never thought I would work for the navy, but they found my résumé on a Web site (there aren't a lot of ergonomists with engineering degrees) and offered me an unbelievable opportunity to build an ergonomics program from the ground up. Today I'm one of just two navy ergonomists; I support navy facilities on the East Coast. Because I work from home, my travel schedule is unbelievable. I'm essentially a consultant, and people call me if they need advice, training, or ergonomic equipment, like anti-fatigue matting for people who stand all day. Sometimes I'll go on a navy base to watch people work and I'll come up with ways to redesign their spaces. I was once on a submarine, where there's not much room to make changes. Still, we came up with a pulley system over a hatch so people didn't have to carry heavy things up and down, in and out. It was such a simple, cheap solution, and they loved it!

Once you look at the world through ergonomics glasses, you can't take them off. I never go to the grocery store without watching the cashier and thinking, I bet her shoulder hurts her at the end of the day. I consider myself to be sort of a preacher of ergonomics. I just love spreading the word.

The preceding women—music supervisor, tour guide and nude model, librarian, camp director, and ergonomist—all work at jobs that already existed in industries that, mainly by virtue of their content, inherently interested them. By contrast, the following women created their working worlds from scratch. Each is, essentially, a small-business owner not because she necessarily loves running a business, but because running her business allows her to be exposed to and support her passion.

Her pet project

Janice Brown's love of animals took years to manifest itself as a work-related endeavor. After college, a lack of confidence and direction made it difficult for Janice, now thirty-one, to extricate herself from a string of at first inspiring but ultimately unfulfilling jobs. She was a personal trainer ("The only thing I learned was how to count and converse at the same time"); a personal assistant to a successful entrepreneur ("I'd take his dog to the vet one day and go on sales calls the next"); and a saleswoman for a software company that sold to car dealers ("Sometimes, the only reason I'd get in to see dealers was because I was a woman").

Although none of these jobs inspired Janice, she always felt guilty about leaving her employer. Such misplaced anxiety only fueled her unhappiness. Finally, after a year and a half doing software sales, Janice hit bottom and sought inspiration from The Landmark Forum, a seminar that encourages people to live their lives fully. "The course reminded me that life was just too short to do something I hated," recalls Janice. Still, she lacked the courage to quit her job immediately, so she stayed employed, began exploring other opportunities, and meanwhile tried to bolster her spirits with hobbies, such as photography courses and playing with her dog, Luna. Walking the White Shepherd mixed breed in the park near her home became the best part of Janice's day. It was only in those moments that she felt completely present.

While walking Luna after work I discovered a cool underground dog-owner community. About thirty people would gather at the local park to walk and exercise their dogs. There were big dogs and little dogs. No one knew any of the guardians' names, just the names of their pets! Slowly, I got to know people and we'd talk about training, feeding—even city laws that dictated where dogs could and could not poop. It was amazing how much there was to discuss.

One day I arrived at my weekly seminar and told the instructor I saw nothing in my future. "Congratulations!" she said. "For the first time you have nothing in your future!" I actually understood what she meant. I felt like I'd spent my whole life seeing what other people wanted me to be. I was trying to be the perfect salesperson, the perfect friend, the perfect daughter, the perfect wife—whatever I thought others wanted—so I would feel good about myself. I even changed my personality when I was with different groups, and it was like I had these separate lives. But people just wanted me to be myself. That moment I thought, I can just be Janice. But it was scary, because I had no idea who Janice was. But at least I'd realized all this and could finally look for the authentic me.

A few days later I was watching Oprah on television at the health club and thought, I want to edit Oprah's magazine. Out of nowhere this is what I wanted to do. I sat with the idea for a while. A few days later I was out with a friend after my photography class and said out loud, "You know, it would be really cool if there were a magazine in Chicago for pets and animals, because there is so much going on in that community." We started brainstorming, and it got me really excited. I did some research and discovered a local pet magazine already existed, which made me miserable because someone already had my idea. But I surprised myself, and instead of going into my usual life-is-over spiral, I called the magazine's editors. They didn't need another person on their staff of two, but it was okay, because I realized that their magazine wasn't my magazine; I had a unique vision. In my heart I knew I wanted to create a one-stop resource for Chicago-area pet guardians, and a fun magazine that helped animals through promoting adoption, rescue, and proper care. My family thought I was crazy, but when my beliefs and actions were finally aligned, when I finally believed in myself and had a passion, I was no longer stopped by other people's opinions.

Janice was also practical, and a lot of her newfound confidence came by networking in Chicagoland's community of pet owners and educating herself. She attended a new-business workshop and volunteered for animal-related activities and fund-raisers, and she sought out pet-related opportunities. For example, when a fellow pet owner introduced Janice to a writer in need of a research assistant for his book about urban doggie haunts, Janice volunteered for the job.

I don't know whether you believe in fate, but when you put yourself out there, things just start happening. People seemed to show up when I needed them. My dad offered to share his marketing expertise. A woman who randomly popped into my life offered to transfer my whole database to Microsoft Access. People wrote articles for free. My first instinct was to not accept help, because I wanted to do it all—I think women have a tough time accepting help. But when people offer, when help comes, take it! They want to contribute, and when you shun them, it's just bad karma.

Janice put the newspaper's printing fee on her credit card—with her husband's blessing and support—and, seven months after her epiphany, she and her husband distributed 15,000 copies of the whimsical *Chicagoland Tails* throughout the city. They stacked free copies in pet stores, coffee shops, and health clubs, and carefully recorded how many copies were taken from each location. That readership data was used to woo potential advertisers for upcoming issues.

Twenty-three issues and more than 100,000 readers later, advertisers now seek Janice out, and *Chicagoland Tails* is profitable. A regional version, *Twin City Tails,* exists in Minneapolis–St. Paul, and Janice has plans to launch magazines for several more markets. A recent thirty-two-page issue was packed with articles about how to keep pets healthy, take dogs camping, and follow "pet etiquette" at the beach. There were ads for obedience trainers and dog collars as well as groomers and pet photographers. And in every issue there's a letter from *Chicagoland Tails*'s very busy, very happy, and quite confident editor and publisher, Janice Brown. In her picture, she's smiling.

Once I decided that I wanted to help animals, it seemed like such a natural choice. My whole mission was to make a difference for animals in Chicago, and each issue has a call to action, something people can do to help their pets. That mission has become my passion. When I was young I used to dress up my dog in overalls and ponytails. Everyone knew I loved animals—everyone except me! Now I take my dog to work with me, and my daughters, too. Of course, there are days when I freak out and say I'm not superwoman and I can't run a business and have a baby and have a life. Remember that scene in the movie Private Benjamin, *when one night during basic training Goldie Hawn walks around in the rain, just hating military life, and cries out, "I want to go out to lunch, I want to be normal again!" Some days, that's how I feel.*

Here's a big part of why I love what I do: The magazine's mission is not about me—it's about the animals. My job is not about how I look or how I feel or how much money I make or what others think of me. And thank God it's not about me, because the whole "all-about-me" thing really wasn't working.

She can look a grizzly bear in the eye and kiss him on the lips.

Lynne Seus is also an animal lover, albeit of a wilder breed than the domestic pets Janice favors. Lynne, fifty-six, and her husband, Doug, train wolves and bears to appear in movies. The couple live and work in Heber, Utah, about forty-five miles from Salt Lake City, where they run Wasatch Rocky Mountain Wildlife. There, at the base of a sprawling mountain range, the short, cherubic Lynne and the scruffy, bearded Doug are ensconced in a seven-acre compound. Their little company is indeed an extreme example of how to turn a passion into a career, but it's also a telling example of how creative Lovers can be.

We began thirty years ago with a crazy dream and started our little company with lots of little animals, like wolves, skunks, bobcats, and raccoons. Our parents freaked out and told us to snap out of it and get real jobs. But it wasn't that easy for me. I love animals and was the kind of kid who was always playing in the woods, dragging home an interesting toad or a baby robin with a broken wing. When I was sixteen, I got in trouble when I secretly cared for an orphan fawn in our basement for several weeks.

Over the years, Lynne and Doug's animals got bigger, much bigger, and the little company grew large enough to support the Seuses and their three children. Not an easy or always lucrative business, training animals for film had its dry spells. In the early days, Lynne's "dirt-poor family" drove beat-up cars and shopped at thrift stores for clothes. To bring in more money, Doug fought the acting establishment for residuals—a financial benefit reserved for human actors—arguing that animal actors should be valued on a par with human actors. Despite opposition from the actors' union, Doug and Lynne didn't let up and eventually secured a federal tax identification number for their most famous four-legged actor, a big-hearted dark brown Kodiak named Bart. Bart was becoming known as the John Wayne of bears, working with dozens of well-known actors, including Daryl Hannah in *Clan of the Cave Bear* (1986), Brad Pitt in *Legends of the Fall* (1994), and Anthony Hopkins in *The Edge* (1997). In 1998, Lynne even escorted Bart to the Academy Awards in Beverly Hills, where he presented an award. But just as business was looking up, Bart's career—and health—came crashing down.

In June we noticed a lump in Bart's paw and when we took him to the vet, the doctor gave him only a month and a half to live. There was only one thing for Doug and I to do: We quit working and nurtured Bart, fed him organic products three times a day, and treated him holistically because—my goodness—he'd taken care of us for so many years! We were able to extend his life eighteen more months, but eventually the last good thing we could do for Bart was put him down.

So, in April 2000, we called the veterinarian to do just that.

An angel must have stepped in, because right after talking to the vet, the Alaska Department of Fish and Game called us. It needed to find a home for two orphan brown bear cubs that had just lost their mother. Apparently, a local hunter shot her dead. It was so sad, but at the same time it was as if Bart had waited until the cubs arrived at our home before he left us. The little cubs are now two years old. We call the female Honey Bump because she runs so fast that her legs can barely keep up with her and she bumps into everything. The little male just had to be called Little Bart. He's precocious, bright, and naughty, and a full 900 pounds! I don't know how big he'll get.

Note that it is a love of animals, and not a love of Hollywood, that intrigues Lynne. The rhythm of her daily routine—the process—truly fulfills her. That's important because the amount of time she spends on the set, or on the red carpet, pales in comparison with the hours she spends with her husband and their animals behind the scenes.

I like the training process because the animals also enjoy it. Their intelligence is truly amazing. I think wild animals today are the result of a natural selection process; the animals that weren't so bright didn't survive. Bears can actually learn to do tasks with only one repetition. For example, we were training Bart for an aspirin commercial and Bart had to put his paw on his forehead as if he had a "bear" of a headache. We thought, How can we get him to do that? Doug had Bart sit down, and he put a clothespin on Bart's fur, like a little barrette. Bart took his big paw to wipe it off, and as soon as he did, we shouted, "Good boy! You're good!" and fed him a piece of fruit. It didn't take long for Bart to realize that whenever he wiped his forehead, a piece of cantaloupe would come flying through the air into his mouth! I often think that if the animals weren't in active training, they'd get really bored.

Even though our animals have a good and safe life, I always feel like— damn it to hell—they must miss something by not being truly wild and free. This is why it's my responsibility to do everything in my power to make it okay that they've spent their life like this. Thankfully, the back of our property abuts a hill in a valley, and there's a nice stream with good water flow and a swimming hole. It's pure joy when the bears run down that hill and do a flying belly flop into the pool. It's like watching your five-year-old kid on a hot summer day. They run around and do little jumps in the air for pure joy. That's what it's all about. Playing with our animals is the joy of my life. The whole reason we started this business— and were maniacal enough to stick with it—is because we can get up in the morning, look a grizzly bear in the eye, kiss him right on the lips, and give him a hug. The wolves are so happy to see us in the morning; they wag their tails and roll on their backs and kiss me on the face. There is such joy in being able to share our lives with these truly magical creatures that—through no fault of their own—were orphaned or born in captivity and grew up in our human world.

The sense of purpose Lynne feels by providing orphaned animals a safe, comfortable home is key to her on-the-job happiness. Lynne and Doug have earned the respect of animal rights groups, they are fully licensed by the USDA's Animal and Plant Health Inspection Service, and they donate a portion of their income to run a not-for-profit organization called Vital Ground, which helps preserve land for wildlife across the country. As for the Seuses' own little plot of land in Utah, "It's heaven," says Lynne. Indeed, she has done her best to create heaven on earth for her animals, as well as herself.

In her own words

MaryLouise van der Wilden, 64
Boutique Owner and President, Le Papillon
Rumson, New Jersey

MaryLouise is a lover of fashion accessories—jewelry, belts, handbags, scarves, shoes—and has operated her own boutique for more than thirty years. The 4,400-square-foot store, Le Papillon, with its hushed elegance, sells four-dollar cocktail napkins, twenty-dollar pillboxes, pants, sweaters, purses, furniture, and home accessories for up to $2,000. MaryLouise, a widow of several years now, earns between $50,000 and $75,000 a year—enough to keep her happy and keep up her own appearance.

My own style has always been very Chanel—I usually wear gold jewelry, a large pin, and always a scarf. When I was little I'd tie scarves around my waist as a belt; in high school we tied scarves around our necks like a dog collar. I was always experimenting. Maybe I'd put a couple necklaces together and twist them. I loved handbags and hardware. Not my mother—she liked things plain, nothing more. Her theory was always to take off one piece of jewelry so your look is not excessive; my feeling is add another piece, the more the better! My first job was in high school, at Bamberger's, a huge department store. I loved playing with the jewelry, doing displays. In college I majored in business administration with a slant toward retailing, and later I worked as a buyer at Bendel's and Bergdorf Goodman in Manhattan. My husband was transferred, and we moved to New Jersey. I commuted for years into New York to work, but one day, after my merchandising manager came to visit me in the suburbs, she told me I should open a store where I lived. I thought she was kidding, but she and my husband eventually talked me into it. More and more women were moving out of New York with their families, and they needed fashionable places to shop.

My true love is accessories, and I love building an outfit around something very basic. You either have an eye for style or you don't; it is kind of a sixth sense. I can tell by looking at people and watching them shop. If people put a hat on the back of their head, I know they don't have a clue, but if they pull the hat down in front, I know they're in synch with what's going on. Most of the women who come in here are accessories-handicapped, and helping them make the right selection for their situation is very gratifying.

I never spend all day standing behind the counter, because I hate sitting still (I figured that out as a kid, when I hated piano but loved dance). Now, I keep moving: I'm either on the floor selling or fiddling with displays; in back unpacking orders; organizing fashion shows; traveling to gift shows to buy accessories; or going into New York City to buy product. Every day is something different. We don't have a cash register, just calculators and a little cash drawer. The one thing I don't like is bookkeeping—maybe because I hate sitting. I used to do it, but now a great gal comes in a few hours every week and does it in a quarter of the time it took me.

Actually, my husband did my accounting before he passed away, and there is no doubt that working at my store helped me cope with his death. It gave me a reason to get up every day, get dressed, and focus on something other than how much I missed him. Now that I think about it, the job I love helped me get through the pain of losing the love of my life.

Her true love

The love of Diane Warren's life is not a person, but a piano. At forty-six, Diane is the songwriter behind some of contemporary music's biggest hits, and from her Hollywood studio, the short-haired brunette has composed lyrics and music for more than eighty movies as well as hundreds of performers, including Celine Dion ("Because You Loved Me"), LeAnn Rimes ("Can't Fight the Moonlight"; "How Do I Live"), Aerosmith ("I Don't Want to Miss a Thing"), Cher ("If I Could Turn Back Time"), and Toni Braxton ("Unbreak My Heart") as well as Faith Hill, Trisha Year-wood, Gloria Estefan, Mary J. Blige, and Eric Clapton. Remember

Laura Branigan's "Solitaire" in 1983, or "Rhythm of the Night," by De-Barge in 1985? Those were the first of some ninety top-ten hits for Diane.

Like other Lovers, Diane started her own company and founded Realsongs after she quit another songwriting house and, for legal reasons, could not work for a competitor. Diane remains the company's core producer of its singular product: hit songs. Yet despite her fortune, despite her two houses and her awards, it's the music itself that consumes Diane every day, six days a week, from 8:15 in the morning until, well, whenever. In fact, her actual composing studio is anything but glamorous: Diane works in a tiny room she calls "The Cave," which is a small space cluttered with multiple keyboards and littered with song sheets, tapes, and, she says, unknown small creatures. The room has not been cleaned in eighteen years. Even the window shades are disintegrating. But Diane makes no apologies for the state of her creative annex. "My studio is my safe haven. I'm happier in this room than in my beautiful houses."

Unlike some of the other Lovers, Diane is much more married to the process her work requires. An admitted sufferer from obsessive-compulsive disorder, Diane is almost addicted to writing songs that, for the most part, are about love. New love. Unrequited love. Love in peril. Love lost. That said, Diane is not a Lover of romance, per se. Rather, she loves the craft of creating music with mass appeal, and to that end she understands that love is the most universal of themes—even if the shy, single songwriter has yet to find it for herself.

As a kid I loved music. It was very healing and like a friend to me. I was basically a lonely kid who lost herself in the radio and subconsciously learned about what makes a hit. When my dad, who was an insurance salesman, bought me my first guitar, I started making up my own songs. I'd look on all my sister's records to see who wrote what, and I even got a subscription to Billboard *magazine. I was probably the only little kid who knew who wrote and produced every hit song. By fourteen, I was pretty obsessed with it.*

I was going to drop out of school, but my dad said he'd only support me if I stayed in college, so I took classes that didn't require much effort— anything short of basket weaving. Usually I'd sit in the back of the classroom and write songs. My mom was worried I would not be able to make a living at songwriting, and that I'd be hanging out on street corners with a guitar and cup in my hands. Despite her concerns, I just moved on, as I always do, and didn't let opposition get in my way. In the song I wrote for the movie Legally Blonde Two, there's a line that says, "Put up a roadblock, we'll just run right through it." That pretty much describes my career. I would knock on publishers' doors and be rejected . . . which just sucks! Acceptance is a way of feeling loved. When someone loves your song, they love you on some level. All of the hits I've had don't make rejection hurt any less. But I have a thick skin, and the fire in my soul kind of keeps me going. I always knew in my heart I would be successful, but I had to have a lot of persistence and knock on a lot of doors. My first break came in 1983, when I started working as a staff writer for Jack White, a producer for Laura Branigan. He asked me to prepare English lyrics for a French song, which is how I came up with "Solitaire." Unlike some songwriters who can't make it as a singer and fall back on writing, I never wanted to perform. I'm not a good singer; plus, I'm totally shy and have really bad stage fright. Really, I just dread going onstage, even for a second. I've been nominated for Oscars, and the times I didn't win I was actually relieved because I wouldn't have to go onstage to accept the award.

I don't think I really know my process. I show up at my piano and just become the person I'm writing about. Almost like method songwriting, I feel it when I write it. I rarely write songs with myself in mind, although "Because You Loved Me" for the movie Up Close and Personal was my chance to thank my dad, even though he was no longer alive to hear it. I love coming up with new ways of saying something that's been said a hundred times, or writing an original melody. I can't put too much thought into how I come up with the melodies. For movies, I like to sit down and talk to the director so I know where his head is. I usually watch the movies at my house or studio, then sit down at the piano and it's like my mind is a computer. I just go to work.

I just love the process of coming up with the songs. There is a challenge in that for me. To be a hit, a song has to get on the radio and go all the way up the charts; but I don't love a song any less if it's not successful . . . if your kid doesn't graduate Harvard, he still may be a great kid. My songs are my kids. To go to a concert and see the whole place singing a song I *wrote, or to pull up to a stoplight and see people in other cars cranking up my song, that is fucking great!*

I don't consider myself a famous person. The money is nice, and for the past fifteen years I haven't had to work a day in my life, but I still do. It's weird, I finished a great song yesterday, and today it's like, "What have I done lately?" I haven't taken a vacation in years. Why? I'm never as happy as when I'm creating.

Fact: Few women can spin a hobby into a multimillion-dollar endeavor. But that's not what's so appealing about Diane as a Happy 100 member. Diane doesn't love work because it makes her rich and famous. Were that the case, she'd spend a lot more time in the public eye than in a dark, cluttered "cave" composing love songs.

In her own words

Keri Wright, 34
Travel Coordinator, FitzBradshaw Racing
Mooresville, North Carolina

Keri loves NASCAR, the National Association for Stock Car Auto Racing. As the travel coordinator for FitzBradshaw Racing—three teams of drivers who race cars sponsored by the Navy, Supercuts, and Hot Tamales in what's known as the Busch Series—Keri arranges travel and accommodations for some forty team members who travel to thirty-four different races a year. She is a great example of someone who learned that just because you burn out at one job does not mean you must leave an industry you love. Sometimes, all you must do to stay happy is switch jobs.

Ten years ago, when I got a two-week temp job at the Talladega Superspeedway in Alabama, one of the NASCAR tracks, I'd never seen a stock car race in my life. I thought, Where's the fun watching people drive in circles? I was offered a job as a full-time secretary with the speedway's public relations department, and after working there for six months I finally understood what makes NASCAR so exciting. There are so many different levels of competition and strategy going into a race. Each driver knows what place he has to finish to get so many points for his team and for himself, and exactly what he has to do to advance to the banquet, where top teams receive awards and money at the end of the season. There might be two or three drivers on a team, and sometimes you watch and wonder if one driver will give up a win for himself to help his teammate win and get more points. Other times teammates try to beat each other to the finish line. The competition is not just among teams and drivers, but car makers like Ford and Chevrolet, which is why it's so important for a car that gets into a wreck to get back on the track as fast as possible.

But what caught me most off guard about NASCAR was the family atmosphere. Each week, thousands of people come together to compete. When they're on the track they're competitive, but off the track they have so much fun together. Between the drivers, the crew members, and the support staffs, there is not a lot of turnover in NASCAR, so even if folks switch teams you still see the same people all the time, and you get to know their families. Eventually, NASCAR becomes an extension of your own family.

For several years I worked as a publicist and my client was Team Yellow. Much of my job was about building a fan base for the drivers and getting them in front of the public and the press. I worked out of my house and spent Monday through Wednesday preparing press kits for whatever track we were scheduled to go to. I usually arranged media interviews in advance, but once our team got to the speedway, I'd often just wander around a track and look for reporters to come and talk to Yellow's drivers.

Because there are NASCAR races every weekend, I traveled a lot . . . too much. I enjoyed the job but just got so tired. Even when you love something like I love NASCAR, traveling all the time takes a toll. It got to the point that I had to make a decision: I could keep doing publicity knowing it would eventually turn into just a "job" rather than something I loved, or I could find something else in the industry that did not require travel. I put the word out that I was looking for another job, and a friend told me that another team, FitzBradshaw, needed a travel coordinator.

I'm an organizing fanatic and that's really what this job is, handling all of the teams' travel arrangements, from plane reservations to rental cars and hotels to maps. (I also handle the teams' show-car program, sched-uling our two promotional cars for 560 showings a year at places like malls and Wal-Mart.) I walk a fine line: The teams have to stay within their budget, but during race weeks many hotels raise prices. I don't want the guys to stay in a place that has roaches running across the floor, but I also don't want to upset the sponsors, who pay the bills. The trick is to find accommodations for many people in a good price range, about $100 per room. I always try for a Super 8–type of hotel because it's clean but not $200 a night. I am extremely lucky that the group I work with is not as spoiled as a few of the other teams, which would only consider staying at a Sheraton. This group is very flexible, and they appreciate whatever I can get them.

I no longer attend the races like I did when I was a publicist, and I really don't miss it, especially on days when it's raining or really hot at a track. Besides, in this job, I have the benefit of the NASCAR family atmosphere without having to deal with all the elements! I still get to interact with so many people in NASCAR and see my friends. My office is in the same building where the race cars are built and maintained, and I work closely with all the teams' crew chiefs.

NASCAR is all about the team, and most people in this sport understand that the team is only as good as its weakest link. And even though I don't go to races or work with the cars, I am still an important link. The drivers and crew trust that when they get off a plane their rental cars and their hotel rooms are going to be ready for them, and it's so nice to hear the guys tell me so. Plus, I have my life back. My hours are eight to five, and so I finally have weekends and holidays free—most important, I still work in the sport that I really love.

One of the most common traits among Lovers is that their love, their passion, is rooted in childhood. That's important. If you still do not know what your own passion is, childhood is a smart place to look for it. And if in the process of reflection you identify a risky—or risqué—passion that you assume you're too old or too conservative to pursue, just close your eyes and picture Lover and model Mary in the buff at age fifty-three, living out her nude-modeling fantasies.

If she can do *that*, perhaps your passion isn't so far-fetched after all.

Chapter Two

The Thinkers

**Private banker, broadcast journalist, personal
financial planner, business consultant, product
distribution manager, retail entrepreneur,
advertising agency CEO, not-for-profit foundation
consultant, and research scientist**

Recall the last time you felt lost in an activity, when your concentration was so intense, you thought of nothing other than the task at hand. Whatever activity you were engaged in (keep it clean, please), it was likely physically, emotionally, or intellectually challenging, if not painful at times. Yet, you knew you could eventually reach the goal, and there was probably some form of feedback that let you know whether you were making progress. If the activity did, indeed, meet the above criteria, you were likely in a state some call "flow."

Flow is a highly desirable state of mind, and its relationship to happiness challenges traditional assumptions about when people feel their best; mainly the conventional wisdom that they are "happy" when at ease or relaxing as opposed to engaged in challenging activities. The concept of flow evolved out of research by Professor Mihaly Csikszentmihalyi while at the University of Chicago. Csikszentmihalyi tried to answer a basic question: When do people feel happy? He and his team interviewed thousands of people all over the world about how they felt while doing a variety of activities, and his theory is based on the notion that people are *not* happiest during leisure or downtime, but instead when engaged in an activity so engulfing and engaging that nothing else matters. A flow experience is so satisfying that people will do it even at great cost and discomfort just for the sheer sake of doing it. While some extreme examples include rock climbing or running a marathon, experiencing flow is not limited to physical tasks, and in his book *Flow: The Psychology of Optimal Experience,* Csikszentmihalyi writes that some of the most exhilarating experiences people undergo are "generated inside the mind, triggered by information that challenge our ability to think," such as completing a crossword puzzle or writing computer programs.

For an example I'll turn to myself. After I read *Flow* in my early twenties, I realized I was in flow when I was writing. I find the writing process mentally trying and often emotionally painful, but time always flies when I write, my goals are usually clear (to complete an article or a book), and I receive feedback from editors and readers. I have often described the writing process as trying to put together a jigsaw puzzle after someone has thrown away the top of the box: The final picture reveals itself only once a piece of writing has been completed, and the process of snapping together ideas, paragraphs, sentences, and words just engulfs me. To be happy at work, I concluded, I should be in flow as many hours a day as possible, which meant I had to be writing.

The Thinkers—and I consider myself one—are working women who seek out and engage in mental flow. Their activities tend to be restricted to the "mental manipulation of concepts," as Csikszentmihalyi puts it, as opposed to physical or logistical tasks. Thinkers tend to research, collect data, listen, analyze, synchronize, coordinate, pull together, figure out, assemble, distribute, disseminate, deduct, and decide. To achieve a mental state of flow, you must be skilled in the rules of a specific activity's "symbolic domain." For example, a writer must understand grammar and effective narrative structure; a poet must be familiar with the tenets of poetry; a computer programmer must know C++ or Java. The more familiar with and skilled at a particular domain or topical area a person is, the more engaging the activity becomes. Thinkers like to play with ideas, solve problems, and create new ways to describe reality. They are happy at work when they can get lost in the flow of thought on a daily basis.

The bulk of a Thinker's work-related activity happens in her head as she listens, processes, calculates, or synthesizes disparate bits of information. Although there is usually a business-oriented goal at hand—for example, the Wall Street banker must analyze financial markets to make money for her company—it is in the very act of synthesizing and problem solving that these women find true fulfillment. Many of the Thinkers are not intellectuals in the academic sense, but they are smart, creative experts in their particular field (or, rather, in their symbolic domain).

While Thinkers are not necessarily in flow 100 percent of the time, most of their jobs offer opportunities for intense thought process. Writes Csikszentmihalyi, "Great thinkers have always been motivated by the enjoyment of thinking rather than by the material rewards that could be gained by it." Indeed, a key element of flow is that an activity is an end in itself and is intrinsically rewarding, even if initially undertaken for other reasons. For example, investing in the stock market to make money is not a flow experience, but analyzing and synthesizing economic trends is.

Thinkers illustrate how the state of flow—and the form of happiness it engenders—can exist in the workplace. True, the flow theory requires people to recast the conventional notion of happiness, which assumes work is a means to an idle end rather than an end in itself. If you automatically assume work is not something to be enjoyed, you may be ignoring the fact that you're already in flow at work and, thus, quite content. Csikszentmihalyi's advice: When it comes to work, heed the evidence of your senses. In other words, embrace immediate experience; don't let yourself fall back on stereotypes of happiness and assume it will find you only at a later date in retirement, at home, or on weekends. For Thinkers, joy resides in the very act of working through problems and mental puzzles, with all the inherent pain and challenge.

Mornings are crazy; that's why she loves them.

From her sixth-floor office in Manhattan, Mary Callahan Erdoes not only overlooks bustling Park Avenue but oversees more than $250 billion in assets for wealthy individuals. Each of her clients is worth, at the very least, $25 million. That's a lot of money for anyone to be responsible for, and as head of investments for JPMorgan Private Bank, Mary, a thirty-six-year-old married mother of a newborn, is also one of the firm's youngest people at her level. For Mary's willingness to invest huge sums of money on behalf of the well-heeled, she earns a seven-figure salary. Yet contrary to stereotypes about rapacious Wall Street executives, getting rich is not Mary's primary motivation or source of happiness at work.

This Thinker's daily rewards are much more cerebral.

In order to make investment decisions, Mary's expertise and intellect are called upon each day to help interpret how events around the world—elections, terrorist attacks, consumer spending, corporate earnings—might affect the economy and her clients' investments. The process of gathering and connecting disparate data is an intellectual exercise that completely consumes Mary from the moment she wakes up.

My mornings are crazy, but that's why I love them. The day starts at six A.M. when I read the newspaper, watch CNBC, and get e-mails off my BlackBerry to prepare for our global team's morning conference call, which is when we assess what happened in the Asian and European markets overnight. After the call we tell everyone around the firm what we expect to happen in the coming weeks and decide what to advise our private banking clients to do with their money. It's not that clients move their money around every day, but they want to hear what we're thinking. Anyone can tell them that an analyst upgraded a stock; that's just information. We have to tell them what to do, and every morning we must offer advice. There's a lot of pressure. The stakes are high when dealing with this amount of personal wealth.

Although it's exhausting, I love pulling together very complicated bits of information from economists, analysts, news reports, and government statistics. We synthesize and work toward the bottom line: What does it all mean for our clients' investments? It's not that my clients aren't smart—many have built very successful businesses—but they may not know much about the financial markets, and drilling down into the basics is part of my success. I find it rewarding to boil down the many events that happen on Wall Street and explain them to others.

Mary could apply the same synthesizing work at a variety of well-paying jobs in the financial sector, but not all of them would satisfy her to this degree. That's because there is an underlying emotional element inherent to managing individuals' money that, simply, makes Mary feel good. That personal connection was absent when, in a previous job, Mary managed money on behalf of faceless companies. Dealing with people is more fulfilling and tangible, and Mary truly feels her efforts make a difference in others' lives. "Every client has unique needs and goals," she says. "Some want to pass money on to charities, others want to make money for their children and grandchildren. What I like is helping all my clients keep perspective about what they want to do with their money. It's all too easy to get caught up in what I call 'Monday-morning-cocktail investing,' which means wanting to buy stocks based on something you heard at a party on a Saturday night. I do a good job making sure my clients stay grounded in their long-term goals." Not only does Mary want to get up in the morning and *perform* her job, she feels good about *why* she does it, "helping people inch toward long-term goals."

Mary is a Thinker whose daily sense of flow is reinforced by an overall sense of purpose. However, if she worked at a firm whose practices she considered unethical, she would likely not be as content. The point: A job that provides both flow and meaning can yield greater satisfaction. That said, even Mary has had moments when she questioned the purpose behind her work.

In the past few years, Wall Street has been especially challenging for investors and people like me who advise them. There's been so much negative news, which can wear on the spirit. On the first anniversary of September 11, I thought to myself, Am I spending my time doing the right things in life? I help rich people. *But still, I wake up every morning and can't wait to get to work, and I probably stay much too late. I couldn't have gotten through the past couple of years if I didn't love what I do.*

We can't let Mary slip away without inquiring how her multimillion-dollar salary contributes to her work happiness. So, what about the money? Says Mary, "Sure, I enjoy going to my clients' homes for dinner and getting to know them, but I don't go on their boats and fancy planes, and I won't go on trips with them. That could compromise my ability to think objectively. But I'd be lying if I said that money doesn't matter. It would be very different to work as hard as I do, and for as many hours, for only a little pay.

My salary and performance bonus make up for some of the life I give up to do this job, and I hope I can make up for the lost time later in life."

Her synthesizing mind

"You know, it's not cool to be happy," broadcast journalist Lesley Stahl stated point-blank. "It's cool to be *cool,* laid-back, entertaining." Fair enough, but Lesley recently told an auditorium full of people that she loved her career, so, cool or not, I wanted to know why.

Lesley has been an on-air journalist since the 1970s. Before her current jobs as coeditor of CBS's weekly newsmagazine *60 Minutes* and anchor of *48 Hours Investigates,* Lesley covered the White House through three presidential administrations. With an interviewing style that's at once pointed and personable, Lesley has reported on events as wide ranging as Watergate, the assassination attempt on Ronald Reagan, and the 1991 Gulf War. She's covered economic summits and political conventions and reported live from every presidential election night since 1974. More recently, Lesley has been investigating the events surrounding September 11, 2001.

At first I pegged Lesley as a Determinator, but after reading her autobiography and talking with her about why she loves what she does, I decided Lesley, while undeniably ambitious, is first and foremost a Thinker. The pleasure she takes in journalism is less about power or public praise than about the daily process of down-and-dirty reporting.

At sixty-two, Lesley Stahl still likes to ask questions.

Lesley grew up with a stay-at-home mother who impressed on her that a "career, not just a job" was the true route to happiness. Her mother also believed—even more than her blond, blue-eyed, cerebral daughter did—that looking good was crucial to professional success. Meanwhile, professors at Lesley's college repeatedly told the all-female student body "that they could do anything with their lives," and Lesley grew up believing she could. Journalism, however, was not on her radar, and she actually stumbled into the profession in her mid-twenties.

I was working for the mayor of New York on his speechwriting staff, and I was always wandering into the press office. One day I asked a reporter what he did all day. He told me every minute of his day—how he made phone calls and synthesized information—and it clicked! I had never worked for my school newspaper, but I loved synthesizing, and here was someone who did that professionally. In that moment I said, "That is me! I have to be a journalist!" I actually thought I would be a science reporter and applied to The New York Times, but the only place I could get a job was as a researcher at NBC's election unit. I was not wedded to TV, but I had always loved politics, and because I just wanted to be a journalist I took the job. So that was how I started, back in 1967.

When the Equal Employment Opportunity Act passed in 1972—which essentially forced companies to diversify their workforces—Lesley applied to the three major networks and was hired to work in CBS's Washington Bureau. In *Reporting Live*, Lesley's autobiography, she freely acknowledges that she was among a cadre of women and minorities "raked in" by affirmative action. Writes Lesley, "I knew my colleagues saw me as a lightweight, unqualified to join the Super Bowl champs of TV news. I had to find ways to convey my seriousness, to send out signals that I was resolute and earnest, not what the wrapping said I was. So I wore my glasses and worked around the clock. I also promised myself I would never blame my setbacks on sexism." Lesley's goal was not to prove herself as a *woman*, but as a *journalist*.

In those days [the bosses] told women in journalism they would not be promoted, and I think many of us were just happy to be inside the newsroom, our expectations were not high. I was just so tickled that I was doing what I wanted to do, just happy to be there. I never saw a ladder, I never looked up, it was not about climbing. I was just happy to stay in the game, and that meant getting the good assignments, covering stories I was interested in, and stories that made a difference. My ambition was not to get a bigger job, but to get good reporting assignments.

One of Lesley's first assignments was to cover, as it was explained to her, "the arrest of some men who had broken into one of the buildings in the Watergate complex," and it was by reporting on President Richard Nixon and the Watergate scandal in D.C. that Lesley, with a combination of moxie and self-doubt, was thrown into political reporting. She diligently cold-called as many as thirty sources a day, asking dozens of questions in search of scoops. She learned not to smile on camera so she'd come across as authoritative, and she suppressed her "urge to weep" when the network's contemptuous male camera crews ignored her. And despite her own reservations, Lesley became a "stakeout queen," hurling questions at high-level government officials as they left their houses to go jogging or pick up the morning newspaper. Yet for all her nerve, she was vulnerable and routinely called her parents after every broadcast for affirmation regarding her on-air performance. "So much of my young adult life was determined by my mother, and I admit that openly. I am not proud, but it is just true," says Lesley.

After Lesley herself became a mother in her mid-thirties, she only took a three-week maternity leave, fearful that having a baby would mean she'd be assigned easier stories. The opposite happened, and when her baby was six weeks old, Lesley began anchoring the *CBS Morning News*. Not long after, she was named CBS's official White House correspondent, where she faced new challenges, such as breaking into the Carter administration's inner circle. But Lesley also attended White House press conferences and traveled abroad with the Washington press corps, and she loved covering conventions—often as the only female reporter. Slowly, she started to scoop her competitors and excel at her craft.

The 1980s were a tougher period, for even as Lesley became more experienced she lived in constant fear that competitors, such as reporter Sam Donaldson, knew something she did not. Then there were the stereotypes that continued to dog female journalists. Wrote Lesley in her book, "When I persisted, I was badgering; when Sam [Donaldson] persisted, he was pursuing." Lesley continued to cover the White House through the first Bush administration and the Gulf War and went on to host *America Tonight* with Charles Kuralt. Then, in 1991, with twenty years of reporting in her wake, Lesley was offered a job at *60 Minutes*, where she quite happily works today.

What is so interesting about Lesley's story is that, unlike most women at the peak of their careers, the actual job duties Lesley performs daily have changed very little since the day she started. From day one she has reported, questioned, cultivated sources, and written and rewritten copy.

And she essentially does the same thing at *60 Minutes*. That's why enjoying *process* is so critical. If Lesley did not like synthesizing facts and wrapping her mind around new information, she probably would have quit long ago. "You can never make enough phone calls," she still says about her work. Of course, her skills have improved. Lesley is more confident than she once was, and her priorities have shifted from breaking news to providing more in-depth insight. When Lesley conducts an interview, be it with Paul Newman or the president of the United States, she wants her audience to see her subjects thinking, not just responding.

When I first got to 60 Minutes, *Don Hewitt [the show's producer] was very concerned I was so myopically involved in D.C. that I would not be able to become the well-rounded reporter he wanted. Don describes the show as a repertory company, and over the years I have played all parts. Every week I do a different story, and I don't think there's ever been one that has not interested me. Sometimes I do investigative pieces, other times I interview a quirky person or tell a story no one ever dreamed they'd be interested in. Each story has its own purpose. Sometimes the purpose is to entertain, sometimes to take people into a world they never knew existed, sometimes to introduce them to an inspiring person. Sometimes it's to clean out corruption.*

Lesley always viewed journalism in somewhat idealistic terms, believing the Fourth Estate exercises a necessary role in our democracy. Yet, and perhaps she is just being modest, Lesley also wonders aloud how big a difference she really makes. "The number of times I have actually effected change is minute," she says. If that is truly how she feels, then power is certainly not a primary reason why Lesley loves her work, but a side dish. Lesley also insists her chemical makeup has something to do with her generally happy state of mind. Just as some people are innately prone to depression, Lesley says she is somewhat hardwired to overcome hardship.

As for her original opinion that it's not cool to be happy, Lesley's right—at least in the context of journalism, where a reporter's job is to sniff out and dwell on problems. After all, if everyone is happy, there usually isn't a story. In the case of Lesley Stahl's career, however, there certainly is.

Every client is her puzzle.

"My husband has known me ten years and says he's never seen me this happy," says Lisa Lynn into her cell phone as she maneuvers through Denver's morning rush hour traffic in her red Acura. At thirty-three, Lisa has just completed a major career shift, leapfrogging from industrial engineer to personal financial adviser. The latter job caters to the problem solver within.

In Lisa's newfound role at American Express, the body of knowledge she is learning to master includes tedious topics many people avoid until absolutely necessary. We're talking universal life insurance, fixed annuities, mutual funds, tax-free savings bonds, real estate investment trusts, 401(k)s, IRAs, 403(b)s, and 529 college savings plans. "I'm a little twisted," admits Lisa, laughing heartily. "But I just feel everything I've done up until now has prepared me for this role. It's a very good fit."

Each of Lisa's clients, she says, is like a puzzle, and a financial adviser's role is to first identify the picture—life goals—and then determine the best investment and savings options that will make that picture a reality. The mental process is about not just the numbers game, but people. "My job is really about getting into a client's skin and figuring out what they really want. Most people don't walk into a financial adviser's office and say, 'I want to retire in twenty years and here's how I want to do it.' If they knew, they wouldn't need us. There are lots of different ways to reach a goal."

There are also lots of different ways to find work you love, and Lisa's own path to financial planner reveals some simple lessons in career hopping, as well as insight into her newly chosen profession.

When I moved to Colorado from Oregon I planned to get a master's in engineering while working full-time at a circuit-board manufacturing company. I researched local engineering programs and found them too specialized for my taste; they got deep into areas that just didn't interest me. Instead, I went to night school to get a master's in business administration. About the same time that I was taking finance courses, a position in my company opened up that mixed finance and engineering. I took the job, which entailed determining costs and preparing proposals for custom-built circuit boards, a process that required an understanding of materials, manufacturing costs, inventory needs, and profit margins. I did that job for about three years and eventually managed about seven people . . . people who used to be my peers, and I discovered something about myself: I am not good at managing others. I tried, but realized that while I may be able to motivate myself, I was not good at motivating others. I just did not bring out the best in people. I could see talent in others, but I couldn't tap it. My tendency was to jump in and help them do the work when they had trouble rather than teach them so they could figure things out for themselves.

Meanwhile, I began to consider personal finance as a career, but my life got busy: I got married, work became all-consuming, and so I forgot about my future career aspirations until my husband and I took a four-week-long financial planning course together. He had no interest in it, but I really liked it, and the passionate feelings about my career resurfaced. One day when my husband returned from a business trip, I announced I wanted to become a personal financial planner. He asked if I could make any money at it, and I said, "I don't know, but it's what I want to do." [Laughs.] I immediately started a four-month research effort to learn about the profession, and what I discovered helped steer my career. I learned that there was little regulation about who can call themselves a financial planner, and planners generally fall into two categories: investment professionals, who just care about finding rich clients and investing their money; or insurance experts, who call themselves financial planners so they can sell insurance.

Eventually I found a third camp of financial planner. A friend in Oregon has a financial planner from American Express who is part of a group of planners that concentrate on a client's whole financial picture; they don't recommend products or solutions until they have a full understanding of the person's financial needs. Several companies have these types of planners, and I interviewed with many of them, but no one was hiring—except American Express. I went to an open informational session at the company, and it turned into a formal interview.

When I told my family I was switching careers they thought I was nuts to quit a job and start over from scratch. But the more I explained to them how financial planning would use my analytic skills and my ability to work with (not manage) people—two activities they knew I enjoyed—they came to understand the job was a good fit. Now, as I go through the *employee training process, I feel as if I'm becoming the person I always wanted to be.*

The analysis uses the engineering part of my brain, and I like examining different investment and savings options. One of my clients wanted to start saving money for their daughter's college tuition, but the couple was in a high tax bracket and didn't qualify for certain savings plans. They also wanted the freedom to get their money anytime and use it for expenses other than college. I researched different types of savings plans, and in the end we settled on putting some money in a state-sponsored college savings plan (where the money can only be used for college) and the rest in tax-exempt bonds (so they can cash out whenever and for whatever they want). I was pretty proud of our plan because it gave them flexibility and gave them peace of mind. I really feel this job gives me a channel to express myself and help people in a way that I not only enjoy but that I am good at. It just feels right.

Lisa still has much to learn in her career, and her toughest challenge at this point is to become more comfortable with uncertainty. "My mentor reminds me not to spend ninety hours trying to get each client's plan exactly right, because circumstances are always changing. In six months the economy will shift, tax laws will change, and as a result I'll have to change each client's plan a bit. Being so flexible is new and tough for the engineer in me, but the doer in me—the one who had trouble managing people—loves to jump in and make changes when the time comes."

As a Thinker, Lisa is more effective managing ideas than managing people. The strength of her story lies in how she transitioned from one career to another: She was honest with herself about her weaknesses, and rather than rush blindly into a new field, she methodically researched and interviewed others until she identified a niche where she felt truly comfortable. Not surprisingly, a Thinker tends to be as methodical about her career path as she is about her work.

She asked, and she received.

It seems oxymoronic that a woman who spends every day engulfed in problems would be happy. But some Thinkers consider solving problems their primary job description and are at their intellectual and emotional peak when something broken must be fixed. As supporters of the "flow" argument suggest, happiness arises not out of a state of ease but instead out of a state of intense engagement.

A Thinker who is primarily a problem solver, a fixer, is called upon when things go awry. Her job requires her to think through a quandary, dissect a dilemma, or disentangle a client from an undesirable or even impossible situation. The solutions may be strategic (devising a marketing plan) or operational (deciding how to display a product in a store). Like firefighters, these Thinkers don't necessarily want anything to go up in flames, but when it does, they thrive.

Many problem solvers tend to work as independent consultants. In Detroit, Mary Ann (M.A.) Hastings owns MHG Consulting, a two-person firm that solves business problems which, more often than not, result from human behavior. "Companies' problems are rarely quantitative in nature," says M.A. "There is almost always a psychological aspect and an emotional component which must be addressed."

M.A. intercedes when coworkers fight, when employees quit, when executives falter, and when workers act in ways so destructive that their colleagues can't cope. Usually, the problems boil down to a lack of communication, so M.A. tries to reopen blocked channels by listening, and she encourages people to express themselves so she and others can understand what they are really saying and feeling. Think of M.A. as someone who corrals and analyzes qualitative information—emotions, opinions, preferences, human behavior—to fix broken businesses. For that deceptively simple assignment, M.A. commands upward of $2,000 a day. Her brand of problem solving is expensive, yes, but the rewards can be priceless.

One family-owned business hired M.A. when the company president— and family patriarch—was on the verge of retiring. Although he planned to hand the company over to his grown children (who already worked for him), he patronizingly referred to them as "the kids" and never discussed major business or financial issues with them. To cure the dysfunction, M.A. met with the family members away from the office and gave everyone a personality test to assess individual skills and interests. She then helped the family restructure the company and change each of the children's job descriptions to match his or her skill set. The exercise forced the father to see his children as talented adults and simultaneously helped save the business from falling into chaos.

"It's my job to pose the questions no one wants to ask," says M.A. When a Warren, Michigan, school superintendent wanted to develop a long-term strategy for his school district, M.A. gathered 900 people in one room—administrators, teachers, students, parents, even local business owners—and asked everyone to provide input about their city's schools. People shared their thoughts aloud until all 900 opinions had been accounted for. M.A. compiled the various complaints and suggestions and presented them to the superintendent to incorporate into his plan.

M.A. turned her ability to synthesize into a career back in 1981, when she was an event planner for a department store and her father's sudden death plunged her into a what's-the-meaning-of-life spiral. "I wanted to do something more meaningful with my work." Confounded, she took a battery of personality tests, after which a career counselor suggested she consider employee training. She worked for another company teaching time and stress management until she was ready to work for a large corporation. M.A.'s experience provides a great example of what can happen when Thinkers take initiative.

I did my homework to find a local Detroit company whose values meshed with my own—I am very values driven—and that's how I heard about Comerica Bank. The chairman had begun a bank-wide initiative on executive leadership and team building, and when a friend told me about it, I called the head of training, who told me he already hired an internal trainer. "No, you're making a big mistake," I insisted. So he invited me to lunch and afterward said he'd give me a chance to interview for the job. "Come in tomorrow and give a presentation for my team," he told me. I put a presentation together that night about how to train people in conflict management, gave it to four people the next day, and got the job.

Most people who have been told a job has been filled back off and move on. While M.A. says the position—which she held between 1984 and 1995—seemed almost fated to belong to her, she acknowledges that without her own initiative, she never would have landed it. "You must go after what you want, or someone else will," she counsels.

At Comerica, M.A. fostered the bank employees' so-called soft skills, such as teaching managers how to deal with difficult employees, and how to work well with others. At first, no one took her seriously.

Then one day, about three years into my job, I looked up from my desk and the bank's CEO was standing there looking at me. I'd never met him in person before. He said, "I've heard a lot about you and wanted to meet you." Then he asked, "How have you managed to get all these guys to listen to and respect you?" I knew he expected me to say that I went to Harvard, or that I had an MBA, or something impressive like that, but I told him: "I listen to them. I pay attention to what keeps them up at night, what they're worried about, their hopes and dreams." That was the truth. Listening is key to why I loved my work then, and to why I love it now.

I wasn't always a listener; in fact, I learned the hard way. I was once at a seminar and the attendees were given a group task to complete. I kneeled on my chair and started delegating orders. Ours was the first team to finish the activity, and afterward a man said to me, "Mary Ann, you're a kick-ass, jump-on-'em broad!" He thought he was complimenting my management style, but I certainly did not want to be a "kick-ass, jump-on-'em broad," so I signed up for a listening course. It turned out to be the most important class I ever took. Listening, I learned, engenders trust, and trust establishes relationships, and it is relationships that make a consultant successful. After all, I'm in a business where people open up their closets and honestly tell me what's not working in their jobs and at their companies.

M.A. left Comerica in 1995 and held a variety of different jobs before she met her former business partner, Dan; today M.A. runs the business herself, which brings this Thinker's profile full circle. Some people peg M.A. as a "feeler," or a Counselor, because she deals in those softer business issues and is a good listener. But the task of translating behaviors and preferences into business solutions is a job for the mind, not the heart. Because M.A. loves the mental challenge of solving business problems, she's a Thinker. "I know when I finish my work, people live better and easier lives. They are more successful and less stressed because of our interactions. What else is more important than making a difference in others' lives?"

In her own words

Richele Scuro, 29
Process and Methods Manager, CVS Pharmacy
Fredericksburg, Virginia

Toothpaste, shampoo, vitamins, and aspirin at the drugstore don't just magically appear on store shelves. Oh, no. There are complicated, behind-the-scenes maneuvers that determine how each product is transported from its manufacturer to a store in the least expensive and most timely manner possible. At retailer CVS, Richele Scuro is a manager who brings military precision to product distribution for 1,800 outlets.

Each CVS store has over 24,000 items to choose from, and I help make sure that the shelves are always filled, and that each store gets two of this or three of that. I manage three distribution facilities that receive product directly from manufacturers and then store, pack, and ship products directly to stores. All told, I support about 2.8 million square feet of facility space, and about 2,000 employees. I have a very high-visibility job, and it's pretty intense. We serve some stores up to three times a week. The more routine a delivery, the more laid back the environment. The less frequent a delivery, the more aggressive the environment.

I'm often called when things go wrong and need to be upgraded, fixed, or improved. When certain stores in Indiana were getting late deliveries, I analyzed the warehouse and discovered there were bottlenecks in the conveyor systems. Like cars waiting in line for a tollbooth, there was a product traffic jam on the conveyor belt because too many products had to pass through a single point to have their bar codes scanned. I suggested redesigning the whole system into six different lines and multiple scan points so the conveyor could run at a faster pace. The project cost about $5.9 million, and we just finished it a few months ago and are already seeing benefits.

Meanwhile, I'm managing multimillion-dollar projects at two other warehouse facilities: At one we're replacing equipment and upgrading the office, and at the other we're making the systems more efficient. I also handle daily operational stuff, like product volume projections and budgets, analyzing sales data, and reorganizing each warehouse so the most popular items are more accessible to our workers, who fill store orders by hand. For example, we try to make sure that every tote a picker fills includes only items displayed in the same aisle of a store. That makes it easier and faster for store clerks to stock shelves once they get our delivery. I've always been someone who loves to improve processes—at every single job I've ever held I always wanted to reorganize the files or do something like condense three reports into one.

I honestly never thought I could solve problems for a living, and it took a while for me to realize jobs like this existed. I studied electrical engineering in college and had a two-year scholarship through the navy's ROTC program. After college I worked in the military for two and a half years—I spent one year on a ship in the Mediterranean—and then bounced from job to job for about five months, just trying to bring home a paycheck. I got my CVS job through a headhunter in 1998, and I've been here ever since.

My engineering background gives me analytical and number-crunching skills, and my military experience taught me a great deal about the real world, like how to be extroverted when necessary. The military taught me to just get the job done, and that I can't always be a nice guy and make buddies. I became thick-skinned and learned not to take things personally, a lesson that helps me deal with contractors. I make my expectations very clear up front and if I don't get the results I want, my contractors know they'll hear from me. I have no problem calling someone to get what I need. Obviously, I try to keep the peace as much as I can, but in this job you can't care whether people like you or not; too many people depend on me to do the right thing. Earlier in my career it was more important for me to be liked, but that can burn you out, especially when you have a lot of responsibility and teams of people who rely on you. Feelings become irrelevant at one point. When one recent project wasn't going well, I was up the contractor's butt every week. The guy would sit across from me and I read him the riot act again and again.

One of the great things about my job has been my mentor, Duane. He's entrusted me with huge projects even though I'd never done them before. A mentor is so critical for anyone's career. When someone has faith in you, it gives you more courage and confidence. I guess project management comes naturally to me; it's not stressful to do the right thing. At the end of the day I'm a problem solver, and what's more fun than that? Not everyone wants my job, but I do love it!

She was the last one standing.

Entrepreneurs create companies that never before existed, which often means solving problems for which there is no template to follow, no prior experience to emulate. That suits Marla Malcolm Beck, who is building a chain of cosmetic and skin care stores, just fine. Unlike women who start a company because they love a particular product (such as Mary-Louise van der Wilden, who opened her fashion boutique because she loves accessories), Marla founded Washington, D.C.–based Bluemercury, Inc., because she loves analyzing data and business processes and making decisions based on her findings. Tasks such as financial modeling, managing inventory, dissecting sales numbers, and solving personnel problems not only put Marla in a state of flow but are more critical to her work happiness than anything about the actual product she sells. "The analysis and inventory management that the business requires fit my skill sets, but I could just as easily sell envelopes instead of lipstick." That said, Marla is proud of the high-end skin care products Bluemercury provides—"It's a good feeling to be able to cure skin problems or acne"—and would probably not have the same sense of satisfaction selling stationery.

Marla, thirty-three, founded Bluemercury because she wanted to be a chief executive, with the role's many responsibilities: growing sales, making profits, raising capital, hiring employees, merchandising products, and others. The college economics major and Harvard Business School graduate figured the quickest and surest way to attain the chief executive position was to leave her rank-and-file job at the white-shoe consultancy McKinsey & Co. and strike out on her own. "Look how long it took Carly Fiorina to get where she is today at HP," says Marla. "Besides, when I looked around at McKinsey, all the women who made it to senior positions left a year after they had a baby. It's unfair on some level, but I also understand that at a professional services firm like McKinsey, people are the unit of production, and the only way a firm can be successful is if its people are willing to go anywhere and work anytime."

So, with plans for children and antsy to be the boss, Marla chose not to return to McKinsey after business school and, instead, spent a year helping an entrepreneur acquire small companies. She began Bluemercury in 1999 as an Internet company during the dot-com boom. But not long after Marla stared selling online, she opened a store on the streets of Georgetown as a way to sell more inventory and prop up online sales.

I fought my investors tooth and nail to open the store. They'd call me in the middle of the night furious and tell me how stupid I was. But my husband was my support system, a serial entrepreneur who'd been through tough times—he'd been bankrupt, he'd been sued—and who ultimately convinced me that the game of entrepreneurship is about being the last one standing. If you survive long enough, then good things will happen. I now believe a business's first couple of years are about survival and cash flow, and just making sure the business simply exists. Opening a retail store was a way for me to ensure we stayed alive. Meanwhile, all those Internet companies blew through their cash and aren't around today. Bluemercury? We have sales of $10 million.

My job requirements fit my skill sets, exactly. I'm good at incremental innovation, at growing and improving things, making them bigger and better. I love taking things to the next level. I can help people figure out what they must do to make their division and the entire organization more successful. I am able to steer others in the right direction because, I think, I'm a logical rather than emotional manager. Every time we need to change the company's structure—maybe something isn't working—I look at all the pieces of the puzzle and figure out what to do. When our stores were getting low on stock, I discovered our buyer was overwhelmed with work and just could not keep up. Rather than throw money at the problem and hire someone else, I sat down with her and together we identified tasks to take off her to-do plate.

Problem solving is the nuts and bolts of running a company. In our first year I could not figure out how best to motivate salespeople. I didn't want to offer huge commissions because money was tight, and I feared the staff would promote products that customers didn't really want (I personally hate pushy salespeople at department stores). The problem I had to solve was how to get my staff to deliver great service without high commissions. The solution I came up with was, first, to hire naturally friendly people who did not need financial inducement to be nice to customers. Second, I pay commissions on a team basis so salespeople must work together. So, while Bluemercury's 1 percent commissions are much less than the retail industry average, they are low enough that salespeople aren't enticed to sell a customer a lipstick that doesn't look good on her. But when all the employees' 1 percent commissions are added together, it makes for a nice payout. These are the kinds of problems I like to solve.

Entrepreneurs and business leaders such as Marla solve grandiose business problems, and their solutions set a company's course, defining where employees spend time and focus attention. These types of Thinkers must be comfortable with the high degree of responsibility and risk their jobs demand. On the flip side, there are less high-profile Thinkers, such as financial planner Lisa Lynn and manager Richele Scuro, who are no less happy even though their synthesizing and problem solving are more isolated to a particular task or issue. The point: There are jobs for Thinkers at all levels of an organization. Marla Beck chose to be the boss; any less responsibility would leave her less satisfied.

In her own words

Shelly Lazarus, 56
Chairman and Chief Executive Officer
Ogilvy & Mather Worldwide
New York, New York

Considered one of the most powerful women in business, Shelly has worked at this global advertising agency for more than thirty years. She started managing a shampoo account and later moved laterally to work for Ogilvy's direct response division. Promotions followed: Shelly was named president of Ogilvy's New York advertising agency in 1991; president of Ogilvy North America in 1994; chief operating officer and president in 1995; and chief executive officer in 1996. Two interesting twists regarding Shelly. She never had a career plan, and says that her job today requires the same activities as when she first started working at the agency: synthesizing marketing tools to improve a company's business. As you'll see, this is one Thinker who never predicted happiness at work would come from running a company.

Growing up, my father worked and my mother didn't, and it was assumed I'd go to college, get educated, and then get married and work until I had kids. Women couldn't get into Yale and Harvard at the time, so if you were smart and capable and academically strong, you attended an all-women's college like Smith, which I did. I picked Smith because it was the happiest campus I visited. There was so much energy. The women were warm and caring and fun and capable. Wellesley felt a lot colder, more ice-maiden-like. Since I was supposed to get married, it didn't matter what I studied, and so I was a joint political science and psychology major. My college boyfriend went on to medical school, which meant if we wanted to get married, I had to work. But when I went out and looked for a job, I quickly realized that the only jobs available were typing positions. Sure, I could pick where I wanted to type—a law firm or a business—but I'd still be stuck typing.

Someone told me that if I had an MBA I wouldn't have to type, so I went to business school, and that's when things started to click for me. I loved the whole intellectual puzzle of marketing and business strategy and putting pieces together, trying to make an enterprise work, drive sales, get consumers to believe in a proposition. I did a summer internship at Kraft, where something happened that became a theme in my life: I got an opportunity that I was much too young for.

At the time, the two men I was supposed to work with at General Foods had been called into the Army Reserves, and I, a low-paid intern, was asked to do their jobs as well as mine on the national roll-out of Maxwell House freeze-dried coffee. I didn't even know what language all the marketing people were speaking, but my boss begged me to do the job. So I cut a deal with him. I agreed to go through each day and pretend I understood what everyone was telling me, as long as he sat down with me every night at 6 P.M. and went over any questions I had about what had happened that day. He agreed, and each night my list of questions got a little shorter. It turned out to be a great opportunity. Everyone's expectations for the intern with no practical experience were so low that they were over the moon if I performed even slightly well! But the most important thing about that experience was that I found marketing totally engaging. I never had time to eat, and I never even knew what time it was. I just did it. First experiences like that are very telling, and the positive feedback reinforced my interest in marketing.

General Foods offered me a job after school, but instead I went to work for Clairol, until a headhunter called and told me about a job opening at Ogilvy. I wasn't interested, but I went to the interview because I had friends at the agency I hadn't seen in years and I thought, What the hell, I'll never take this job, but it would be fun to say hello and give them a hug. *But when I went on the interview I was seduced. The people were great, and agency work let me focus on things that most interested me, the idea side of product management (like product positioning) instead of tactical work, like manufacturing. It also occurred to me that everyone at Clairol's marketing department came to life when the ad agency came to visit. So I left Clairol for the agency and my first account was Twice-As-Nice shampoo. My task: Get eighteen-to-twenty-four-year-old women to try it for the first time. I never intended to spend more than two years at Ogilvy, but here I am, more than thirty years later.*

I've always been extremely instinctive about the way I approach client work, and as an account manager at Ogilvy, working closely with creative people was instinctual for me, and I spent a lot of time with them, often helping them reframe the business question to spark their creativity. No one told me to do that, and in that sense I actually don't think my job has changed much to this day. I still probe and suggest different ways to do things, whether it's an ad campaign or facilitating an acquisition for our company. From the beginning of my career I've been thinking about how best to bring together all the agency's resources to come up with an idea or a solution. My job was—and is—absolutely about bringing together those resources. But whereas before I worked with a handful of product managers, now I work with CEOs and bring them ideas to move their businesses ahead, just as I tried to do for Twice-As-Nice shampoo.

There are a hundred ways to build a brand—advertising is only one—and our job is to figure out the other ninety-nine. Consider American Express. When we began a new campaign with Jerry Seinfeld to promote the card, someone noted that TV commercials were too contained because we had to make Jerry funny in thirty seconds, but Jerry is really funny in three minutes. Expanding American Express ads to the Internet allowed us to lengthen the ads and showcase Jerry's humor. When Hershey asked us to design a billboard in Times Square, we noticed that the store underneath the billboard space was empty and for rent. We told Hershey, "If you really want to promote Hershey at the world's crossroads, bring it to life in a store." That's how the Hershey Store in Times Square came to be. When we worked with BP to transform its brand from old, big oil company to leading energy company, our creative team not only used television ads, outdoor advertising, and public relations but even designed disposable cups for use in the new convenience stores at BP's new gas stations. The cups had little logos and sayings on them that promoted BP's new image, such as, "Of course it's hot, it's solar." When you can bring a brand message down to coffee cups, that's effectively taking advantage of all the resources available.

How do I deal with the stress of running a multibillion-dollar company? I think people can easily lose perspective, and so I always tell this story: I had a boss early on in my career named Charlie, and one day Charlie saw this woman we worked with running in circles because she was supposed to present a media plan and the computer was down. Charlie watched her, then he got up and stood in her way and grabbed her shoulders to stop her. "What do you think they are going to do to you, take your children away?" That phrase still goes through my head about once a week. What's the worst thing that can happen? I think that philosophy has a lot to do with who I am. I never had huge ambitions, and I certainly never expected to have this much fun.

From street to strategy

In doing her highly specialized work, Sharon Edwards, at once blunt and sensitive, straddles extremes. On one day she's meeting with residents of a low-income housing project, and the next she's seated in a cushy office talking with executives at the nation's largest foundation. Talk about a dichotomy, but Sharon lives to bridge such disparate worlds. This fifty-four-year-old's job is to tell charitable foundations how to spend their money in ways that will best help needy populations. Periodically, Sharon will be sitting among clients, hashing through a problem or doling out advice, when she notices someone, usually an older white man, looking at her askance from the corner of his eye. "I know what he's thinking," laughs Sharon. "He's trying to figure out how that black woman got to be where she is!" Sharon takes such attitudes in stride, as long as they don't get in the way of the work at hand.

The work at hand is, in short, solving social problems. Sharon's Houston-based company, The Cornerstone Consulting Group, helps foundations and not-for-profit organizations revitalize impoverished communities by implementing health and human services programs for children and families. "Foundations are basically entities created by the rich to give back in various ways to all types of causes," says Sharon. She and her ten-person staff are primarily hired to help foundations figure out how best to spend donated funds to achieve a particular mission, such as reducing teenage pregnancy. "If you want to start a pregnancy prevention program, you can either randomly hand out contraceptives at schools, you can talk to parents, *or* you can hire me and I'll cut to the chase and tell you which programs work, which are a waste of time, and who you need to target." Although she is a specialist in adolescent reproductive and health issues, Sharon is not an expert in all areas of social reform. No matter. "When I don't know something, I'm never intimidated, because I know how to *think!*" And it frustrates her when others don't.

Too often people believe they have to be "experts" to make good decisions, but people usually know more than they realize. You don't have to know everything about accounting, for example, to make certain financial decisions for a company. All I do is bring in thought processes to help people think outside the box. There are some tangible tools you can use to solve problems. First, you must ask the right questions. The wrong question leads them to the wrong answer. Second, you must listen, I mean really listen, to what people are trying to say but may be frightened or incapable of expressing. I respect all people for who they are, and I can communicate with both welfare mothers and company presidents. My staff calls me the social chameleon.

Some assignments require Sharon to visit poor urban neighborhoods and rural counties and speak directly with residents about their lifestyle. "We go to churches and schools and get to know people in the places and organizations where they already feel comfortable." For example, in the midst of the nation's welfare-to-work efforts, Sharon helped one large foundation better understand exactly what the "working poor" needed to effectively migrate from government subsidies to self-sufficiency. "The foundation assumed people needed child care, but we found out that they needed transportation," says Sharon. Once she understands a particular population's needs, Sharon recommends ways her client can best use its resources to meet those needs. "Real-life examples help me do my job," she says, "yet while I like talking to people on the street, I also like the mental challenge of trying to figure out how foundations can best serve folks without wasting time and money."

Shifting gears from street to strategy is critical for Sharon, who, like most Thinkers, gets bored easily. As a young girl she dreamed of being a classical musician, but her mother, a single parent, drilled independence and self-sufficiency into her daughter's mind. "My mother just did not see how a black girl in the late nineteen sixties was going to make a living playing the bass violin!" she laughs. During a high school career day, a black female pharmacist who talked about her job left an impression on Sharon, who went on to attend five years of pharmaceutical school and practiced for many years. After her daughter was born, Sharon left the pharmacy where she worked for a more flexible job with the public health department, where she learned about government health and social programs. Another job at one of the nation's largest foundations gave Sharon an insider's understanding of the politics that affect how foundations spend donated dollars. Finally, in 1994, she cofounded Cornerstone to be an intermediary between social programs (groups that need money) and foundations (groups that dole it out). Throughout her career, Sharon has remained fascinated with people in an intellectual, "but not touchy-feely," sense, which is why she prefers the role of the problem-solving observer.

Despite her success, "issues of race and gender are always there," says Sharon. "Race shouldn't matter, but it does, it matters all the time. My business partner is a white Jewish man, and for years we've had our own dialogue about how race affects business relationships. I think we all ought to work toward the ideal that it should not matter if a CEO or anyone is black or female, or whatever . . . the first focus should be whether a person does a good job." That's not to say Sharon isn't proud to be a role model for other African-Americans and women, but at the end of the day she loves her work because of the messy, knotty process of trying to solve social problems. "While I find stereotypes fascinating, I mostly love getting past them and focusing on the issues at hand. I take personal pleasure when it's just two people working together to accomplish a common goal."

In her own words

Felicia Mann, 28
Research Scientist, Battelle Memorial Institute
Columbus, Ohio

Felicia has an undergraduate degree in industrial engineering and a master's degree in information management and since college has worked for Battelle Memorial, a large manufacturer and researcher whose main customer is the U.S. Department of Defense. Felicia is hired on a project-by-project basis to assess and refine new weapons, tools, and software. As a Thinker, her job is to find problems before they even exist.

I was in fifth grade when the Space Shuttle Challenger *exploded, and I think that sparked my interest in science and NASA [the National Aeronautics and Space Administration]. I didn't know anything about the space shuttle, and I started reading about it and other space programs, as far back as the Apollo and Mercury missions. For a while I wanted to be an astronaut—I even did a summer internship at NASA—but I grew out of it because, I think, I wanted to be more hands-on, more mechanical. When I first got to college I thought I'd be an aerospace engineer, but as I read more aerospace textbooks, I found it too theoretical, not hands-on enough. I eventually discovered industrial engineering, which is an* application of math and science that involves people. Most engineering programs leave people out of the equation; they're just concerned about how to make things work. Industrial engineering is concerned with the human element and how machines affect people, and vice versa.

Some folks think defense work is narrowly focused, but that couldn't be further from the truth. Throughout my employment I've participated in so many different projects and worn many different hats, from safety engineer and computer programmer to statistician and program manager. One of my current projects is to assess something called the joint biological detection system, which is a box the size of a small refrigerator that samples air for biological contaminants. I have to check all the internal components to make sure there is nothing in the equipment itself—a sharp edge or a voltage cord—that could harm whoever operates it. I have to physically manipulate the equipment to predict how someone might accidentally hurt herself. My goal is to figure out the worst thing that could happen to someone if they make a mistake. I participated in another project for the Marine Corps, in which we had to assess what equipment Marines would use during a very specific situation. Our goal was to eliminate any equipment that the Marines would never need— which means we had to predict every type of scenario they could find themselves in—so they did not have to carry extra weight.

At some level, all of my work is about the human factor—how people interact with machines—although my specific responsibilities change from job to job. The diversity is one of the main reasons I'm so happy with my career. I also like the impact my work has on our national security, and I'm honored to work with a group of people who are exceptional not only in their areas of expertise, but who are willing to give a helping hand whenever asked.

One of the biggest lessons I've learned since leaving college is that the real world is not like a textbook. Whenever we were asked to solve problems in school, we always had to provide the absolute best solution— money and personnel issues aside. But in the real world I have to concern myself with my budget and time constraints. I can't always come up with the ideal solution, but rather one that's best given the limitations of a specific situation. That's the challenge I'm still learning to deal with, but I think that's life.

From an employment perspective, the future for Thinkers is bright. Indeed, the business landscape promises a never-ending flood of unpredictable problems to solve and data to analyze. While technical innovation and the so-called information or knowledge economy may have decreased the number of manual labor jobs, they have spawned a category of worker that Robert B. Reich, former U.S. secretary of labor, author, and professor of social and economic policy at Brandeis University, calls symbolic analysis. According to Reich, most symbolic analytic work involves "analyzing, manipulating, and communicating through numbers, shapes, words, and ideas"—the very activities through which Thinkers find flow. Job categories for symbolic analysts include journalists (*60 Minutes'* Lesley), scientists (Battelle's Felicia), engineers (CVS's Richele), marketing executives (Ogilvy & Mather CEO Shelly), investment bankers (JPMorgan's Mary), and all types of consultants (M.A., Sharon, and even financial adviser Lisa). Other related jobs include lawyers, senior marketing executives, composers, writers, teachers, and designers. "Apart from recessions," Reich wrote in the *Wall Street Journal* in December 2003, "demand for symbolic analysts in the U.S. will continue to grow faster than the supply."

Jobs for Thinkers may be plentiful, but the onus still falls on individual women to proactively search for and identify the specific job that not only puts her in flow but also provides a sense of purpose and surrounds her with people she respects. Such proactive behavior brings to mind another passage from the book *Flow*, which researched the universal state of happiness: ". . . happiness is not something that happens," wrote Mihaly Csikszentmihalyi. "It is not the result of good fortune or random choice. It is not something that money can buy or power command. It does not depend on outside events, but, rather, on how we interpret them. Happiness, in fact, is a condition that must be prepared for, cultivated, and defended privately by each person. People who learn to control inner experience will be able to determine the quality of their lives, which is as close as any of us can come to being happy."

Remember: Flow can be found in the most unlikely of workplaces.

Chapter Three

The Determinators

National sales manager, product development director,
investment banker, head of corporate communications,
public relations practitioner, chief executive officer,
truck driver, senior technology executive,
marketer, and corporate lawyer

Ambition is such an intrinsically American characteristic that it's easy
to forget it's also a relatively new, hard-won concept for women. In her
book *Out to Work: A History of Wage-Earning Women in the United States,*
Columbia University professor Alice Kessler-Harris writes extensively
about the emergence of ambition in the post–World War I generation. In
particular, Harris examines the social, technological, and economic
trends that gave rise to "a new generation of female wage workers . . .
whose job-related hopes extended beyond economic survival . . ."

For Kessler, ambition is defined as wanting to work—and realizing that
one could work—for more than just money. She notes how, during the
war, women took over men's jobs and discovered new skills. And after the
war, domestic innovations—from coal fires and running water to easy-to-
clean linoleum floors—reduced time required for manual housework,
which freed up women to pursue activities outside the home. Meanwhile,
birth control, loosening sexual inhibitions, and the right to vote fueled a
new sense of possibility among females. All told, the increased exposure
to job skills, free time, and social confidence helped mold a generation of

women for whom the notion of professional choice took root. Writes Kessler, "Women, like men, demanded their share of the world's rewards. Ambition crept into their vocabulary. To aspire, to achieve, not merely to do a job, became at least a possibility for daughters as well as for sons."

Over the course of subsequent generations, ambition among women in the workplace—whether expressed as Rosie the Riveter during the Second World War, the women's movement in the 1960s, the rise of women-owned businesses in the 1980s, or the celebrity status of influential women such as Hillary Clinton and HP chairman and chief executive officer Carly Fiorina—has become synonymous with the primary definition of "determination": striving toward a particular end. For many contemporary women, the very act of striving is itself the source of happiness.

I call these women Determinators.

Determinators drive themselves to succeed at whatever they put their minds to, be it running a company, raising a family, driving a truck, or selling cosmetics. The process of excelling, in and of itself, provides great fulfillment. Determinators do not, however, define success in stereotypical, one could say male, terms: mainly power, prestige, and wealth. In lieu of power in a dominant, controlling-of-others sense, these women desire control over their own destinies, their daily activities, and their ability to influence business decisions. Instead of prestige for the sake of fame, Determinators want to have a visible impact with lasting effects. In essence, they want to make a difference on a grand scale. And rather than money for the sake of Donald Trump–style glitz, Determinators perceive money as a means to self-sufficiency and a just reward for work well done. In fact, few if any Determinators cite money as their primary motivator. Yet at the same time, they expect salaries that reflect their accomplishments, and thus they are more likely than other women to insist they be paid what they're worth.

In interviewing these women, I recognized Determinator-like traits in my own work habits, and they brought to mind an essay I wrote in high school about how I envisioned my own future. At the risk of exposing my Holden Caulfield voice circa 1986, I'll share this excerpt:

It's kind of embarrassing, the image I have of myself in twenty years: I'm wearing this formal, very high fashion suit, heels, and my hair is pulled back in a perfectly pinned bun. I am carrying a briefcase and walking down a crowded city sidewalk. The best part is that I've got this great look on my face, very determined, but not like stone, more subtle, like a soft confidence. I don't even know where I'm walking, to a meeting maybe, or to my office. The point is that I know where I'm going. I think that's what I see in my future . . . a future.

As young women, many Determinators had similar visions of their futures. They had a gut feeling they were going places, even if they didn't know where. That said, Determinators are not annoying over-achievers. Confident but not cocky, they don't brag about their accomplishments. But—and this is significant—neither do they minimize them. Indeed, public recognition in some form is desired by both ambitious men and women. In her 2004 book *Necessary Dreams,* psychiatrist Anna Fels writes that the motivation behind ambition is a combination of mastery of skills and the desire for public recognition. But by recognition, Fels does not mean empty praise or compliments but rather ". . . being valued by others for qualities that we experience and value in ourselves. . . . recognition affirms a person's individual experience of accomplishment." In that vein, Determinators do not seek raw prestige, but a more meaningful, individualized attention.

Determinators also do not seek money in and of itself. It's tempting to assume Determinators love their work because many earn high salaries. But the money-yields-happiness assumption is erroneous. We see women with six-figure incomes, roll our eyes, and say, "Of course they love their jobs—look how much money they make!" While money can make life easier, high salaries are rarely the primary reason someone loves her job. Consider that about one-third of the women in The Happy 100 make less than $50,000 a year. Sure, they'd like to make more, but they still love their work. Flip the money-causes-happiness assumption and you'll come closer to the truth: Many high-wage earners achieve that level of income simply because they love their work and, as a result, perform well and earn promotions. When it comes to the high-wage earner, the key is to understand *how* the paycheck brings her happiness. Does it give her stability and independence? Does it pay for her children's college? Let her support herself and her family? Fill a closet with Manolo

Blahniks? Give her the freedom to indulge hobbies? Or is it just icing on the cake? Unless you know the individual and her motivations, it's almost impossible to know the role money plays in her life.

A better way to identify Determinators, rather than by impressive salary or job title, is how these women pilot their careers. In short, they take control. They take initiative and overcome obstacles—from disapproving parents to corporate layoffs to discrimination—with enormous self-confidence. Nothing deters a Determinator. As you read their stories, notice how each takes charge of her workplace and her working life. Being proactive—rather than reactive—is a Determinator's most telling trait.

Knock, knock. She's there.

The Determinator mentality—particularly a desire for independence and control—often takes root in childhood. Such was the case for Maria Peninger in the 1970s, whose mother's mantra, "Never depend on a man; you have to be independent," was reinforced by the clients who visited her father's family law practice, usually distraught mothers and wives who were abused or abandoned by husbands. "I would hear my father talking to his clients about custody battles or alimony, and I just knew I didn't want to be in that position, ever," recalls Maria. That may explain why, when the young Maria was left to her own devices in her small, middle-class town of Forest City, North Carolina, she'd knock on neighbors' doors to sell random items she'd collected: Christmas cards, cookies, even household gadgets she'd bought from a wholesale catalogue. Says Maria, "I loved the entrepreneurial spirit of being able to make a living." From that desire for self-sufficiency sprang pleasure. "I sold because I wanted money, but it was also fun." A shy girl, selling gave Maria a reason to approach strangers. She developed a competitive spirit and felt proud when customers said yes. A no never shook her confidence.

Coincidentally, the 1970s was also the era of the Avon lady, and whenever the effervescent saleswomen knocked on the Peningers' door, it was Maria, not her mother, who chatted with them. At fifteen, a determined Maria and her friend drove twenty-five miles to an Avon meeting, where they signed up using their mothers' names and birthdates and became (unbeknownst to Avon) two of the youngest Avon saleswomen in their rural county.

Maria's interest in business grew while attending Appalachian State University. In her marketing and sales management courses, she devoured the corporate case studies her professors assigned, including one about Avon, which she read during her senior year. Maria thought, *I can do this. I can make these decisions.* Still, when her father told Maria about a woman he'd met in Forest City who had a job opening in sales management at Avon, Maria was reluctant. The last thing the newly minted graduate wanted was to return to her small town.

After the interview, though, her viewpoint changed.

"The woman who interviewed me painted such a vivid vision about my future and said if I did well in my district I could move anywhere within Avon," says Maria, who instantly saw beyond the immediate job description to future job possibilities. Despite the move back home and paltry starting salary of $13,500, Maria became a district manager responsible for managing and recruiting Avon saleswomen. "I offered women at all ends of the economic spectrum the opportunity to sell Avon, which would make them money at a time when there were not a lot of jobs around. Avon was an entrée for women into the workforce, and I found that very rewarding," she says.

Exactly twenty years later, Maria is still at Avon. As vice president of sales, the woman who at twenty-one years of age managed 250 door-to-door sales representatives now oversees about 330,000 sales reps—half of Avon's U.S. sales force. Maria earns a healthy six-figure salary and while she has not sold makeup directly to customers since her teens, she's responsible for motivating women who do. The role taps both her maternal and stringent management styles and requires her to constantly set higher goals.

Avon expects you to perform, and if you don't, you won't have the privilege of working here. I like the pressure of being directly responsible for bottom-line results. I never had any special tricks or did anything terribly creative, but I do hire really good people . . . if I hire bad people, I let them go quickly.

While I think I am a nurturing leader who works well with her people, I also have zero tolerance for nonperformers. I raise the bar every year. I don't think people are scared of me, and I really feel like my district managers understand that I work hard to make them smarter and better. I also don't allow them to get distracted by anything that will not drive the business. Some folks can get derailed, but I don't let that happen to my team.

Pay-for-performance definitely motivates me, and when I was a division manager I encouraged my district managers to buy a car, get a second home, buy a diamond ring. Together we worked out how they could pay for it. I never put anyone in financial jeopardy, but we'd sit down and do the math to see how she could make her dreams come true. I'd ask them, "If you could have anything, what would that be, and how much does it cost?" Then we figured out how to get there. I always had a calculator with me.

Today I'm responsible for creating a sales plan that my organization can deliver on. Say, for example, I have to increase the prior year's sales by 7 percent. I help create initiatives and incentives to get me to that 7 percent. For example, I help decide if Avon should spend half a million dollars on sales incentives for a skin care product or a fragrance.

Another way to grow the company is to hire more salespeople, and so we created a unique way to motivate our sales force to recruit other women. I always look forward to Thursdays because that's when we get a report that shows how many new reps we added that week. Yesterday I found out we grew by 2,400! To see results come in reminds me of when I was a little girl, when you could see that the right decisions caused good results.

Although Maria has been married for nineteen years, her youthful desire for independence remains strong: She and her husband keep separate finances, only recently signing up for a joint checking account. "I've always had something in my name only," says Maria, stressing her belief that married women maintain their own credit cards and bank accounts in case they ever need to demonstrate a credit history. Despite her accomplishments, childhood notions of independence still linger in Maria's mind.

Under her skin

For Annie Carullo, senior vice president of corporate product innovation at Estée Lauder in New York, the desire for independence—and control—stems from her parents' divorce. Now forty-three, Annie grew up in a cramped, narrow apartment on Mulberry Street in Little Italy, then a relatively poor, ethnic enclave of New York City. Her father left home in the 1960s, and her mother's daily struggle to provide for and raise four children formed Annie's early notion of the woman she wanted to become.

After watching my mother get out of bed and go off to work every day, I came to realize that I couldn't ever allow another person to provide for me in life. If I did that, I might not be able to manage if the rug was pulled out from under me. What if the person I depended on for food and rent wasn't there anymore? I was going to be independent, and if a man came along, he would be the cherry on the cake.

Television also shaped me. I grew up in the 1970s and spent hours watching popular television shows like Mary Tyler Moore *and* Charlie's Angels. *These women became my ideals. I was imaginative and envisioned myself living a glamorous life. Yes, I was going to be in a corner office with a fabulous career and a Day-at-a-Glance calendar and a phone in one hand. . . . I was going to be a powerful executive and supermodel woman. Remember Revlon's fragrance Charlie? I was going to be the woman in the ads. I had ambition and a vision of success—but no idea how to get there from Mulberry Street.*

Ironically, Annie loved everything about what the Charlie brand symbolized except the actual primping and makeup. In fact, despite her mother's daily effort to transform herself "from a woman with four kids into a stunning lady" with lipstick, eyeliner, and mascara, Annie shunned cosmetics for herself. Her teenage beauty ritual consisted of dotting color on her cheeks and tinting her lashes, which begs the question: How does a woman *not* obsessed with makeup rise so high at one of the world's largest cosmetics companies?

"I was motivated by success," says Annie, who actually stumbled into the cosmetics field when a friend found her an administrative assistant job at Revlon. Annie was, by her own admission, "the worst secretary in the world, who couldn't even write down a telephone number correctly." Still, she was inquisitive and memorably animated and always accepted new assignments. Fortunately, companies such as Revlon that specialized in women's products actively helped their female employees excel. Eventually, Annie took a trainee job in product development at Revlon and, to the plain Jane's surprise, the cosmetics business got under her skin.

I love everything about product development, but most of all I love inventing something new. Luckily, the cosmetics industry gives me a platform to be creative without too many restrictions. I can travel anywhere I want to find out just about anything I want to know. If there is an herbalist in Madagascar researching the root of a green leaf thought to have healing properties, I'm off to Madagascar! If I want to ask an engineer to develop a new makeup applicator that looks like a Swiss Army knife—which I did and which comes out next year—I can do that. I can bring ideas to life any way I choose. I love having the freedom to pursue an idea.

Once we get the green light to go ahead with a new product, the real labor begins. The research and development team must find the right materials and formulate them in just the right way, so that, for example, a red is red enough but a yellow isn't too yellow.

I also love figuring out packaging by reading what's going on in the world and seeing which images are permeating customers' minds. We have to create a product image that's consistent with the brand's image. Some brands are rule breakers, but Estée Lauder is more traditional. Customers must feel at home every time they use our brand. When we finally put the product in the field and test it with customers, we learn what works and what doesn't. We make changes. Then, just when we think we have everything perfect, the legal department calls and says the name we chose means something dreadful in Russian! [Laughs.]

Because I'm so passionate about the work, because I give birth to these products, I go nuts over every detail! Sometimes introducing a new product is as painful as childbirth and raising a kid: You name them, dress them, and essentially you fall in love with them. Sometimes they go out into the world and just don't do as well as you hoped. Other times, they perform better than you ever imagined.

Maintaining a degree of control—over her own career, over her company's future products, and even over improving other women's physical appearance—gives Annie tremendous satisfaction and pleasure. Her most recent product at Estée Lauder is a wrinkle serum that diminishes the appearance of facial lines by essentially filling them in and healing them, like a wound. While Annie may never develop a cream to, say, completely erase the lingering childhood pain of one's parents' divorce or perfectly repair the inevitable cracks in life, she believes that a beautifully painted face has its place. "It's truly a gift to make a woman smile when she looks in the mirror," says Annie, who, as a little girl, watched her mother do just that.

She shall rise up.

Grace Vandecruze, thirty-nine, is a happy investment banker in New York City. Although she earns a relatively impressive income, her love of work is rooted not in the salary that her job yields, but in the integrity, the intellectual rigor, and even the competitive nature she brings to her work. Despite this banker's comfortable compensation, her spending habits are relatively minimal: Single, she owns a one-bedroom, 1,000-square-foot apartment on Manhattan's Upper West Side. She is always looking for sales and owns only two pocketbooks: a plain, black leather Louis Vuitton bag she carries to work, and a small Coach bag for weekends. Her priciest purchase to date has been a Steinway baby grand piano.

Grace is a managing director at investment banking firm Fox-Pitt, Kelton Inc., a wholly owned subsidiary of Swiss RE. Her specialty is the heavily regulated yet fragmented insurance industry, and it's Grace's job to advise insurance companies and insurance regulators about company valuations, or rather, what insurance companies are worth. Grace is also responsible for raising capital and advising industry executives on mergers and acquisitions, from identifying acquisition targets to negotiating the terms of a deal. Determining company valuations is not an exact science. Although there are standard valuation methods, Grace is constantly called upon to apply—and defend—her expertise and judgment.

What's important is to make sure my answers have an intellectual honesty to them. I have to stand by whatever I advise. Just last week I was in court testifying about the value I gave one of the largest insurance companies in the world, Conseco, which is going through a bankruptcy. Conseco disagreed with my valuation and I was on the witness stand for two days straight defending it. All day, Conseco's lawyer hammered me with questions. It felt like they were targeting me personally and trying to discredit my methods. There I was, just sitting on the stand, and the lawyer just kept pointing at me with an open, red pen in his hand: "Now, Ms. Vandecruze, why did you do this . . . why did you do that . . ." He carried on and on with aggressive antics and it built to a crescendo! I refused to break. I remember thinking, Does he really think I'm made out of feathers and will just cave? I refuse! The mere fact I'm even testifying about a company valued at about $5 billion is such an accomplishment after all I've been through in my life!

Here's a snapshot of what Grace has been through: When she was four-teen years old, her nine-member family emigrated from Guyana to Brooklyn, where her parents both worked as nurses. Poor but close-knit, the Vandecruze family lost everything they owned in an apartment fire and had to live in a homeless shelter for several months until Grace's parents could purchase a new house in Queens. Grace went on to col-lege, worked two jobs to pay for school, earned her MBA at the Wharton School, and once employed on Wall Street worked eighty hours a week, excelling as one of the few women and African-Americans working in high finance. Sitting in her fortieth-floor office, which overlooks Man-hattan's East Side, Grace reflects on how the values she learned dur-ing her childhood remain with her today:

My strong spiritual beliefs have a lot to do with how I conduct myself professionally, and integrity is incredibly important in my line of work. Companies want to work with people whom they can look in the eye and trust what they are being told. Whether negotiating a fee for services or discussing the valuation of a company, honesty is exceedingly important. The integrity I bring to my job brings me tremendous pride.

I also have to say, growing up in a family of seven children, I find the competitive aspect of my work very intriguing. When I was a child I would play chess and checkers with my dad, and he never once gave me a head start. I had to master the game along with him and try to beat him. Because I grew up in a large family and with a fighting spirit, I am always assessing and reassessing my competitive position in business, and I am always elated when I win. In many ways my work is very much like my hobby, sailing. When I sail, I have little control over things like the weather, wind, and waves, and I am constantly looking at the navigational tools, the direction of the wind, and trying to adjust the sails to the elements. As an investment banker, I also have little control over things like the markets or the economy, but I am in the driver's seat because my opinion affects a company's strategy. I always focus on a company's future, not its past. When a company's chief executive officer calls me in, he really wants and needs my input. The power I have is about leadership: I'm in the boardroom and the door is closed and the directors are looking at me and honestly asking, for example, how they should be maintaining their position in the equity markets or valuing a company.

I've always survived by believing I could accomplish what I set my mind to and calling upon my psychological strength and stamina. When you live your life knowing failure is not an option, you just keep pushing.

Grace's expertise and integrity allow her to influence business not as a pompous, money-hungry Master of the Universe, but as an honest, well-respected professional. As for that pricey piano Grace purchased, she recently put it to good use. In a rare extravagance, Grace invited her entire family to a private room at the posh St. Regis Hotel in Manhattan. With her mother as guest of honor, Grace thanked her relatives for their support, and then she played a piece she'd been practicing on her home piano. After the private concert, Grace gave her mother a silver serving tray from Tiffany & Co. inscribed with a passage from the Bible: "And her children shall rise up and call her blessed." Names of her mother's children and grandchildren followed the quote. "It was a glorious evening," recalls Grace, beaming. No doubt it was also priceless.

Her inexplicable fire

Located a few blocks west of Grace Vandecruze's office, in a suite on an equally high floor, sits Anne Janas. It's no coincidence to find more than one Determinator working in New York City. Manhattan has always attracted the ambitious, and Anne felt the city's magnetism forty years ago and 800 miles away, growing up in Savannah, Georgia.

At fifty-six, Anne is vice president of U.S. corporate communications for Hachette Filipacchi Media, an international publishing company that prints, among other titles, *ELLE, Premiere, Road & Track, American Photo,* and *Metropolitan Home.* Anne reports to Hachette's chief executive and oversees the company's public relations, corporate sponsorships, charitable affiliations, and trade relationships.

Externally, Anne has a soft southern lilt to her voice, and her short auburn hair and petite features might be considered perky were she not so polished and genteel. Internally, Anne harbors an "inexplicable fire" that was lit by a childhood visit to New York City.

Mother and Daddy were always good about taking their three children on individual trips, and my special trip was to New York City. I was about fifteen, and as we headed to New York in a cab from the airport, my parents talked to me about the city like they had previously talked to me about sex: "Well, it's really wonderful, but you have to be very cautious." It was very funny, and as we got closer to the city, my heart actually sped up. Unfortunately, Mother got the flu and stayed in the hotel room to recuperate, so it was just Daddy and I. "Whatever you want to do, this town is yours," he told me. We ran from one side of the city to another that day. I was just so thrilled to be there—New York City was in my soul, and it felt like a place I did not have to make my own, because it already was my own. When we returned home to Savannah, I told people I was going to live and work there one day.

Anne put her dream on hold when she dropped out of college to support her first husband in graduate school in the late 1960s. The couple lived in South Carolina and had a baby when Anne was twenty-one. Knowing she'd eventually want to work, Anne took night classes in art and creative literature, which led to a marketing job at a local television station. She went on to work for Cox Communications in Atlanta for ten years before being offered a job as vice president of corporate communications at NBC—in New York City. By then, Anne was on her second marriage and her daughter was off to college. Anne's husband, John, was willing to join her, and she was finally ready to live out her dream.

My philosophy about how to get what you want is simple: Say it out loud. When I first dated my husband, John, in Atlanta, we talked very practically about what each of us felt was important in life. I told him it was part of my life plan to live in New York and Paris one day. That was his desire, too! So when the job at NBC came through, John was ready to quit his job and move with me. It's so important to verbalize your desires to everyone because, slowly, you'll start to make decisions based on that destination.

Once in New York, Anne could not believe her luck. With an office that overlooked the Empire State Building, she was in the hub of Manhattan. But that luck changed just six weeks later, when GE bought NBC, and subsequent changes caused many people to lose their jobs. Disappointed and nervous, Anne was out of work. Determined to stay in New York, she turned her marketing expertise on herself. She analyzed her skills, researched what industries were growing, and networked heavily with people in the publishing business. In short, Anne took control of her predicament and, after more than 100 networking meetings and interviews, landed yet another dream job, this time as head of public affairs for *Time* magazine. The move from broadcasting to magazine publishing was a carefully crafted career switch. Even more than broadcasting, the magazine industry allowed Anne to combine her organizational and communication skills with her intellectual and cultural interests. After *Time,* Anne went on to work for publishing juggernaut Condé Nast (*Vogue, The New Yorker*), from where Hachette's chief executive recruited her himself.

Back home in Savannah, friends often ask Anne how she handles the pressures of corporate life in Manhattan. For this Determinator, pressure is part and parcel of why she loves what she does.

*I tell them that if you really want to stress me out, put me in a small
town with limited resources, little stimulation, and in a repetitive job.
Then I'll age quickly, break out in a rash, and suffer sleepless nights.
Stress, you see, is relative. I have an emotional relationship with the city,
and if you are not in love with and committed to New York, life here can
be difficult.*

*Last May I was one of 300 executives from around the world at the
Global Magazine Conference in Paris. One evening, at a private black-tie
dinner party for 700 at Versailles, I stood in the formal garden wearing my
designer gown and overlooking the private fireworks display. I thought,*
This is better than I ever thought it would be.

Such glamour is icing on the cake for Anne and other happy working
women of her stature. Indeed, the number of nights Anne spends in a
ball gown sipping champagne pales in comparison to the number of days
she wears a suit and eats lunch at her desk. While such perks satisfy
Anne's childhood dreams about a career in the big city, it is her job's variety of activities and intellectual content that truly fuels her happiness.

In her own words

Jacqueline Chen, 26
Account Director
Ogilvy Public Relations Worldwide

Jacqueline oversees about $1.2 million in public relations work for finan-
cial services companies. The high-pressure job requires that Jacqueline
communicate her corporate clients' financial information to the media,
analysts, and investors via press releases, briefings, interviews, articles, and
annual reports. A consummate professional, Jacqueline seeks out complex assignments, preferring to be challenged than to coast comfortably.

*I'm a multitasker, a self-starter who performs best under pressure. I've
always been that way. In college I put a lot on myself, working forty-hour
weeks, attending school full-time, and doing extracurricular activities.
That's the way I work best.*

I am definitely type A, and my family has a lot to do with that. My mom came to this country from Korea and met my father, who is Chinese, at the University of Maryland. My parents got divorced when I was two, and my mom always had her own business. She ran a restaurant and retail chains, and I grew up watching her work as she raised two daughters, always doing three things at a time. I admired her work ethic. She was a big influence on my life and always taught me to speak my mind, take a position on things, and be independent.

All of my cousins are very much of the same bent. We have very strong personalities and are very independent . . . it's just in our bones. My mother always said to me, "I'm so proud of you. I never once had to tell you to practice the piano, do your homework, or go to cheerleading practice." My mom wanted me to be the next Connie Chung. We have a home video of me interviewing my stuffed animals on the couch! So I think I wanted to be an on-air reporter before I knew what it was like. But in college, when I worked at News 12 in the Bronx and Fox 5 in D.C., I realized that broadcast reporters must start out in a small market, in a small city, and at a salary around just $20,000 the first year. I decided journalism was not for me. I wanted to be in New York, with the hustle and bustle. I wanted to be in the financial capital of the world!

My first job out of college was at a small agency, and my title was PR manager. Can you imagine! It was great for me, rather than to be an assistant at a big company, I came out of the gate and could work with the heads of companies. Because our firm was so small—it was ten people— we had to take every and any piece of business we could get. It was a great experience because it was so broad. I did everything from take out the garbage to help clean the bathroom to work with senior executives. Small environments are a great place to start working, because you do everything.

One thing I learned from the boutique firm was how to market myself. I joined associations and went to conferences, and by the time I went to the Ogilvy interview I had learned how to package myself. I came in with media clips, sample writing, press releases, bylined articles, even a letter from a client. I later learned that Ogilvy wanted to hire me during my first interview because all the other people they saw didn't come in with anything; I was the only one who had! It really worked!

Packaging yourself doesn't end once you have the job. For me, I'm young and very self-conscious about how young I look, so I tend to dress up more to fight stereotypes. I usually wear suits, usually black, navy, or gray. I hate to say this, but I think appearance and the way you present yourself at work is huge, whether people want to admit it or not. You never know when a client will pop in and want to see you.

I worked at Ogilvy for two years in the technology practice, and when the economy got bad and layoffs started, I never knew if I'd walk in and more people would be laid off. I decided to look for other work and was hired to be PR and marketing manager for a hedge fund. I had a very candid, but positive, exit interview at Ogilvy and was told the door was always open for me to return, so I was able to explore a new opportunity with a great feeling of comfort that I could return to Ogilvy if I wanted. At the hedge fund I'd get a bonus for every article I placed—$4,000 for a feature, $2,500 for a tier-two publication, $1,500 for tier three—and I was a media monster, on the phone pitching every day. But after a year I realized that agency life, not working directly with just one client, was for me.

I'd kept in touch with my former Ogilvy bosses and colleagues, and one person was just starting to build the financial communications practice. During one of our phone conversations I was asked if I would ever consider coming back, and the answer was yes. In a matter of weeks I returned, definitely having made the right decision. Still, I'm glad I took a chance and explored the "other side."

I always want to be learning. People sometimes say I should be in consumer PR, but I chose financial communications because it's more challenging and I always want to be challenged. Some people like selling Tide and SnackWell's because it fits their style. Me? I prefer to write earnings releases, deal with complicated mergers, acquisitions, and IPOs. It's all very sensitive and legally challenging, and very exciting.

She is Daddy's not-so-little girl.

Not all Determinators make it in New York. Indeed, one of the 1970s' greatest symbols of female ambition, Mary Tyler Moore, made it "after all" in Minneapolis. Chief executive officer Christine Jacobs made it in

Atlanta. Now fifty-two, Christine's journey took her from a hospital emergency room laboratory to the New York Stock Exchange, where in 1998 she was the first female company chairman to ring the opening bell. Then, as now, Christine was chief executive and chairman of Theragenics, a biotechnology firm known for developing a radioactive seed that, when inserted via a needle into a cancerous prostate, emits radiation and kills cancer cells.

Christine is extremely dedicated to Theragenics and its mission. As the self-dubbed "maven of prostate cancer," she recalls a career path fraught with hurdles, such as wooing investors and convincing skeptical doctors to try Theragenics's treatment on their patients. But it's a more intimate anecdote that best illustrates Christine's proactive nature.

I'm the oldest of nine children, and my father put us all through college. When he heard I was leaving my hospital lab job to take an entry-level sales position, he was really disturbed and stopped talking to me! It was painful for my parents because they thought that, as a profession, sales was beneath me. He was a loving father but wasn't comfortable watching his kids take risks. In his mind, the hospital was a safe environment that gave me a great retirement package and insurance. While those things were important to him, they weren't to me—at least at age thirty-four.

Meanwhile, I had a boyfriend at the time who told me to go for the job. When you're in your thirties and your boyfriend says, "Go," and Dad says, "No," you tend to listen to the boyfriend. [Laughs.]

For about six months my dad wouldn't speak to me. Eventually I was promoted from the entry-level position, and around that time my family was having a cookout. On a whim it occurred to me that maybe my dad was having such trouble with my job because he couldn't visualize my new life. So on the day of the cookout, even though I had the day off from work, I dressed up in my navy suit, carried my briefcase, and showed up at the picnic looking like I had just come from work in order to let Dad see his professional daughter. My family was used to seeing me in a lab coat and had never seen me so dressed up. That's how I did it! It was a defining moment that changed everything.

About ten years later, after I had switched biotech companies and risen to be Theragenics's chief executive, I invited my entire family—Mom, Dad,

*my brothers and sisters—to New York the day I rang the opening bell at
the Stock Exchange. I also brought the company's lawyers, accountants,
and consultants—anyone who'd helped the company and me since I
joined back in 1987. It was a small group of fifty! Dick Grasso [then
chairman of the NYSE] was so overwhelmed that my family showed up;
he spent the entire morning with us.*

*That day my dad turned to me and said, "Honey, I'm really glad that
you didn't listen to me, because every time I told you what not to do, every
time I told you no, you defied me, and you were right." I cried!*

If you've ever been Daddy's little girl or have had a parent disagree with
your career choice, you have to get a kick out of the creative way Christine handled her skeptical father. For many women, the need to please
can make familial expectations hard to dash. Yet Determinators have the
confidence to move on despite their critics—even tough ones like dear
old Dad.

She's in the driver's seat.

Margaret Peterson may never attend black-tie affairs in Paris, work with
pop stars, or sit in an office overlooking the Empire State Building. No
matter. For twenty-five years Margaret's been quite happy sitting behind
the wheel, in control of a huge tractor-trailer, with a view of the open
road. Margaret, forty-seven, is a professional truck driver for Roadway
Express, out of Bloomington, California. Her office is the two-seater cab
of an eighteen-wheel Volvo truck.

Margaret is a Determinator because she has persevered against odds
and was never content to simply drive from one place to another and arrive on time. Margaret always looked ahead, spending her twenty-five
years in trucking building a career on and off the road by constantly expanding her knowledge of the commercial transportation business. As a
result, she's been able to support herself and save for retirement.

The yen to motor across the country began because Margaret couldn't.
The daughter of a construction worker who never took a vacation, Margaret grew up in the confines of a small, northeastern Minnesota town
called Hovland. "It had a gas station, a beer bar, a church, and a post of-

fice. The nearest movie theater was sixty miles away. I didn't know a world existed outside Hovland," recalls Margaret. During college her father suggested she get a trucking license, but Margaret—who majored in communications—ignored him until she traveled with a friend who happened to drive trucks. One night, when her friend got tired of driving, Margaret reluctantly took the wheel.

Says Margaret, "He watched me drive and shift gears for about ten minutes and then crawled into his bunk and went to sleep. I drove through the night and my adrenaline started flowing. I don't think I blinked once, because I was so excited! The feelings of freedom and responsibility were indescribable." Her parents lent her money to attend the ABC School of Driving, and she graduated only to face her next bump in the road: a male-dominated industry fraught with sexual discrimination and harassment. Back in the late 1970s and early 1980s, Margaret was one of the only women driving trucks.

At one of the first trucking companies I worked for, they paired me up with a newly divorced man in his mid-thirties. So there I was, a twenty-two-year-old kid with a veteran driver who told me he knew everything there was to know about trucking. He smoked, and he hit on me. This was before the age of political correctness, before people were educated about harassment in the workplace.

Looking back, I probably didn't handle it the best way, but I survived and grew stronger. Rather than complain to someone or request a transfer, I just refused his advances. Of course, that created some hostility in the truck, but I had a goal and I was not going to let him get between me and my goal: I needed to ride with him for six months so I could learn enough to drive a truck myself. I was determined to be the best I could be in the trucking industry. Finally, our boss assigned me to do short runs on my own, and soon I was driving across the nation.

I was like a kid in a candy store! To sit behind the wheel of a huge truck and visit places I could only imagine from books was amazing to me. Back then my truck had no radio or tape player, so I listened to the CB radio. My CB name was High Pockets because I'm tall, and so my pockets are high. It wasn't easy being a woman driver. I couldn't get served food at truck stops or even pay for fuel, because they didn't think or believe I was a driver. Back then spouses or girlfriends were the only women around. Basically, I didn't exist in their eyes. Women were simply not respected in the industry, and those of us who have been driving for years had to work a bit harder than some of the guys. Every day I went to work I had to prove I was as good or better than the guys.

I stuck with it because I have always been focused on my goals. The goals change over the years because I'm always eyeing something bigger or better. I always have to be moving toward something, and I guess I'm just stubborn enough to say this is what I'm meant to do and am determined not to let someone get in my way.

As the novelty of sightseeing waned, Margaret grew frustrated with the job's lack of intellectual stimulation. There was no radio in her rig, and she couldn't strike up conversations with colleagues about current events or books because "back then, many of the other drivers didn't pick up a newspaper or read a book."

Intent on exercising her mind, Margaret took control of her career and ran for job steward in her local union. Once elected, Margaret became the liaison between drivers and the company. Unfortunately, the post's dirty politics proved too nasty for Margaret's tastes; she chose not to run for reelection and settled back into driving. Then in the early 1990s, Roadway increased its commitment to driver safety training, and Margaret volunteered to help, often acting as an internal spokesperson. In 1996, Roadway management formed teams of drivers to lecture RV groups and high school students about highway safety and driving careers, and Margaret was among the lecturers, a role that jump-started a dual career as driver and public speaker. She felt good enlightening people about seemingly small details, like avoiding blind spots, and she smiled when students' eyes lit up at the prospect of a trucking career. Today, she also teaches courses in defensive driving and how to properly handle hazardous materials.

After twenty years at Roadway, Margaret no longer enjoys traveling for weeks at a time, but her seniority allows her to bid on daylong freight-hauling jobs and return to her own bed and her two dogs each night. The off-road work—speaking, teaching, even writing articles—keeps Margaret engaged. "I can no longer just sit behind the wheel and veg out. I have to have things to think about," she says. "Trucking has allowed me to channel many interests into something positive. I never turn away a chance to learn more or gain additional knowledge. I embrace every opportunity and always look forward to what's next down the road." Whether sitting behind the wheel, teaching a class, or mentoring colleagues, Margaret is drive, personified.

Her emancipation

Patricia Sueltz is a hardwired Determinator, but even strong women such as she need a little help from friends—or at least from their significant others. Pat's story illustrates that it's tough to be a superhero at work without a super-understanding spouse by your side. Of course, this is something men have known for years. Pat and her husband just turned the tables.

Pat, fifty, spent twenty years climbing the corporate ladder at technology behemoth IBM. Until recently, she was one of the top sixteen executives at the $11.4 billion technology services company Sun Microsystems, in charge of one of its largest divisions, Sun Services. In spring 2004, Pat made another leap, leaving Sun to be president of technology, marketing, and systems for a much smaller technology outfit, salesforce.com. Her new employer may be tiny compared with IBM and Sun, but that only means Pat has more control over its future. Says Pat, "I am now higher up in the business hierarchy, no longer compartmentalized at a large company, but able to make decisions about overall operations. That is very satisfying."

Like her job at Sun, at salesforce.com, which sells sales software, Pat is traveling a great deal, meeting with CEOs and other business leaders. A primary reason this mother of two is able to maintain her high-powered work lifestyle is because her husband, Steve, is a stay-at-home dad, a role he volunteered for back in 2000. The story of Pat's romance—with both her husband and her career—begins at Occidental College in California, back in 1974.

I was just walking across campus and a friend ran up to me and said, "You have to go see this recruiter. She's interviewing for jobs at Pacific

Telephone and Telegraph and paying $550 a month!" So I just walked into the interview, wearing a T-shirt and shorts, and they asked, "How do you feel about working outdoors?" In my deepest, most mature voice, I said I loved it. "How do you feel about working with men?" I said no problem. "How would you like to be an installation foreman?" I said I'd like that. They paid me $710 a month; I was on scholarships and needed the money.

It turns out that the phone company had agreed in court to put more women in management positions as a result of a discrimination lawsuit. I was one of those women. But there was still a lot of harassment in those days, and for two summers I worked side by side with guys who rolled their cigarettes in their shirtsleeves and drank a lot of beer, but I loved the job. I learned how to wire phones and climb telephone poles, and while the technology was very simplistic, I saw how phones made our lives better.

I got married to my boyfriend, Steve, after college, and while he went to Stanford to get his MBA, I continued to work for the phone company, where my liberal arts education served me well. I could apply logic to my environment, and I had good get-along-with-people skills. I became a middle manager running what was then the first computerized prepaid service operation. Then, Steve got an offer from IBM to work on the East Coast, but when IBM refused to fly out me, his spouse, to visit New York, my husband said moving across the country was a joint decision, and unless I could come out, he'd have to turn down the offer. Long story short: IBM flew us both to New York, where I ended up having a long conversation with the man who recruited Steve, after which IBM wanted to interview me for a job in information technology. I started as a systems analyst, working on satellite transmission and then application development, and I absolutely fell in love with IBM. The company seemed vast to me, like I could do anything there.

For the next twenty years Pat did, well, almost everything. A rambunctious voice in a bureaucratic corporate environment, Pat was called by IBM's CEO uninhibited and unmanageable, "and then he said to hire more people like me," she laughs. Pat was rewarded for her problem-solving innovations over the years, and by 1999, when she was a general manager, Sun came calling with a job offer she could not refuse. Pat and

Steve agreed that since they had moved to New York for Steve's career twenty years ago, it was time to move back to California for Pat's.

I can't say I grew up wanting to do a specific job, but when I got into corporate life I knew I wanted to be the person who could manage a lot of different areas and assimilate a lot of information and make decisions. I can't explain it. Perhaps it's because I was a Korean War baby. My birth mother was Japanese and my father was American, and I was born out of wedlock, and my birth mother placed me in an orphanage where she knew Americans adopted children. By doing that she gave me an opportunity. My [adoptive] parents always told me I could be anything except president of the United States, but that if I could change the Constitution, then I could be president. When I was three I would stand in the closet preaching (I don't know who to), and later I ran for student body president and won. I always get very into whatever I'm doing. My friends say that whenever I play tennis on a clay court I think I'm at the French Open, or when I bike I think I'm in the Tour de France. I always wanted to be chosen—maybe it has something to do with being adopted— but I always wanted to make sure I was in a position to either get picked or have an opportunity, and to be in that position requires a lot of preparation. Although I get a real kick out of what technology makes possible, I don't think my love of the job is content-dependent.

About six months after moving to California, Pat and Steve noticed a disturbing sign. They were consistently traveling or coming home late only to relieve their nanny, who cared for the younger of their two daughters.

If you peered into the window of our house late at night, everything looked perfect, but we noticed that our youngest daughter just looked sad. We went to bed one night and talked about it, and we talked about it some more for about five months. Finally Steve said, "We have to make a decision. We don't want to lose our daughter at age nine. That was not the pact we made when we had children; we didn't have kids so we could yell at them to do the dishes." [Laughs.] Then Steve said, "This is your time. I think you have to go for what will make you happy. How can we tell our daughters to be all they want to be if their mother is not all she wants to be?" Steve graciously said he would stay home full-time. He gave me the caveat that, yes, he might be grumpy sometimes, and there were other challenges. Women in the community who stayed home were not exactly welcoming to him, and even our daughter worried about what she was going to tell her friends. "Tell them I stay home with you," said Steve. It got easier when Steve began tutoring students in math, and our daughter's friends called him for help with their homework—she got a kick out of that.

Meanwhile, Pat charged ahead at Sun. Her goals as a leader: grow her division's revenue, sustain its profitability, and maintain a fair and challenging workplace environment. She spent almost half her time visiting Sun customers and the other half running Sun Services. "To me, power means authority and responsibility. Sometimes a leader facilitates, sometimes she dictates. But power can't be abused, it has to be treated gently." Because Pat also believed that, if she "quit learning, I would die," she was open-minded when an executive search firm called about an open position at a small technology company. "I scheduled a forty-five-minute lunch with the CEO, and two and a half hours later the meeting was well worth the cost of my parking ticket," says Pat.

While Pat was hardly unhappy at Sun, she was open to opportunities that would further push her limits and expand her knowledge. Plus, salesforce.com had plans to go public, and helping usher the company through its initial public offering had attractive financial as well as educational potential. "Everyone at Sun assumed I left for more money, but the fact of the matter is, my move had more to do with taking a risk and trying something new." Pat believes that salesforce.com's technology and business model, which essentially lets customers subscribe to its software and support services, is going to change the software industry. In her new role, Pat has more control than ever over how the business grows.

For this Determinator, size doesn't matter: "It's not about prestige, but about learning. Now is my chance to tie together my experiences and skills from three large technology companies and apply them to a team of 480 folks. Instead of just singing in the chorus, I can put together the whole aria! It's emancipating!"

Pat admits the new role might not be as easy to pull off if her husband were not also free from stereotypical gender roles. "Steve is quite an emancipated man and has been for twenty-seven years," acknowledges Pat. "My partnership in marriage has embodied the spirit of 'together we're better.' Taking turns jumping into the ring has worked out very well for us, and my husband is my biggest mentor, companion, and friend."

She's not afraid to ask.

Many Determinators, I found, are motivated more by overcoming obstacles than by honing a particular craft. These women leap from challenge to challenge, just as competitive athletes move from game to game. While athletes are also perfecting their skills, their greatest joy comes while playing: Each game is a chance to test and prove themselves yet again. And just as soccer players need teammates to score, so too must women in the workplace seek assistance from colleagues to reach their goals. Yet asking for help is not always easy for women, who, as truck driver Margaret Peterson put it, must work harder than men to earn respect. But as Courtney Harris is learning in Woburn, Massachusetts, those who ask, excel. Courtney's experience illustrates that Determinators addicted to challenge succeed because they aren't shy about soliciting assistance—and admitting what they don't know.

Courtney manages communications for U.S. Genomics, a start-up biotechnology company that develops highly specialized scientific tools to help scientists study DNA, RNA, and proteins. Courtney's job is to inform investors, the media, future customers, and the scientific community about U.S. Genomics's plans and products. With the company's nascent reputation in Courtney's hands, the job would be challenging even if she *had* practical scientific and marketing experience. But at age twenty-five, she doesn't. Courtney's confidence and intellect help offset that lack of experience by giving her the strength to admit that, sometimes, she doesn't have all the answers.

I think that I have always trusted my gut and been a person who wants to do things herself. When I was sixteen years old, I didn't want someone else to change my car's oil. I did it myself. I just wanted to be self-sufficient and be able to trust my own instincts. My mom was a great role model. She trusted her own instincts and was a hippie free spirit and traveled around the world in a VW bus. I figured if it worked for her it would work for me. My mom is also a two-time survivor of non-Hodgkin's lymphoma, and she was saved by monoclonal antibodies, which were a breakthrough drug in biotech and health care. That has a lot to do with why I like U.S. Genomics; it makes products to help scientists make discoveries, and that feels good.

Intellectually, I like trying to understand the products and then figuring out how to turn the science-speak into human-speak for investors and journalists. It's not easy, what I do. I don't have a portfolio of experience, and I can never say, "The last time I did this . . . ," so when I come up with a new idea, I have to justify it. Since I have no track record I can't just say I think it's a good idea, which forces me to analyze my opinion and ask myself why I want to do whatever it is that I want to do.

I didn't ask for a lot of help when I first started, because it was hard for me to even admit to myself that I didn't know things. But eventually I learned that asking others for input or advice actually took pressure off me. It's a nice relief to be able to say to myself, Okay, I don't know this, but I know I have the skills to get to the right answer.

Right now I'm working on one of our first product brochures. This is very different for me. It's not like I am a typical customer—in fact, I've never bought anything like what we sell. Yet I still have to convey the benefits of our products to people who are experts. My solution to this problem was to gather scientists from around the company and brainstorm. "Tell me," I said to them, "why would someone buy this, and what does a customer need to know that will convince them to buy it? What do I need to say in the brochure?" It was hard to understand everything they told me, but I just kept asking basic questions and really enjoyed the challenge of it.

I still have to stand my ground a lot. When people disagree with me they say, "Let me check with your boss to make sure you can really do this. . . ." And then, of course, my boss just says, "Sure, whatever Courtney says." I'm such a driven, type-A personality that I need the fast pace of a start-up. I expect to reach a higher level in my own career more quickly than if I worked for a big company. In some ways I even like the failures because, as long as I analyze them, failures propel my learning curve.

Determinators know that admitting what they do *not* know is not a sign of weakness but a sign of strength. For Courtney, acknowledging she's not always in control is the optimal way to maintain it.

Her trials

Many people need to ask explicitly for what they need if they want to get it. Yet women more often than men opt not to ask, assuming they won't get a raise or more time off. We want to be transferred to a better account or work for a different company, yet instead of requesting just that, we complain about why it will never happen. That's why the Determinators' chapter ends with Judy Harris, a happy working woman whose story is an empowering reminder that when we ask, we often get.

A lawyer and managing partner at the Washington, D.C., office of Reed Smith, one of the largest law firms in the world, Judy, fifty-four, has quit and been rehired several times. Do not be intimidated by Judy's credentials or make the mistake of thinking that her Ivy League education gets her what she wants. Instead, be impressed by her courage, her honesty, and her ability to express her needs.

I graduated Yale Law School in 1973, in the same class as Bill Clinton. The prevailing feeling among the twenty-five or so women I graduated with was that we carried future generations of women on our backs. Staying at home to raise children was not an option for us. It never even crossed my mind, because I felt I'd taken up a chair at Yale, a chair that could have been occupied by someone else who would no doubt make something amazing of her life. There was a tremendous sense that we had to succeed or Yale would never admit another woman.

But while I harbored this ambition, I also had an innate sense of moderation. I knew I wanted to succeed, but I also did not need to be the best lawyer at the fanciest law firm. While I got incredible job offers after law school—I was the first woman in Yale's history to win its annual trial competition—I eventually chose a small firm that would let me combine various things in my life, like travel and family. Even as the firm grew into one of the twenty largest in the world, I've always been very clear with myself about how much free time I was willing to give up.

One of my weaknesses is that I am a terrible decision maker; I get paralyzed staring at thirty-one flavors of ice cream. [Laughs.] But the few times in my career when I've actually identified and articulated what I really wanted, I always got it.

No one has ever really said no to me.

The first time I left Reed Smith was in 1979, before we had kids. My husband had a yearlong job opportunity in Palo Alto, California, and I wanted to join him. My firm offered me a leave of absence, but I didn't take it because I didn't want to sit idle for a year. So I looked up every government agency that had an office in San Francisco and eventually I called the antitrust division of the Justice Department and said, "Here's the deal. I'd love to come work for you for a year in San Francisco." We negotiated, and they agreed to let me spend a year in San Francisco if I took over a troubled case against Texas's utility companies. I agreed, and when my husband went to San Francisco, I joined him and continued to get legal experience.

Two years later, when my husband and I moved back to D.C., I asked Reed Smith if I could return. The firm said yes.

The next time I left Reed was when I was offered a job with the Federal Communications Commission during the Clinton administration heading the legislative office. At the time, all the laws regulating the communications industry were about to be rewritten. I knew nothing about Congress, but the friend who offered me the post kept pushing me to take it. When I told my then-thirteen-year-old son that I was thinking of going to work for the government again, he asked me why I would leave the law firm. I gave him a big talk about serving the public interest. "Plus," I added, "who knows where it will lead!" Matthew looked up at me and said, "Mom, do you really think at your age you should take a job because it might lead somewhere?" At my age? I was only forty-six at the time! [Laughs.]

Despite her son's doubts, Judy quit the law firm again and went to work for the Clinton administration for less money and, it turned out, longer hours. Battling the Republican-dominated Congress to pass legislation in the hostile anti-Clinton environment proved exciting but trying. "It kept me gasping for air," Judy recalls. One day, after the bill Judy was hired to help pass was passed, she looked at her calendar and realized her other son's bar mitzvah was coming up. Judy couldn't even find time to brush her teeth, let alone plan such a huge affair. She told her boss that, with her original mission accomplished, it was time for her to move on. Despite her boss's offer to find her a party planner to handle the bar mitzvah, Judy walked away and, instead of returning to work immediately, took the summer off to be with her sons.

I loved the summer and thought I was doing all this great bonding with my kids. Then one day I overheard my younger son say to a friend, "You know, my mom used to be this big-deal lawyer and now she's our maid." When I asked him about his comment, he told me how he had always been so proud of me for working. "It seems like you're wasting your life," he said. "We're okay, go back to work." And so I did. Once again, I asked to return to Reed Smith. I could have chosen another high-powered law firm—many made me offers—but I preferred to go back to where I already had a track record of success.

One Friday night, after being back at Reed Smith for several years, I was at work late and started to feel very sorry for myself. Both my sons were now in college but planning to spend the summer at home. I figured this was one of the last times I would get to spend an extended period of time with them. I thought, Why don't I take the summer off? It was like lightning had struck, and I just began to write a lengthy e-mail to my managing partner telling him that I was taking July and August off to be with my boys. I said the firm would not have to pay me, and I promised my work would not suffer, because I would tell my clients that I would be on vacation and would come in for meetings as needed. Don't get me wrong, it was not an easy thing to ask; I was very nervous and I even cried a bit because my firm had already allowed me to come back to work several times, but in my gut I knew I wanted to be home. It was close to midnight by the time I pressed the send button. When I came in Monday morning the managing partner had responded: "I'm envious," read his e-mail. "Have fun and see you in September." It was a wonderful summer. And when I returned to work in September, not only was I able to pick up where I'd left off, but I was asked to become managing partner of the Washington, D.C., office. I said yes.

While Judy's profile does not focus on her legal work per se, she is completely engaged by it. And because she is also effective, she has been able to command the flexibility she desired. Judy's story is important because it illustrates how Determinators—and, for that matter, all working women—can exert control over their careers. Passivity does not pay.

As many Determinators' paths show, happy careers rarely evolve out of dormant desire, blind fate, or mere coincidence. Instead, they evolve from careful planning, vision, and confidence. Regardless of a Determinator's motivation—a quest for independence and control; the joy of honing a skill; a lifestyle preference; or addiction to challenge—a Determinator takes control of her future. She plots, she plans, she takes steps to improve her condition. Just as Judy called up the Justice Department and declared she wanted to work there—and asked to return to her law firm after leaving—other Determinators go after jobs rather than wait for jobs to find them. Bravely bucking family expectations, financial marketer Jacqueline and CEO Christine both pursued careers for themselves, not for their mothers or fathers. Truck driver Margaret volunteered for management roles at Roadway in addition to her driving duties. And U.S. Genomics's Courtney knows that asking for assistance only makes her more successful. When Southerner–turned–New Yorker Anne was out of work, she styled a job-transition road map that she still follows to this day. Says Anne, "The difference between whether you or another qualified person lands the job you want is often a matter of getting in front of the right people and explaining to them how you are going to solve their needs." To figure that out, Anne forces herself to answer five seemingly basic but telling questions: What do I want? What can I give? What is going on in the marketplace? What do the companies need? And, finally, to whom do I need to speak?

Anne and other Determinators offer an overarching lesson: Those who take control of their careers simultaneously take responsibility for their own work-related happiness. While you don't have to be ambitious at work to love your job, be ambitious in the quest to find work you love. The latter is among the noblest forms of self-determination.

Chapter Four

The Heroines, Healers, and Sisters

Singer-songwriters, state representative, humanitarian
aid activist, auto shop owner, biomedical research scientist,
county judge, physical therapist, kindergarten teacher,
chef, hospital clown, flight attendant, doorperson,
massage therapist, cancer-prevention fund-raiser,
nonprofit program founder, college professor, financial
educator, erotica boutique owners, and nurse

From 1943 to 1968, about half of The Happy 100 women were in the throes of childhood. How many read the series of books about a nurse named Cherry Ames, I do not know, but what a career this young, fictional medical practitioner had. In the first book, Cherry Ames was seventeen, a pretty brunette attending nursing school. Years of job-hopping ensued, as did at least two dozen more books. There were *Cherry Ames: Senior Nurse; Cherry Ames: Army Nurse; Cherry Ames: Flight Nurse;* as well as *Cherry Ames: Veterans' Nurse; Cherry Ames: Private Duty Nurse;* and even *Cherry Ames: Cruise Nurse.* Cherry Ames got around, treating ailing patients in all parts of the world, even solving a mystery or two.

Despite their charm, the Cherry Ames books are indicative of a time when most girls believed nursing was one of the few occupations open to females. Indeed, many Happy 100 women told me that, as girls, they saw only four career options in their future: nurse, teacher, social worker, or secretary. Expectations have no doubt evolved in the twenty-first century. Young women now grow up with basically unlimited career options, and their participation in the workforce has grown significantly, at least in the U.S. In 1950, about 34 percent of women over age sixteen worked. By 1998, almost 60 percent did, according to the Bureau of Labor Statistics. Still, many Happy 100 women told me their motive for choosing their particular line of work has a "caretaking" aspect. Quite simply, women still want to help others. What's more, almost all Happy 100 members agree that "making a difference," or purpose, in some form, is critical to their job satisfaction. For the women in this chapter, it's the cornerstone of why they love their work. And as you'll see, there are unexpected ways in which women improve the lot and lives of others. Depending on just how, they are classified as Heroines, Healers, or Sisters. There's only one nurse, and one teacher, in the group.

Heroines, Healers, and Sisters are catalysts for productive change for the people they influence and help. Their tools are broad and diverse: managing, cooking, counseling, educating, coaching, songwriting, singing, clowning, motivating, massaging, selling, hand-holding, networking, speaking, and fund-raising, to name just a few. Heroines have an activist nature, exerting their opinions, creativity, and intellect to quash the status quo. The Healers are less rebellious and more cultivating of one-on-one relationships with people in need, preferring to work closely with others. As for the Sisters, these women are Heroines and Healers who are specifically focused on saving *other* women from sickness, from social stereotypes, and even from themselves. Sisters have a feminist bent.

Despite their differences, the women in this chapter all agree that lifting other people's spirits and circumstances inevitably lifts their own.

The closer they are to fine

First, the Heroines. These women are the activists, the reformers, determined to administer aid on a grand scale. In that vein, the Indigo Girls know that few things move the masses as effectively as music. Amy Ray, thirty-nine, and Emily Saliers, forty, are the folk rock band's singing-songwriting duo. Together they've produced nine albums, won a Grammy, and spawned a devoted fan base. For many listeners, Amy's and Emily's songs—intelligent, introspective lyrics set to hard-rock rhythms and sweet melodies—play like background music to their own personal stories of self-discovery. Listening to the Indigo Girls is like hearing a more poetic version of your own internal voice's confusion, anger, heartbreak, or silent musings. At concerts, audiences belt out words to each song with the passion of a church choir. Much more than typical pop-song fare about love and romance, the Indigo Girls' songs address the internal life and its vagaries, empowering listeners to take control of their circumstances and find peace within. I refer to this as an "inner-activism" on behalf of the band.

While Amy, a brunette with a deep, raspy voice, and Emily, a shaggy blonde with a more melodious style, appreciate this gift to touch others, such inner-activism is not the primary reason why these women love their work as musicians. "That is not necessarily our mission," said Emily when I met with her backstage before a concert in New York City's Central Park. "We just write reflections of our own thoughts and what we see others going through, just as all writers do." Adds Amy, "Songwriting is like therapy, just like when you sit around with friends and talk about your problems. It's about sharing. It's not like you write a song to specifically help someone else."

That, however, is not the case when the issues at hand are social or political, such as banning nuclear weapons or opposing the death penalty. Leveraging the power of music and fame to undo injustice—*outer-* as opposed to *inner*-activism—is the primary reason Amy and Emily are happy working women. In addition to enjoying the process of singing and writing—both began playing guitar as young women—they give voice to the disenfranchised, such as Native Americans or the gay community. Through song, public speaking, and their Web site, the Indigo Girls rally for gun control and human rights and against war. As Emily explains, just being true to themselves is often example enough.

Emily: There is a lot of homophobia in the music industry, and early on in our career I had a lot of fear about it and did not want to be known as just a "lesbian band," which in the end we were identified as. I think it's held us back to a certain extent, but it's worth it to be part of a movement, and I am grateful we have the courage to be part of that movement. We don't take crap from people. If someone makes a sexist or rude comment, we address it immediately. We won't put up with being mistreated, and we try to live our lives in a way that represents the things we stand for. I know the fact that Amy and I are "out" has been helpful for a lot of gay youth, and I am grateful for that and don't take it lightly. But attitudes take a long time to change, and this country still has a long way to go. Look at what's happening in the church now, the uproar and how people are so freaked out over gay people. I find it appalling.

Emily's activism—born partly, she says, of socially conscious, liberal parents—extends beyond the gay community. She recently helped produce a CD for a woman on death row convicted of a crime that, says Emily, the woman did not commit. And after September 11, Emily channeled her antiwar sentiments into, among other things, a song titled "Our Deliverance," which decries the U.S. war in Iraq.

> *They're sending soldiers, to distant places;*
> *X's and O's on someone's drawing board.*
> *Like green and plastic, but with human faces, and they want to tell*
>   *you it's a merciful sword.*
> *But with all the blood newly dried in the desert, can we not fertilize*
>   *the land with something else?*
> *There is no nation by God exempted;*
> *Lay down your weapon and love your neighbor as yourself.*

Compared with Emily, Amy is a bit more radical, and her songs have a tougher, more rock-and-roll edge. In a letter to fans on the Indigo Girls' Web site, Amy writes, "The laws we have set up to protect the earth and to protect our communities are being gutted by the Bush administration. . . ." This Indigo Girl does not mince words.

Amy: Yes, I'm angry about certain things . . . but I am not angry to the point that I am paralyzed. Anger is a tool I use, that I've harnessed. A lot of times I make more room for political work than other stuff. I may turn down a gig if it interferes with some political work I am doing. What drives me to be more popular or to have a song on the radio has, honestly, always been politically based. The better we do, the more money we can give to organizations like Honor the Earth. I'm also motivated as someone who has always seen through a lens of a gay woman. While I am not nearly in the same powerless position of, say, a Native American woman, I can relate to her experience of being disenfranchised. Whenever Emily and I want fame, it's always [in the context of] politics. Fame is about power, and people want power for different reasons. We want it because we know what it's like to be disenfranchised.

Emily echoes this sentiment: "The only reason I'd want to be more famous or wealthy is to leverage more power for social causes."

The two friends met in elementary school and began playing music together in high school. Both live in Georgia but rarely see each other when not performing or recording (Amy also owns a record label, Emily a restaurant). Just as the marriage of music and activism forms the Indigo Girls' product, the marriage of their different yet complementary talents makes them ideal coworkers. They are respectful to the point that they won't edit each other's songs unless invited, and this professional partnership is critical to their job-related happiness. "I've known Amy longer than any other friend in my life," Emily told me as ticket holders for their sold-out concert began to line up. "Plus, we have the best fans in the world."

Proof of that came when hundreds of people showed up for their Central Park concert despite the now infamous blackout that hit New York City in 2003. While the electricity failure caused thousands of workers to stream out of Manhattan's dark office buildings, it also threatened the Indigo Girls' concert that night. Luckily, the stage's generator kicked in, allowing Amy and Emily to play for their fans. So, on a hot summer night, while the rest of the East Coast went without power, the Indigo Girls granted it to their audience, who, of course, sang along:

My life is part of the global life.
I find myself becoming more immobile when
I think a little girl in the world can't do anything.
Distant nation my community, street person my responsibility.
If I have a care in the world, I have a gift to bring.

In her own words

Neva Walker, 32
State Representative
St. Paul, Minnesota

For four years, Neva has represented some 37,000 residents in a low-income South Minneapolis neighborhood. She is the first African-American woman to serve in Minnesota's legislature, despite being one course short of a college degree, and a single mother of a sixteen-year-old son. Neva embraces public service not because she loves politics, but because she loves service.

It's ironic that I went into government, because, as a child, I didn't want to be like anyone in my family, who all worked in social service or in government-paid labor jobs, like sanitation or construction. My grandfather was a deacon, my dad worked for the City of Minneapolis, and my mother was a nurse–turned–social worker. While I loved that my mother helped people, she also brought her work home all the time. Families would stay at our house because they had nowhere else to go, and my mother set up a food shelf where families in need could come and get canned goods. "At some time, everyone needs a hand-up," Mom would say to me. And it was our responsibility to give back. Period. Even if I chose not to go into social services, I was expected to volunteer.

But I did have the organizing bug: In eighth grade I started my own basketball team, and in high school I registered people to vote. I also had a sense that people in government were making decisions about our community—but those people weren't me! I believed in more of a collective power and had difficulty with authority. I asked the pastor questions that I knew he couldn't answer, and because my mother did a lot of civic work, I was around the mayor a lot, and I used to question him.

When I got pregnant in high school it was tough to tell my parents. I decided to keep the baby, but I knew I also had to finish school. My mother was my backbone, and my dad tried to make sure I had a regular teenage life. I kept playing basketball but also brought my son to school with me. When I got into the University of Minnesota, I took my son to college with me and moved out of my parents' house. To pay for his day care I worked at Kmart, at a construction company, and in homes for the mentally and physically disabled. Also, I no longer wanted to be a lawyer but wanted to go into business so I could make money and take care of my son. But in my sophomore year at college I had a dream that showed my whole lifespan: I saw myself in a business suit, sitting at meetings; I was making money in some management job, but I was so unhappy. The next day I switched my major only to realize I was already closer to a degree in sociology than business. Still, I was so busy during school that I ended up dropping classes and picking them up again, and eventually I dropped out of school and continued to work full-time in the group homes for the disabled. I'd feed them, give them meds, take them for walks, and in some cases intervene with their families. I did that for six years and I loved it.

I also volunteered, doing community youth projects. Eventually a neighborhood organization hired me, and I went door-to-door to start block clubs so neighbors could come together and talk about community issues. After that, I became an affordable-housing community organizer, working with homeless folks or low-income families on the verge of becoming homeless. We taught people how to advocate on their own behalf, and we rehabbed the existing stock of low-income housing.

One day, the group I worked with and several homeless families were supposed to testify in front of the state legislature at a committee hearing about the homeless. Minneapolis rents were so high that even working people could not afford the cheapest apartments. But when the group went to testify, we were made to feel unwelcome. They made folks walk into the Capitol hearing room one by one, and we weren't even protesting or causing a scene! The whole thing just rubbed me the wrong way because the Capitol should be open to everyone. Around that time two friends were trying to convince me to run for city politics. They said, "Neva, you know the budget, you know how neighborhoods work." But I didn't care for politics—it was cutthroat, and it seemed elected officials did not get to really work that much on policy. I'm a social justice person who wants to change people's lives, and I didn't want to have to deal with issues like trash removal. Also, I don't like compromise and am one of the most private people I know.

But one day I was watching government hearings on television and *realized that there had never been an African-American woman in the Minnesota legislature. I couldn't believe it! I asked my mom if she could think of anyone. We could name black men, but not one black woman. It was ridiculous. It was 2000! I tried to find someone to run but couldn't convince anyone. Either they didn't have time or it wasn't their "thing" or they had children or didn't want to connect themselves to a specific party. I thought all their reasons were ridiculous, but they were my issues as well. So I thought, If I can get past my own issues I could run.*

I decided it was not about me. Minnesota needed its first African-American woman in office on the state level, and it would at least give me an opportunity to get people to pay attention to policy.

I was twenty-eight when I decided to run—I looked about twenty-two—and someone told my campaign manager that the fact that I'd been a teenage mother would be a problem and implied I should "make my son disappear." But I could not deny my son! I was a mother before I was anything else, so we decided to come at the issue head on, and in all my campaign literature there was a picture of me and my son, and the very first line said, "A mother of a twelve-year-old."

The hardest part was winning the nomination to run on the Democratic Farmer Labor Party ticket. I ran against three other people, and my most surprising critics were elderly black women who criticized me for being young and for being a woman. I was prepared for some criticism, but not from the women I'd grown up with! I also faced every "ism": sexism, racism, and ageism. But I won because I knew how to organize people. To win the nomination, I needed 60 percent of the delegate votes. The more people I got to show up at the convention, the better my chances. So my campaign team focused not only on wooing past delegates, but getting new ones to sign up, people who had never before been involved with politics, whom we trained so they would know what to expect when they got to the convention. On the day of the vote, all my supporters wore green shirts and green buttons and carried green signs with my slogan NEVA WALKER IN THE HOUSE. There were maybe 300 people in the room, and so many were wearing green that one of the candidates threw his support to me after his speech. He could tell I had at least 60 percent, and he was right. I won with 72 percent of the vote. A few months later, after the regular election, Neva Walker was in the house.

Most of the other legislators are older white men, and some embraced me when I first came to the Capitol, but to this day some still don't know what to make of a young black girl from the south side. During my first two years I didn't sleep well and I gained so much weight. My party was in the minority, and I had to figure out how to survive spiritually when issues I cared about lost in a vote, or if I heard a sad story that I could not do anything about, or if I heard a racist comment.

Two of my big issues are reducing teen pregnancy as well as out-of-home placements of children. We need money to help get families back together and, if not, to pay for more foster parents. I've also worked to help bridge disparity issues for people of color. We were able to get $12 million that will go directly to communities to educate citizens on cancer, diabetes, and pregnancy and HIV prevention. We also allocated dollars to try to reduce black-on-black crime. We weren't as successful when we tried to cap application fees for rental housing, or when we wanted to make it mandatory that police officers had to write down the race of people they pulled over. Our goal was to identify the police officers that were racially profiling people, but instead the legislature required only voluntary data collection. That was a tough fight to lose because all the men in my family had been stopped by the police simply because they were black. Recently, it happened to my son for the first time.

My platform has always been community participation. Most people don't know who their state legislators are, and I want people involved in government and I want them to know who represents them. That's why I spend so much time visiting classrooms, talking to students about my issues and why they should be concerned about what I do. I call it planting seeds. I know I'm making a difference because I go to the Target and a sixth-grader comes up to me and says he saw me speak at his school.

I've learned a lot about compromise in this job. I was raised to believe that there are no permanent friends or permanent enemies, just permanent issues. I can't hold a grudge if someone doesn't vote with me, because tomorrow I may need their help. I've come to realize that if you want to make large-scale change, you have to accept that there will be a lot you can't change. But at least I'm here.

Her finest production

"I love the way film can reach a large number of people and have a positive effect," says Caroline Baron. The New York–based film producer is not just talking about inducing laughter or tears, but how film can, quite literally, save lives, awaken dormant spirits, and revive hope among displaced, isolated, or poor populations.

Caroline, forty-one, is a natural leader and manager, two skills that facilitated her career as a producer. She became hooked on movies while working on her first, *The Toxic Avenger*. ("I managed that movie with my summer-camp counseloring skills," she jokes.) For a while Caroline worked on mainstream films, including *Addicted to Love*; *Indian Summer*; and *The Santa Clause*. But these days she opts for headier, heartfelt fare such as the independent romantic comedy *Monsoon Wedding*. Says Caroline, "I've always loved that film work exposes me to different types of people and cultures, and I've been able to travel all over the world."

That said, it is Caroline's second job, which the first helps support, that gives her the greatest sense of purpose and satisfaction. In 1999, Caroline founded FilmAid International, a humanitarian aid project that brings movies to displaced populations, or refugees, in places such as Kosovo, East Africa, and Afghanistan. With the help of funds from foundations, government organizations, corporations, and individuals, FilmAid helps refugee camps select and show films. "After other humanitarian aid organizations meet the immediate survival needs of food, shelter, and medicine, FilmAid steps in with education, information, and entertainment," writes Caroline on FilmAid's Web site. She told me that it was back in 1999, while listening to a National Public Radio report about Kosovo, that she first learned that two of the largest problems in refugee camps were idleness and psychological trauma.

The very night before I heard the NPR report, I'd been lamenting how I felt so helpless in light of the ethnic cleansing going on in Kosovo. As I listened to the radio, I had an idea of holding an outdoor movie screening for children. Basically, I made it happen in six weeks. I went to Macedonia with an international affairs graduate student and a filmmaker friend from London, we hired a local crew and an interpreter, rented a

*truck, and set up screens in the middle of the refugee camp. I soon
realized we could use the screen not just for entertainment, but to deliver
information, and one of the first things we did was videotape the contents
of a UNICEF land mine–awareness pamphlet and projected it. It was
vital information for the refugees.*

In the years that followed, FilmAid expanded its content and scope. The
United Nations' high commissioner for refugees asked Caroline to bring
FilmAid to Africa, where she helped set up screens for refugees from the
Sudan, Ethiopia, Burundi, Somalia, Rwanda, Uganda, and other countries. In Tanzania, audiences reach up to 33,000 people for a single
screening. People are starved not just for food, but for entertainment
and connection to the outside world. Feature films shown on a large
screen bolted to a truck are accompanied by educational films that promote AIDS awareness, safe hygiene, conflict resolution, and women's
rights. "After a couple in Africa sees a film about AIDS, the man can no
longer deny to his wife that the disease exists. How can he say no to her
when she asks him to use a condom?" says Caroline. Screenings of
Winnie-the-Pooh helped boost attendance at a center for malnourished
infants, and more recently, FilmAid was in Kabul, Afghanistan, where a
room full of street children who had never before heard music watched
The Wizard of Oz. Caroline had the pleasure of telling little girls that the
film was not just for the boys to watch, but for them as well, contrary
to what they had assumed. Even more shocking, the movie was about a
girl, unheard of in the oppressed country.

*This is gratifying to me, and it's so basic that it's almost a crime not to
do it. You have to do work that makes you feel good, and FilmAid is
important to my happiness. It has really enriched and changed my life
enormously. It's a wonderful way to have a huge and powerful impact as
a filmmaker.*

There has been public praise for FilmAid (it was featured during the
Golden Globes as well as in *Vanity Fair* magazine) and celebrity endorse-
ments (actor Julia Ormond is Caroline's cochair, and advisory committee
members include Susan Sarandon and Robert De Niro). But for Film-

Aid's founder and chairperson, the traditional lures of Hollywood are important only to the extent that they further FilmAid's cause.

She respects you and your car.

At first blush, it's tempting to peg Catherine Simpson as a Builder. After all, the thirty-six-year-old is a trained car mechanic who owns two auto repair and service shops in Atlanta. As a young girl she was a tomboy who hauled around a personalized green toolbox and built dollhouse furniture. Builder, right? Not so. Catherine is a mechanic with a mission, and thus a Heroine. "I always knew I wanted to do something to help people," says the strawberry blonde who speaks with a slight southern accent. She just had no idea her venue would be a greasy garage.

The daughter of liberal parents, Catherine marched in Equal Rights Amendment parades with her mom and volunteered throughout high school and college. Determined to help others, Catherine moved to Seattle after graduating from Georgetown University and worked as a counselor in a residential facility for troubled teens. Despite her good intentions, dealing with young people in their darkest hours became emotionally overwhelming for Catherine. Their own pain struck a bit too close to home. You see, Catherine needed to tend to herself before she could tend to others. In college, Catherine had been raped, and the emotional pain still lingered. "It was the most depressing time," she recalls of her early twenties. Salvation came from an unlikely source.

I was depressed and eventually stopped working altogether and, for several months, lived off savings and my parents' support. I also volunteered in a bookstore, and a woman I worked with told me about a class that taught women basic trade skills. It was the first thing that had excited me in ages! I interviewed for the class—a government-sponsored program designed to teach skills to women coming off welfare so they could get higher-paying jobs. Although I was not on welfare, I hadn't gotten a paycheck for several months and was accepted into the program.

The class was a turning point for me. Some people said I was wasting my Georgetown degree, but working with my hands was exactly what I needed at that time in my life. It was a great way to get out of my head, especially after working with many troubled teenagers. Building things was so empowering after being at such a low point in my life.

Toward the end of the course we learned a little bit about mechanics, like fixing small gas engines and power tools, and I enjoyed that even more than the construction and carpentry. Mechanical work was more mentally challenging for me because I had to think about how parts worked together and what made something work. It was also physical, not so much in a strength way but in terms of working with my hands, which I loved.

In 1992, Catherine's Mazda started making a terrible noise, and she called auto repair shops for quotes. The experience changed her life. "I didn't like how the guys talked to me or treated me. They used all these words I did not understand at the time, which made me feel like I was being ripped off. And so I got this idea," says Catherine. "I wanted to open my own auto repair shop, a place where women could feel comfortable bringing their cars." But first, Catherine had to learn about cars, and she applied to a two-year program in Seattle that provided a year of classes and a year of hands-on training working at car dealerships. She scored high on the entrance exams, but the instructor in charge of admissions plainly told Catherine that he was reluctant to admit her because she was a woman. "He had never admitted a woman into the program and he wasn't sure how the dealers would react," says Catherine. While the instructor polled dealers, Catherine began looking for other opportunities. "I landed a job in a transmission repair warehouse as a trainee and told the school to forget it."

Her induction into the auto repair workforce was also an introduction to the realities of being a woman in the macho mechanics business. Most of the men Catherine worked with were professional and kind, and Catherine says she would not be where she is today without "all the great men who supported me over the years." But sexual harassment and discrimination remained very real issues. "Everywhere I worked there was usually one bad apple, some guy who would make things difficult for me," says Catherine. There were men who leaned in a bit too close to check her work when she was fixing a car, and men who dropped sexual innuendos without a thought to their impropriety. When Catherine was promoted to manager at one garage, rumors that she was sleeping with her boss subsided only once her performance proved she had the skills for the new job. When she landed a job at a large dealership, Catherine was paired with a male trainer who would shake his head and say, "You'll never make it in this business." At another garage, Catherine would sit at lunch among male mechanics who ogled calendars of naked women. "I could tell lots of stories about horrible things some guys did," says Catherine, who, because of her past, was particularly sensitive. "The harassment brought back that helpless feeling that someone was doing something to me I could not stop." But the good apples outnumbered the bad, and she continued to learn the trade.

Meanwhile, Catherine had moved back to Atlanta to live closer to her family, her dream of opening her own garage still alive. She took a six-month mechanics course to learn even more about auto repair, but when she would call to apply for mechanic training positions, garage owners always asked if she was calling for her husband or boyfriend. No one assumed Catherine was calling for herself. The one summer she worked at an all-woman garage further fueled her desire to open her own shop.

Catherine put the dream on hold for several years while she helped manage her mother's art gallery (a valuable professional experience because she learned how to operate a company) and worked as a nanny for her sister's children (a valuable personal experience because Catherine had no interest in having children of her own). "While I was a nanny everyone thought I'd abandoned my plans. They were all shocked when I went through with them," says Catherine.

She took night courses in business and in early 2000 wrote a business plan while her father cosigned a loan from the bank. After about a year finding and renovating a former auto repair shop at an intersection in Atlanta, Catherine's Auto Repair and Service Shop opened for business.

When I first opened I was the service adviser, which meant greeting the customers, finding out what was wrong with their cars, dispatching work to my technicians, estimating the price, and then telling customers the problem and how much it would cost to repair. After almost two years of that I thought I was going to lose my mind! I had hired four mechanics, and between keeping up with them and running the business, I was too busy. Finally, I hired a service adviser, and today I concentrate on running the two garages I own.

My slogan is "Respect for You and Your Car," which gets across exactly what I want to achieve. We never talk down to customers and always take time to explain what we're doing. We just give people as much information and options as possible so they can make an informed decision. People tell me all the time that my shop is different from other garages, and I think they say that because of how I pay my employees (even though my customers don't know about it). Unlike other auto repair places, I don't pay on commission or the "flat rate" system. There is no individual sales incentive, only an overall profit-sharing plan in addition to everyone's weekly salary. This way, no mechanic has an incentive to sell anything that does not need to be sold. There is never a high-pressure pitch. While other mechanics focus on time and money, I tell my staff to focus on quality and customer service. I also give my staff paid sick leave and insurance, something many garages do not.

For the first few years, hiring and supervising took most of my time. While I originally wanted to hire women mechanics, only a handful ever applied! Recently I did hire a female apprentice, and it felt so good to give her an opportunity. One of the toughest things about owning my own shop is hiring and retaining talented and reliable mechanics. I think I'm a fair boss, but I have high standards and, all told, I've had to fire about ten people since I opened. Personally, money is so unimportant to me that my disinterest in it is almost bad for the business. I am just starting to pay more attention to making bigger profits so I can expand. I do not personally need a lot of money, just enough to support myself and travel, but I am starting to realize that to grow, I need to be more profitable. People joke with me about my idealism, and how I almost feel bad making money off people's car troubles. I have to get past that, especially since what drives me is being powerful in terms of making changes in the industry.

One of the most important things I do is teach car care classes to women, many who drive from miles away. I just love educating the women (and the occasional male) who show up and seeing how empowered they feel when they learn how to open the hood of a car, check the oil themselves, or change a flat tire. Just understanding basic car care makes them feel more in control of their cars, and their lives.

Catherine would definitely not be as happy operating just any type of business. "I love trying to make a difference in the *automotive* industry," she insists. Considering that only half of Catherine's customers are women, she is succeeding in her mission not only by standing up for female customers in the auto repair market, but by standing up for disgruntled car owners everywhere. For that service alone—not to mention her intellect and courage—this is one auto-shop owner who deserves to get rich, and happy, off other people's car troubles.

In her own words

Marina Ramirez-Alvarado, 35
Biomedical Researcher, Assistant Professor, and Scientist
Mayo Clinic and Foundation
Rochester, Minnesota

Marina was born and raised in Mexico, received her Ph.D. in Heidelberg, Germany, and did postdoctoral training at Yale University before joining the faculty of the prestigious Mayo Graduate School, where she teaches Ph.D. students. She primarily studies light chain amyloidosis, or how and why misshapen proteins cause diseases such as Alzheimer's, Parkinson's, even mad cow. Marina knows that the work of scientists such as herself can have profound effects on millions of people.

Back in junior high I actually wanted to have a travel agency, but my friends and a teacher encouraged me to study chemistry because I was good at it. My father never went to college and worked as a consultant in the farming industry, helping people grow and sell crops. My mother was a stay-at-home mom who barely finished junior high. My three brothers and I all went to university, but I'm the only one who no longer lives in Mexico. When I was getting my master's degree my dad always asked, "So, when are you going to start wearing a suit and heels?" "Never," I told him.

"If I'm working in a lab, you don't want me in high heels. It's not safe." I guess he could not imagine a job that didn't require a woman to wear a business suit.

People picture scientists surrounded by colorful flasks and bubbly things, but we mostly work with little plastic tubes and our chemical solutions are always transparent. My specialty is protein biochemistry. I am a relatively new investigator, and most days I work in a lab doing experiments by myself or with students and a technician. In the process of fighting disease, proteins change shape, and sometimes those shapes are harmful and cause other diseases. By understanding why they are misshapen, we can eventually begin to develop medicine. For example, say a protein is like cooked spaghetti, all loose, which is incorrect. Sometimes a very small molecule can be added to bring the two pieces of spaghetti together and maintain their shape. Sometimes we produce proteins in the lab by adding DNA to bacteria, and then we purify the protein and ask some questions about it, like how easily it can lose its shape, for example. We also measure it and compare it to proteins from other patients. By understanding why proteins are misshapen, we can learn how to eradicate them and prevent them from becoming that way in the first place.

The field is very competitive, and everyone wants to discover something desperately. There is great satisfaction when you're the first to do something, and there can be recognition and economic reward if you make a discovery in biotech. You can patent it or start a company, which a lot of scientists do. I have no patents and no interest in that. I don't need the money, and I am very happy with the amount they pay me. When you go to a company, your focus changes. Instead of asking questions for the love of knowledge or to help find a cure for a specific disease, the goal becomes getting more and more money. I guess I'm not that kind of person.

While we do compete in science, we also team up to inspire each other. A huge thing for me is being able to see my students go from knowing nothing to grasping general concepts. Seeing their heads just absorb all of this information and fight through challenges just fills my heart with joy! Sharing the passion of science, day by day, is a very important thing for me.

Discovery is a very slow process. You have to be patient, and there will be numerous disappointments. Some days are very unproductive and you *go home and feel as if you did nothing. You can find yourself in a deep hole and need to be creative to get out. Other times you're on top of a hill and accomplish many things. The day you get something right, even if it's tiny, is such an important and wonderful day. I've seen the face of many people who have been struggling and struggling and all of a sudden the thing works, and they glow! One reason why I keep doing this job is because those days exist. This Friday we were setting off some reactions to mimic the dying process of a new type of protein so we could study it under a microscope. It was the first time we did the process with these particular proteins. Suddenly my tech came into my office, just glowing. "It worked!" she said. It doesn't matter if you had a year and a half of disappointments—what you feel on that day makes a great difference. If we end up improving the quality of patients' lives, curing a disease, or increasing their life expectancy, that will be when I say all those years of hard work were worth it. It's a long process, but I like to quote something I once heard from a medical student candidate. As she put it, "I want to help others through academic work and gaining new knowledge."*

She holds her own court.

M. Sue Kurita's signature can send someone to jail or set them free. As a county court judge in El Paso, Texas, Sue oversees more than 4,000 criminal misdemeanor cases a year, sentencing some people to jail and some to rehabilitation and letting others off the hook. "It's a scary feeling, because this job has so much responsibility. It's awesome, but not awesome in a great way. You have to respect the power of the situation," says Sue. The voters of El Paso respect Sue: They've elected and re-elected her eight times.

Judging is not a life calling for Sue, but an extension of a legal career that this single mother chose to support herself and her daughter. One of five siblings, Sue is part Asian and part Hispanic, and while her mother espoused marriage to "a good man," her father emphasized education. On her mother's advice, Sue married immediately after college, but after five years her husband "found greener, younger pastures" and left Sue with a baby and a job that paid only $15,000 a year. Adopting her father's advice, Sue invested in more education and went to law school.

I did not have a huge drive to go to law school, but it was easier to do than medical school with a three-year-old child. I took the LSAT, applied, and then panicked once I got accepted. I chose a school close to home, and walking to class my first day I literally had to tell my right foot to take a step and then my left foot to take a step. It was the longest walk I ever took.

Sue's goal: Graduate quickly and start making a living. She lived off loans and some money from her ex-husband; she took summer classes; and she treated each school day like a workday, attending class from nine to five while her daughter stayed in day care. She came home to fix dinner and did homework while her daughter slept. During the first year, as if being a single parent were not difficult enough, Sue underwent surgery to remove a benign tumor. Refusing to take time off from law school for fear she'd never return, Sue pushed herself to continue, although she throttled back her expectations. "I was more relaxed after my surgery. When you think you're going to die, you put things in perspective, and I decided I did not have to be at the top of my class. Just finishing law school became my goal." Sue graduated in two and a half years, took the state bar exam, and moved back to El Paso to practice real estate and, eventually, divorce law.

As a divorce attorney, Sue took great pride in being a catalyst for civility and fairness during difficult proceedings, but the rampant pettiness in divorce cases wore her out, and in 1998 she gave up her private practice to become a full-time judge. (She'd been a part-time municipal judge since 1988, handling traffic violations and the like.)

Today, the Honorable Judge Kurita's sixty-by-sixty-foot courtroom houses a jury box and a gallery that seats fifty. Some sixty defendants walk through its doors daily and face the black-robed judge, mainly for cases of drunk driving, family violence, theft, and drug possession. "At my level, it's all about volume," says Sue, who says judging is not as much about punishing the guilty as giving folks a second chance. By upholding the law, Sue says she makes a difference in people's lives by bringing common sense to the bench as she evaluates the merits of each case.

As a result of my court, there is a possibility of successful rehabilitation. What most satisfies me is that I may have a chance to make a difference in someone's life, help them reassess their priorities. If an eighteen-year-old gets caught with marijuana, it's likely he just made a bad decision and I can put him in a program, keep an eye on him, and maybe get him straightened out so he can change. I also teach, and in some ways that's even more rewarding because I directly impact students. As a teacher, my students choose to come to class and learn. As a judge, defendants show up involuntarily; I can tell them to do something, but it's up to them if they're going to change.

Off the bench, Sue is a public figure who sits on the boards of a Holocaust museum and a Catholic school. She also referees volleyball, and after September 11, 2001, she visited New York City on behalf of the City of El Paso to offer support. Sue is a valuable example of a woman who can love her job for heroic reasons without becoming fanatical about the cause—sort of a low-maintenance Heroine. (Indeed, if she were fanatical, she probably could not be an effective, objective judge.) I would not even say Sue is intensely passionate about the law, but simply proud to consistently do a good job. Here is someone who pursued her career for practical reasons but came to love it for more heartfelt ones. And as a single mother, Sue is as much a Heroine on the home front as she is on the bench: By 2002, at the age of forty-eight, she'd paid for her daughter's college education and finally paid off her own student loans. You don't have to save the world to be a Heroine. Sometimes, saving yourself and your family is enough.

In her own words

Nancy Roberge, 51
Physical Therapist
Chestnut Hill Physical Therapy Associates
Wellesley Hills, Massachusetts

As a physical therapist (PT) who specializes in breast cancer survivors, Nancy is frustrated that more doctors don't tell patients how physical therapy restores muscle activity and can prevent postsurgery complications. And she is frustrated that managed care discourages women from

seeking out PTs. So in addition to treating patients in her private practice, Nancy lobbies state and federal legislatures, teaches up-and-coming
PTs, and is getting a doctorate. This Heroine's platform: educate patients,
practitioners, and policy makers about the benefits of physical therapy at
all stages of cancer treatment and recovery.

*Too often when a woman with cancer completes weeks of radiation
treatment, the doctors simply send her on her way and the patient feels
abandoned. She has more questions and is still reeling from the original
diagnosis. As a physical therapist I ease that transition by trying to restore
her quality of life. I ask my patients, "What did you do before you had
cancer? Were you a runner? A swimmer? Do you have three young kids
you used to pick up but no longer can because your arm is so swollen?"*

*Many doctors and other physical therapists do not understand how PTs
can help women after breast cancer. If you have a body part amputated,
PT is automatically part of rehabilitation. But if you have a breast
amputated or reconstructed, PT is not a given. My soapbox is that women
do not get the right education to restore functions or prevent problems like
lymphedema, a swelling of the arm after lymph nodes have been removed
or irradiated. Lymphedema can be brought on by a multitude of factors,
including air travel, a needle prick to the arm, or a wound, and it results
in trouble lifting, decreased flexibility, a lifetime of discomfort as well as
constant and costly medical attention. Most breast cancer patients don't
even know they're at risk for lymphedema, and so they don't take easy steps
to prevent it. Women are extremely upset that doctors are not cautioning
them, and part of why I'm getting a doctorate is to research and publish
empirical results to add to the anecdotal evidence I've seen.*

*I'm also the legislative chair for the Massachusetts Chapter of the
American Physical Therapy Association, trying to make lawmakers aware
that physical therapy needs to be a more autonomous profession and be
given direct-access status so patients don't need doctor referrals to see us.
Advocacy is easy for me because I speak for the patient. If I spoke only for
myself, my knees would be knocking together.*

*I always knew I wanted to go into health care. My mother had multiple
sclerosis, and my father built a special pool where she exercised with a
physical therapist. I thought,* What a cool job. *At first I focused on*

orthopedics but switched to breast cancer when a physical therapist friend of mine was diagnosed with the disease and treated herself to therapy after radiation. Her doctor was astounded at the range of motion she had in her arm and how well she healed, and a light went on for me: I realized breast cancer patients need physical therapists, so I refocused my practice and knocked on doors of radiation oncologists and nurses, telling them what PTs could do for patients. I literally started cold-calling and asked them to refer patients to me!

Now the majority of my clients are breast cancer survivors. Sure, the exercises I do with them every day can get very redundant, but it's so critical to their quality of life that, for me, the redundancy just fades away. There is so much pain in the world, so much we can't control, but when it comes to breast cancer we can minimize some of the suffering by utilizing the PT profession. I just have to get the word out. If you treat, it's for today. If you teach, it's for tomorrow.

Her Three Rs

Teaching can be heroic. Teaching can also be exhausting, underpaid, time-consuming work. But the former can often compensate for the latter. For Holly Rumph, who at age fifty-seven has been teaching kindergarten and disabled children for more than thirty years in rural Wyoming, teaching is about not just what happens in her classroom every day, but about what her children take from that room into the world. Holly is a Heroine shaping future generations.

I believe that children need me, and I believe that there is so much more to give them than the three Rs of reading, writing, and 'rithmetic. My three Rs are respect for yourself, respect for others, and responsibility for all your actions. If children can begin to learn respect at age five or six, they will carry it throughout their lives. Sometimes I think we are living in a valueless society; other times I think people go overboard with values. There is no happy medium, which was how I grew up. Yes, I went to church, but it was not the be-all and end-all of existence. We were also taught to do music and dance and to respect others. My main goals as a teacher are to raise children who want to learn and who will grow up to be responsible citizens, responsible taxpayers.

As for Holly, her childhood was, for the most part, "idyllic." With a father in the navy, Holly's family moved around the country a great deal, and memories of her own schooling are telling: She recalls a beautiful, energetic second-grade teacher as "the most wonderful woman in the world"; she recollects having so much fun in high school that she feared she might not get into college. Once she did, she recalls majoring in home economics until a field trip to a local school to teach seventh-grade girls how to make aprons went awry. "The hormones were flying! Teaching home economics was not at all what I thought it would be. I just knew there was no way I could teach junior high." Later that year, a class in child development brought Holly face-to-face with a more palatable population: preschools. She fell in love with the young children, their open minds, and their hunger to learn. As a result, Holly switched majors and transferred schools to study early childhood education. She taught immediately after graduation, first in the poor projects of St. Louis, and then in a Montessori school for children of wealthy Catholic and Jewish families. "I went from having three-year-olds whose mothers were fourteen, to three-year-olds whose mothers were forty," recalls Holly. But the kids, she says, were always the same. "You could almost see their brain synapses forming!" Witnessing children as they encountered the world was a pleasure that never wore thin.

After her daughter was born, Holly's first husband, a police lieutenant, moved the family west, to Wyoming, "so he could hunt." That was in 1973, and over the next thirty years Holly would divorce, remarry a rancher, adopt a son, become a grandmother five times over, and teach kindergarten and special-needs children in some five different schools. Since 1989 she has been teaching in Gillette, Wyoming, a city with a population of about 20,000. Her husband of twenty-five years lives on the family's ranch about sixty miles away from Holly, and the couple sees each other weekends and one night a week. Holly could quit teaching and move to the ranch full-time, but her family would lose their health care benefits. Holly also wasn't born to be a full-time housewife. "Besides," she says, "the little guys give me a reason to get out of bed in the morning."

The first thing I face in my classroom is a room of twenty children who all want my attention, but they have to learn to get in line and be patient and do their tasks. I also go around and welcome each child. We begin the day with circle time, a coming together, like a community. We go over the day's calendar, and whoever is the helper for that day does her show-and-tell. Over the years I've seen kids show everything from bowling balls to roller skates to pythons. I've even had cows, pigs, and a horse. (Parents know that if their child brings something living, then they have to come to class, too.) [Laughs.]

When someone walks into the room I want them to know the children are the focus, so my students' pictures and drawings are everywhere. The room has a block center, a computer center, a reading center, a listening center, and, of course, a cut-and-paste center. I do most of my formal teaching in small groups because it's hard to teach twenty children the same thing at the same time. There will be ten kids who finish early and ten who struggle. Now they are learning to read and how to add and subtract. A lot of what we must teach today is way beyond what we used to, and it's probably developmentally inappropriate. State standards have changed—a lot is driven by the federal government's No Child Left Behind program—and kindergarten is what first grade used to be. Some of the kids are ready for it, but for the children who aren't, it's a struggle, and they can feel that they're not where they need to be. No matter how hard you try to not make them feel that way, they know they aren't adding, subtracting, or reading at the same level of others. That's hard for them.

The most important thing for a teacher is to have unconditional positive regard for these children. Nothing they do can make you stop loving them for a minute. And you have to enjoy being with them, and get some of your life force from them. Otherwise, teaching would be a daunting task.

Thirty years is a long time to teach the alphabet. But for Holly, work is not knowledge-centric but child-centric. It's about the kids and their futures. "There is an adult growing up in every child," she says. "One little girl I taught came running up to me twenty years later and told me I was the woman who made her know she wanted to be a doctor." Multiply that response by hundreds of former students and there's no doubt that Holly and her three Rs have made a difference beyond the classroom. Helping to form the next generation of adults is this Heroine's sole purpose.

She warms their hearts.

Compared with Heroines' grand ambitions, the Healers tend to be more personal in their altruistic endeavors. Healers find joy in more incremental improvement, in touching individuals and getting up close and personal. Seeing a smile, hearing a "thank-you" is often all the feedback a Healer needs to know she has made a difference.

"I love my job because I get to feed my friends at my house four times a day!" exults chef Sally Ayotte. The declaration sounds simple enough, until you consider that Sally's "house" is actually a huge cafeteria located at the South Pole, and her "friends" are 1,200 scientists, construction workers, and assorted staff. Sally is the executive chef at NANA Services working for the U.S. Antarctic Program's research centers at the South Pole. Although Sally loves food, she loves her job as a chef because of the positive effects food can have on people. In that way, she is a Healer.

It's difficult to fathom why a chef would choose the coldest place on earth to cook. So after I saw Sally, thirty-nine, interviewed during a CNN story about working at the South Pole, I had to track her down and ask, "Why?"

The chipper brunette was educated as a nutritionist and went on to work in nursing homes and hospitals. Small problem: "No one ever declares their love of hospital food," complains Sally, "and I got tired of cooking for people who didn't appreciate what I did. I love food and I love people." Restaurant work didn't interest Sally, who wanted to know her customers' tastes. Problem solved: Ten years ago, Sally began cooking for employees at seasonal venues, mainly vacation destinations like national parks. She spent four summers in Denali, Alaska, feeding up to 400 park workers. In Honduras she cooked for a whitewater rafting company, and she spent another summer preparing meals for guests aboard a large private sailboat. Then, in 1996, Sally ventured to the Amundsen-Scott Pole Station in Antarctica, where she fed 220 people.

When the gypsy lifestyle turned against her—"I had my little thirty-five-year breakdown where I thought I had nothing to show for my life"—Sally bought a house in Colorado, and the piece of land brought peace of mind. For six months a year, Sally lives in Colorado, but from October to February she relocates to Antarctica, supervising kitchens at the continent's three research facilities. Six days a week, from six A.M. to nine P.M., Sally oversees a staff of fifty-six cooks who prepare four meals a day. Among the $1.2 million worth of food at her disposal are 5,000 pounds of hamburger meat, 2,500 pounds of halibut, 2,500 pounds of crab, 12,000 pounds of chicken breast, and enough frozen vegetables to, well, feed a small town. It's the rare chef with such an enormous shopping list, and rarer still the one who dons fleece booties in the kitchen.

There is nothing to do at the South Pole but work, eat, and sleep, which means I get to be in charge of one of the big three! The temperature can be twenty degrees below zero, which means folks need about 5,000 calories a day. We all give up a lot to be here for six months every year. Families are not allowed, and it's never dark; the sun shines twenty-four hours a day. What do you do when you want a little comfort, when you want to warm up, when you miss your family and want to forget where you are for a few minutes and be reminded that someone cares about you? You eat!

I like to make people happy by offering them something that not only tastes good but is also good for them. It's a challenge to plan a six-month menu—more than 700 meals—a year and a half out. Menu changes are rare at the bottom of the world, and if we run out of an ingredient, it's gone—there's no 7-Eleven down the street to pick up some butter or salt. We get food deliveries only once a year, so great care and planning goes into every order. Each year I perfect the menu, and I've established a five-week rotation. Given all the limitations of cooking at an altitude of 10,000 feet and so far from civilization, it takes some serious creativity. We have no cream and only powdered milk. All dairy, like cheese, is frozen. We also have some serious baking and boiling challenges and employ standard altitude baking formulas. A lot of bakers come here and can't make their favorite recipes, and they get all worked up when an angel food cake falls or a Danish pastry doesn't rise. My job is to give them encouragement to make every failed dish into something beautiful that everyone can eat. We never just throw food away, because all the trash is hauled back to the U.S.

I work with the coolest people in the world. People from all over the country want to come here, and we get the cream of the crop—no pun intended. It's easy to make lifelong friends when you spend six months with someone in a kitchen or chatting with them over meals. There is no television here, no radio, and I get to know the scientists and what they're studying: clean air, the earth's creation, the hole in the ozone layer, marine life, the ice, the atmosphere. The only way to make hundreds of people feel special and loved is to treat them as dinner guests, so we throw a dinner party four times a day. We must always be in a good mood and smile when we cook. If we're not, the food's flavor and presentation reflect it. Frown, and the pot roast will burn.

That's the last thing anybody wants, especially at the bottom of the world.

In her own words

Jeannie "Bloopers" Lindheim, 58
Hospital Clown
Artistic Director, Jeannie Lindheim's Hospital Clown Troupe
Boston, Massachusetts

This former acting coach turned her talent for improvisation and intuition into a specialized profession. Since 1997, Jeannie and twenty-two other clowns in her not-for-profit troupe have entertained more than 21,000 sick children. Jeannie's sweet clown voice, big red nose, and bag full of props can be a bit deceiving: she is no displaced circus clown, but a professional healer of the human spirit at its most vulnerable.

Clowning is not just about being funny (although we obviously look ridiculous)—it's about being present. A clown does not walk into an environment, she creates it. I tell my clowns that they are clowning to the light behind the children's eyes. We empower kids and their families because we're the only people they can say no to in the hospital. Patients can't say no to a doctor, they can't disagree with a nurse, and when we visit kids we literally give them a remote control (yes, the kind used for toy cars) so they can turn us on or off—that's very empowering.

We ask our audience questions: What's your favorite food? Would you like to see me fly or do a magic trick? Choices also empower kids, and we always ask their permission before we do anything for the child. A smile is a sign that we're allowed to enter their world. We were visiting a little seven-year-old boy and a nurse took us aside and said he'd just lost his sight and was very depressed. She asked if we could cheer him up. Liz and I walked into his room and slowly approached the bed. He was all curled up in a ball and looked so sad. I said, "Hi, I'm Bloopers and this is Periwinkle. We're clowns. Can I play my harmonica for you?" "No," he said, shaking his head. "Can I play my xylophone for you?" Again, no. Then I got an idea. "What's your favorite food?" I asked. "Chocolate pudding," he said. "Would you like us to make up a story about chocolate pudding for you?" He shook his head yes, which was huge! So we made up the wildest, wackiest story about chocolate pudding. He was flying through it! He was swimming in it! He was taking a bath in it! And all the while he smiled and smiled and smiled. He looked so happy! For those moments when we were with him, we changed the environment in his room, and magic happened.

For two years I balanced clowning with teaching acting at the Boston Conservatory, until something happened that told me I had to clown full-time. One of my students called and said he had a friend whose son had cancer, and could Bloopers go visit the boy at home? I said sure, but I didn't hear from the parents until about four months later, when the clown-office phone rang; it was the sick boy's father. "Can you come see my son?" he asked. "Sure, tomorrow or Friday?" I asked. "You better come tomorrow. I don't know if he'll be with us Friday." The moment I hung up the phone I thought, Why I am teaching acting? I want to be running the troupe full-time. I took one of my most experienced clowns, Beth, to the house with me. The parents, grandparents, and cousins were all there, along with a hospice worker. We did our clowning thing for forty-five minutes: I pretended to get my head stuck in Beth's prop bag, I gave the boy's mom a sticker, we put red makeup on everyone's noses, we sang, we danced . . . the child was in a wheelchair and could barely process our presence, but I think he knew we were there, I sensed that in his energy. The father thanked us, saying, "He'll have that to take with him," and when we left the house, Beth and I stayed in clown character until we got into the car. I didn't really believe the boy would die, but when I called back on Saturday to see if he would like another visit, I was told he had passed the day after we came. True to my new priorities, I finished out the year teaching and after that ran the troupe full-time, fund-raising, training, supervising other clowns, and clowning myself. I did it for three more years without salary.

I used to think anyone could clown in a hospital, but it isn't for everyone. It's intense, and in a sense, clowns are very vulnerable. After each gig we often take about thirty minutes and just talk about our feelings. I personally can't clown every day—maybe just three times a week.

What's not to love about making sick children and their families happy? We change the energy in a hospital room, in the hospital lobbies, in the elevator—everywhere! Even though I am sixty and supposed to be maturing, I feel I'm growing down as well as up. I got breast cancer three years ago, and during my surgeries I put my red nose on when the anesthesiologist came around. It made everyone laugh. While there were also tears throughout my sickness, I got through it with humor. Having cancer, you reflect on your life, and I knew I would always be clowning.

Her sweet spot

When I asked Midwest Airlines if the company had a flight attendant who loved her job, the Milwaukee-based airline held a contest inviting attendants to submit a hundred-word explanation about why they were so happy. From that lot, two women were referred to me; one was Anita Mucci. Anita, fifty-four, has been a flight attendant and supervisor with Midwest since 1991. After we talked on the phone, her deep-rooted passion for serving passengers floored me to the extent of disbelief. As an admittedly impatient frequent flyer who always wonders how flight attendants withstand the monotony of their jobs, I had to meet Anita in person. So one fall day, Anita—cheery cheeked and neatly dressed in black slacks and a beige sweater—served me tea at her home in Burlington, Wisconsin, where she lives with her husband. The quaint house was replete with an American flag out front and pictures of children and grandkids. And on certain days, Anita told me, the rich smell of chocolate permeates the streets. Burlington, it turns out, is home not only to Nestlé chocolate factories, but also to one very happy working woman who landed a job that hits her own sweet spot.

Even after twelve years at Midwest, I get excited just packing my bag, and I look forward to each trip. I just love people, and each day there are new faces on the plane as well as frequent fliers. It gives me such pride to know that a businessman who flies with us often likes one Sweet'n Low and two creams in his cup of coffee and I can start his day off right. I enjoy helping people with whatever their needs may be. Today I might have a mom traveling alone with young children, an older couple celebrating an anniversary (elderly people can be so much fun), or people going to and from funerals (just offering condolences means so much). The events of life pass through an airplane's doors, and I try to meet people and find out if they're going on vacation or to visit family. That's part of my job, to try and make it special for them in the air.

I particularly enjoy the challenge of turning someone's day completely around. They call me the schmoozer and send me into situations that need defusing. Sometimes I have to calm a fearful flier. Part of the whole thing is treating people with respect, compassion, patience, and tolerance—all tied into one big ball. I put myself in their shoes. If people board in a bad mood, they'll be in a good mood when they deplane. We don't know why they're so grumpy, so without knowing that missing link we have to start fresh and put a smile on their face. It's both a job and my personal goal.

It's true, I'm a fanatical people pleaser (my pastor even told me that), and I've always wanted to make someone else's day better. It's very nurturing. If I see a neighbor looking down and I can put a smile on her face, I feel like I've accomplished something. I was like that as a kid, and in high school I was never in a clique, I just had a reputation for being friendly with everyone. Very few people did not like me, I can get along with anyone.

I'm living my dream career, and I'm very fortunate because many people can't. I wanted this job back in high school.

More fascinating than Anita's über-nurturing nature and endless patience is how she pined to be a flight attendant. It took her more than twenty years to muster enough courage to even apply for the position, and in her tale is an example for anyone hesitating to switch careers: Throw your negative assumptions out the window, because they're probably wrong.

Anita had a "burning love" for flying as a young girl, yet it wasn't any notion of exotic travel or adventure that captivated her; she simply thought it would be "fun" to care for people in the air. But when Anita graduated from high school in 1967, the airlines' strict, pre-discrimination-law requirements deterred her. Stewardesses had to be a specific height and weight; they could not wear glasses, be married, or have a family. Even Anita's guidance counselor suggested she forget her high-flying aspirations and instead attend business college for two years. So she did, and for the next twenty years Anita worked as a legal secretary for the same law firm while she and her husband raised two children.

Anita liked her job at the law firm, but the desire to work for Midwest—Milwaukee's hometown airline whose ads boasted "The best care in the air"—reared its head every time she traveled. "I kept seeing ads for Midwest Express—back then, the airline served champagne and meals on china to all its passengers—and I thought, Wow. But the ads were a tease. There was no hope for a forty-year-old!"

Thanks to her husband's prodding, Anita finally called Midwest's 800-number and requested an application. But when it arrived by mail, the four-page document sat in a drawer for *a year* while Anita convinced herself the airline would never hire a middle-aged lady. She also worried the job would disrupt her family's routine. Doubt ate away at her until, one morning after discussing it once again with her husband, she filled out the application and mailed it in. Says Anita, "I didn't want to look back and regret doing nothing at all."

She waited and she waited. Finally, in July 1991, a letter invited Anita to interview. Quite simply, she "freaked out," called her husband to share the good news, and asked her daughter to help her select an interview outfit. Anita settled on a simple white dress and jacket, with hints of yellow and green, and dangly daisy earrings. "Don't ask me why I wore those. I laugh now, thinking how unprofessional it must have looked, but I was trying to look my Sunday best." Anita was a wreck before the interview. But once it began, she felt that "everything flowed." A nail-biting week and a half later, Midwest called Anita back for another interview, and after more meetings and two weeks of waiting she finally heard if she'd be donning Midwest's navy blue uniform and serving shrimp scampi 30,000 feet above the earth.

Every night at dinner, my husband and kids would be, like, "You're going to get it," but I played it down and said the same thing over and over: "They're not going to hire a forty-year-old woman, but at least I made it this far." Then, at eight o'clock one morning at work, the phone rang. "Anita, this is Mary from Midwest Express. We would like to offer you the flight attendant position." I tell you, I get teary-eyed just thinking about it! It was so exciting. I gave a big huge sigh and cried . . . just like I am doing right now.

I am just so proud that I finally had the courage to do it. God had a purpose for me not becoming a flight attendant twenty years ago, and I am definitely better at it now that I no longer have my two kids at home. When I get on that plane, I am needed. Except for my husband, I no longer have anyone at my house who needs me, but each day at work a whole plane full of people do! If I think about it, I probably need them just as much.

Her hours fly by.

Just as flight attendants are lifelines for airline passengers, so are doormen to apartment dwellers, especially in large cities. Vertical living has its challenges, and doormen provide a sense of security, even a sense of family. Their smiles welcome residents home at the end of a long workday, and doormen are usually all that stands between a tenant and her dry cleaning, her deliveries, her leaky faucet, or the Chinese food she ordered for dinner.

Considering it's such a nurturing job, where are all the door*women*?

Well, I found one after reading a blurb in *The New York Times* extolling the virtues of Katherina Kunhardt, a door*person* who works at a 260-apartment building on Manhattan's Upper East Side. Katherina is fifty-three and speaks Spanish and broken English, yet through the translation services of her fiancé—an elevator maintenance mechanic who works in her building, where they met—Katherina told me why she is so happy at work.

In the Dominican Republic I was a lab technician who tested blood samples for malaria. That was a mistake. I should have been a social worker because I enjoy people so much. I also only made 300 pesos a month, and came to this country to make more money after I got divorced and my children were grown. I became a U.S. citizen in 1997 and started working as a security guard at this building. The job was not good because it did not pay very much, and when a doorperson job opened, I made a résumé and they gave me a shot.

I work with another doorman from 3:30 in the afternoon until 11:30 at night, and every hour we switch sitting and standing. All the time I am busy doing something: Opening the door as people leave or come into the building, helping people with luggage, handing people their mail, watching the monitors . . . the hours go by so quickly.

The job itself is very fulfilling and makes me feel good. The people who live here are very educated. I see people from all over the world in our building. One apartment is selling for $2.5 million! There are a lot of elderly and they need help with packages, and sometimes I accompany them up to their apartments. Everyone is very nice and interesting, and I have very good relationships with the tenants. I feel they trust me and admire me a lot. I get a lot of compliments. The people I work with are also very nice and respect me. We all chip in and have birthday parties for each other, we get a nice big cake and soda, and at Christmas the employees have a dinner. I feel very comfortable here.

While Katherina truly enjoys being a doorperson, she agrees that she would probably not be as happy working at just any building. The comfort, familiarity, and respect she feels among her current tenants and coworkers (not to mention her fiancé) make Katherina feel at home. Going to another building would be like moving to another country—and she's already done that.

Her escape

I found so often when interviewing women who love their work, the unassuming applicants—the women with seemingly simple jobs—were the ones who proved to be the most moving. Such was the case with Annette Keith, a forty-four-year-old who by day is an administrative assistant in a bank's commercial loan department, but by night a massage therapist at Mary's Corner, a beauty salon in Amarillo, Texas. The latter job is the one Annette loves; the former, which she's held for twenty-five years, merely pays the bills. Annette has a chirpy, high-pitched Texas accent and humbly describes herself as "plain." The daughter of an Italian-Mexican father and an Indian mother, Annette grew up in Amarillo and only recently began to travel beyond Texas's borders. She has no children—save three cats and a dog—and was recently divorced.

When we spoke, Annette was in the throes of creating a new life for herself, and massage therapy, which her ex-husband did not want her to pursue, is the key to her new kingdom.

Massage therapy was something I was always interested in, but it was not something my husband looked at in the same way I did, so I just let it fall by the wayside. Two years ago, after the divorce, the opportunity came up to take weekend classes, so I said, "Why not?" I've always rubbed people's shoulders and everyone always said, "Annette, you should do this for a living." It's the helper in me. I don't see this as a job at all, whereas my work at the bank is a job. We're in the Bible Belt here in Amarillo, and massage is slowly getting more popular. But there's a difference between being a massage therapist and a masseuse. I am not a parlor girl.

I do Swedish massage and charge thirty dollars an hour. I want to keep it reasonably priced so people don't have to worry about the money. We all need to do things for ourselves, and I know what it's like to want a massage but not have the budget for it. The majority of my clients are women, all ages and all sizes. I see two clients after five P.M. Monday through Friday, and four to five on Saturdays. Some come in just to relax and don't say a word, but for the most part people talk about anything and everything that deals with life. I just follow their lead. If they want to carry on a conversation, I'll chat with them, but I always say up front, "This is my opinion only." If we're not talking I go over their different body parts in my head. I think about how the joints or bones are connected and how the massage is doing them good. I reeducate myself all the time. I also get into the music I play. Mostly I like piano, but I also play a little Yanni and Enya. The room is like a tropical island theme: Posters of beach scenes hang on the wall, and there's a mirror framed in palm leaves. I can wreak havoc on hair when I massage someone's head! The mirror lets them get themselves back together.

Massage therapy has given me a little more confidence in myself and a sense of independence, especially since the divorce. It's something I pursued, completed, and continue to grow with. I want to go back to school for pediatric massage, working with premature babies in neonatal care units; massage stimulates their little nervous, circulatory, and muscular systems. There's something about being able to help a child fighting for its life, who is totally dependent on other people to survive. One day I hope that will be my full-time job, and I'm moving to Colorado soon to attend the Boulder College for Massage Therapy. A lot of people have tried to talk me out of it, and my family does not think it's going to happen. They say I'm silly to be doing this at forty-four, but that's exactly why I need to go with it. As long as I can find a place to live that will have my cats and dogs, I'll be fine.

Unlike her bank job, massage lets Annette touch people in both the literal and figurative sense. Not only does she enjoy the science of her craft, but she feels good about the profound healing a small luxury has on her clients.

Still, Annette does not see her career transition plans as particularly brave. "It's only massage therapy," she insists with a laugh. But to whip the rug out from under one's life and start over, at any age, for whatever purpose, takes tremendous courage. It's also an enormous source of future strength: Annette will forever carry the knowledge that she had the power to change her life once—and can do it again if she so chooses.

She hates why she does it.

While Healers seek to help both men and women, Sisters find particular satisfaction in helping other females overcome obstacles, such as breast cancer, low self-esteem, sexual dissatisfaction, incarceration, even lack of financial acumen. For these Happy 100 women, job satisfaction stems from helping their sisters.

Julie Ratner is an ideal woman to introduce the Sisters. Julie, fifty-seven, and her younger sister, Ellen, were wonderfully close despite their six-year age difference. They chatted on the phone constantly, Ellen vacationed at Julie's summer house in seaside East Hampton, New York, and when Julie ran marathons, Ellen cheered from the sidelines. When Ellen got engaged, Julie ran out and bought every bridal magazine she could find. When Ellen went into labor, she was in Julie's kitchen. But when Julie went through her own painful divorce, Ellen was not there to help her through it.

In 1995, at age forty-two, Ellen—a brown-eyed journalist and mother with a "ready smile" and velvet voice—died of breast cancer.

"Ellen's loss was a bigger loss than my marriage," recalls Julie. "Her death was a huge waste for the world." Since being diagnosed with cancer in her mid-thirties, Ellen had lived bravely and at the time of her death was in the process of disseminating information on the Internet about pain-management techniques for breast cancer patients. After Ellen's death, Julie wanted to carry on her sister's activism by educating and counseling breast cancer patients, survivors, and their families. In a lovely twist of fate, the steps Julie took to honor her sister's life also ushered in a new life for herself.

About when Ellen was diagnosed, I was visiting Brown University with my daughter, who was applying to college, and I fell in love with the campus. I decided I wanted to work in a college admissions department. So I returned to school in 1991 for a doctorate in student development.

Meanwhile, Ellen got sicker and sicker and passed away in 1995. I received my doctorate a year later and assumed, as always, that I would work in academia. But around the time of my graduation I was having lunch with a woman, a near stranger, who said, "Let's start a run in East Hampton to honor the memory of your sister." Of course, I had been a runner, and Ellen loved the Hamptons, which has one of the nation's highest rates of breast cancer. While the Hamptons is known as a vacation spot for the wealthy, there is a huge population of year-round residents there who serve the summer community. These are women who don't get on the social pages, but who work two to three jobs, who live on the Indian reservation, who are African-American, who don't have as much time and money as other people to get mammograms and treat themselves after being diagnosed.

Julie began to organize a five-kilometer run in East Hampton and called it Ellen's Run. Working with a small volunteer army, Julie spent an increasing amount of time soliciting sponsors and recruiting other volunteers. The work ate into her full-time position as dissertation adviser at a teachers college, and Julie says it became clear that Ellen's Run needed her "whole self." Money Julie received in her divorce settlement made it possible for her to quit the college job and operate the Ellen P. Hermanson Foundation full time. To this day, Julie does not take a salary.

The run has evolved into a money-raising vehicle for an often-overlooked aspect of breast cancer. "While other organizations focus on a much needed cure," reads the Ellen's Run Web site (www.ellensrun.org), "the foundation is unique in its commitment to helping breast cancer patients and their families cope with the physical and emotional vicissitudes of breast cancer."

The more than $1 million raised to date goes to educate residents in medically underserved communities about early detection and provide psychosocial support services. Some funds also go to pain-management research. Emotional support for a victim and her family can often take a backseat to physical issues, but as Julie witnessed with Ellen, it is very difficult for a victim to live day to day with a diagnosis after she feels her body has betrayed her. The disease becomes a family affair, affecting a cancer victim's family and friends.

To raise money, Julie seeks out companies to sponsor the annual run and hosts a cocktail party and auction the night before the race. Roughly 1,000 people participate in the race each year. Everything from goody bags to T-shirts must be donated. Raising more money is Julie's ongoing challenge.

I love the challenge of trying to do better every year. I love that we really help people and make a difference in the lives of women and their families. The run certainly does not take the place of Ellen, and in many ways it is really quite selfish of me. Starting and working on the run saved my life after Ellen died and after my divorce. It kept her close, and it opened up a mansion's worth of windows for me, exposing me to all the possibilities left in the world. My life is forever enriched thanks to the extraordinary people I've met. Precious few women have not been touched by breast cancer. I recently went to a concert at Carnegie Hall, and Marvin Hamlisch, the composer, said, "Will everyone who's had a sibling die from breast cancer stand up." I did. "Now, everyone who has had a mother, a spouse, or a partner die from breast cancer stand up, too." By the time he was done you could count on one hand the number of people sitting. It was very dramatic. You know, I love what I do but hate why I do it.

Her fourth-grade self

Running saved Molly Barker's life. Growing up in a middle-class neighborhood in Charlotte, North Carolina, Molly shouldered the burden of an alcoholic mother. With her father often away selling insurance and her older sister off at college, Molly, now forty-three, became the caretaker in an empty house of denial. On days when she came home from elementary school to find her mother passed out in the bedroom, drunk, Molly thought her mother was dead. On days Molly got into the car with an intoxicated mom behind the wheel, she thought they were both going to die.

Although Molly's mother was sober by the time Molly was in fifth grade, Molly's home-life anxieties added more weight to the already heavy afflictions of adolescence. Like any young girl, Molly wanted to fit in. She wanted to be pretty and popular and flirtatious, the image of the perfect girl she saw on television and in magazines. The irony is that Molly, thin and blond, resembled the stereotype, but in her mind she never measured up, and so at age fifteen she followed her mother's footsteps and began drinking to avoid the mounting pain. In the years that followed, Molly also became a serious runner. Miraculously, she competed in triathlons and earned a master's in social work even as her alcoholism escalated.

I was a high achiever trying to cover up what was going on at home. One night, July 6, 1993, I was ready to kill myself. I called my sister, and she talked me out of it and convinced me to just go to bed. I did, and the next morning I woke up and went for a run and had a spiritual awakening. It was a weird morning: A thunderstorm was brewing, and as I ran, the wind whipped and swirled the leaves around. The weather. The running. It was a very physical experience that culminated as my life crashed down on me. I stopped at an intersection and just burst into tears because I knew I'd arrived at a critical juncture and had to stop drinking. That moment remains an inexplicable mystery in my life.

In her early thirties, Molly finally joined an alcoholism support group, which not only fostered her sobriety but also introduced her to the field of alcohol and substance abuse prevention. She took a job at a drug education center, where she met an "emotionally secure" woman who became her mentor. Eventually Molly married and had a son and daughter, and just as her own life was improving, Molly began working to improve the lives of others.

Everything began to click. I began working at the drug education center part-time, and one day I honest to goodness had a vision: I was running and hundreds of little girls were following me up steps, like I was Rocky! So in 1996 I began working part-time at the local Y developing athletic and self-esteem programs that I did not yet have a name for. The part-athletic, part-counseling programs evolved into a character development course that used running as a catalyst to teach wonderful life skills to little girls. I envisioned my programs for the left-out girl, the loner lost in the classroom and on the playground.

That course is the basis for what is now an eight-year-old international program called Girls on the Run. Its motto: "To educate and prepare girls for a lifetime of self-respect and healthy living." By training girls for a three-mile running event and leading workouts that enhance self-esteem, Girls on the Run strives to give girls enough confidence to turn down drugs and alcohol, avoid pregnancy, prevent eating disorders, and ward off depression. Most important to Molly's mission is timing: Girls on the Run reaches youngsters in third to eighth grade, when they're on the cusp of peer pressure but still receptive to adult influence. Each running event is coordinated locally, and to date, about 20,000 girls have participated in forty-three states.

Molly's story does not end there, for she was yet to be truly happy in her work. She had a tough time finding her niche within the very organization she created; passion alone was not enough to bring Molly joy on the job. For the first few years, Molly hated—and was lousy at—the management and administration duties the not-for-profit demanded. "Managing was not my gift," jokes Molly, who preferred being out and about with young girls as opposed to sitting in front of a computer. But Molly felt guilty delegating office work and felt obliged to do it herself. ("I could not imagine that anyone would want to do a spreadsheet.") Once again, the little girl inside Molly put the weight of the world on her shoulders until the stress wore her down to the point that she confronted her board of directors. "I told them they were going to lose me, and then, just as I was stepping down, Elaine appeared as if by magic." Elaine was a fed-up corporate attorney who heard about Girls on the Run and was willing to take a pay cut to manage it, which was her forte. Molly, meanwhile, could hand over the reins and focus on what she understood best: little girls in potential times of trouble.

While drinking is no longer a problem for me, other stuff is. I have no memory of my fourth-grade year because my mother's drinking was so bad and my anxiety was so high that I blocked it out. Girls on the Run allows me to revisit that fourth-grade year over and over. Showing up for a race, I visit with the girls, help them train, start the race, and just hang out with them. Working with them helps me celebrate the fourth-grade girl inside of me, the one I can't remember. I'm still healing myself.

Crying as she shares this revelation, Molly says her goal is not to *remove* pain from young girls' lives but rather give them skills to cope with discord in healthy ways. The ten-to-twelve-week program preps girls not only to run three miles but to pace themselves in the marathon of adolescence. The by-products of sport—self-esteem and critical-thinking skills—help girls stand up for themselves, say no when they need to, and celebrate their bodies, even if they're not of the Britney Spears variety. Encouraging girls to talk about and experience their pain prevents it from being expressed in dangerous ways, says Molly. "Society tells girls that they're not supposed to be angry, but we say anger is okay. It's what you do with it that counts."

In her own words

Ann Folwell Stanford, 52
Professor/Director, Women, Writing and Incarceration Project
DePaul University School for New Learning
Chicago, Illinois

Ann has a Ph.D. in English and teaches adult students in the interdisciplinary liberal arts program at DePaul University. In addition, Ann founded and directs the DePaul Women, Writing and Incarceration Project, a program that trains students to teach creative writing to women in prison. Her personal history plays an integral part in her present work happiness.

I have two memories of my youth: My grandmother was a nurse, and I used to dress up in her old nurse's cape. It was heavy wool with red on the inside, and I wore my father's stiff white clergy collar on my head as a cap. The other thing I remember doing was going through our neighbors' trash piles and collecting pens and paper to set up my own little office. I loved to play office; it never occurred to me that it was work.

I married an Episcopal priest, like my dad. It was the early 1970s, and my husband and I were both very much into working with street kids and runaways through a nondenominational ministry. That's what brought us together. I was really young, and when we had a son, staying home all day drove me crazy. I still did not have a college degree, so I went to work at a Catholic grassroots funding agency, which was very progressive for the time. Before that job I had always felt very incompetent, always pitched for the lowest job possible. But for the first time I began to understand that I was competent, and within three months I was promoted from secretary to office manager. I began to understand that I could do things, a huge turning point.

My husband and I relocated to Roanoke, Virginia, where he had his first parish. I took a job as a social worker dealing with neglected and exploited elderly people and just hated it. Even though they kept telling me how good I was, I'd come home for lunch every day and cry; I am not a real extrovert, and I had an extrovert's dream job. A woman I met at a cocktail party suggested I take her course in women's journal writing. I did, and all of a sudden the veil was torn and I became this raging feminist! Here I'd been very involved in social justice but it had never occurred to me to think about feminism! And I was mad! I'd been trying to make Christianity work for me, but it didn't. I just took my Episcopal prayer book and ripped it in half and threw it across the room. (That was a bit over the top.) But I continued to take other classes in the English department, did really good work, and received a lot of affirmation. My husband was a little worried about my disintegrating spiritual life, but he was very supportive and did a lot of cooking and caretaking while I attended classes.

I also began to sense something. There was a name for something that was bothering me since the third grade: lesbianism. All I knew was that lesbians and homosexuals were people who were mentally ill, and that I could never allow that part of me to surface. At the same time, I just wanted to be with women more than men. I grew terribly uneasy and scared, but in my classes I learned that it was not a sickness. I was blown away and also kind of excited to learn that homosexuality was something to admire in many ways. I read voraciously and ended up having an affair with a female teacher, which turned out to be short-lived but lifted another veil. Eventually I left my husband and son and lived alone for a while, until I realized I wasn't emotionally ready to leave my family. I was in my early thirties, but emotionally I was probably thirteen. My husband and I actually dated for three months before I moved back in.

I went to graduate school and loved it. School was like this huge dessert bar and I could choose whatever I wanted without consequences. I worked as an editor for a research magazine and did some writing and had about forty articles published. I was learning like crazy. Sure, we'd complain, but I had worked as a maid and a secretary and now I was getting paid to write! Compared with manual labor, this was a treat. It was not all easy, but eventually I graduated with a Ph.D. in English.

Meanwhile, my husband and I had stayed together. We really worked hard at it and were married for a total of twenty-seven years, although we ended up having very separate lives. Still, there was a lot of affection. We assumed I was bisexual and left it at that. Eventually I got sick and tired of leading a double life, and so I called it what it was: I was a lesbian. I told my husband I loved him and cared for him but just could not be with him anymore. It was a huge relief. Even if I was never, ever with a woman, I knew being alone would be better than trying to make myself into a heterosexual.

When I was ready to apply for jobs, I applied for a position at DePaul University's School for New Learning, which provided interdisciplinary liberal arts for adults. I was an adult by the time I went to college in my thirties, and I wanted to help other adults expand their minds and define their goals, negotiate the complexities of school, work, and family. That was thirteen years ago, and I got the job, and tenure, and eventually they asked me to be the associate dean. That was when I decided to come out. I no longer wanted to compartmentalize my life. I was almost fifty and was tired of hiding. After a stint as dean, I decided to return to the faculty.

Seven years ago I was on a fund-raising walk and happened to start talking with a woman who was a volunteer in the library at Cook County Jail's women's division. At the time I was being challenged as a white woman teaching African-American literature at DePaul, and I thought, What am I giving back to this community? *The majority of people in jails and prisons in the U.S. are poor and people of color. The women in the Cook County Jail were charged with crimes like drug possession and murder, but they were not yet convicted. The library was a place where discussion could happen, and I was invited to come in and lead a group talk and began going once a month to discuss poetry. The women really liked it. While their educational level was often different from that of the adults I taught at the university, the woman's group seemed to have a bit more hunger and excitement about reading and thinking and sharing ideas. I saw they wanted to write, so I began bringing paper and pencils. We started with very basic exercises, which were explosive! We'd all read our work out loud, and the atmosphere became electric, full of laughter, tears, and creative silences.*

The very act of writing in a place as dehumanizing as jail, a place of confinement, is an act of resistance and courage. These woman are being treated like criminals but have not been convicted, and some will go home. While society is trying to shut them up, these incarcerated women are saying, "You can lock me up, but you cannot lock up my creative voice." Teaching them is different from teaching a regular college writing course, where I approach writing as a craft. In jail, the situation is more short-term, and I just try to get the women to open themselves up as thinking, creating human beings. I introduce them to poetry and to literature by and about women in prison, as well as Shakespeare and short fiction. The course has evolved over the years, and the women still teach me so much. They tell me they want homework, they tell me which exercises don't work for them, they truly want to be a community of writers. When I take my students with me to the course, it just blows their minds! They expect the media's version of angry, sinister, brutal women— not women who are so eager to write.

There are probably parallels between incarcerated women and myself. I certainly felt trapped for a lot of my life, and writing helped me, absolutely. Teaching these women just makes so much sense to me. My life feels very much all in one piece.

She's all about the money, honey.

When it comes to professional networking and self-education, women have perfected the craft. Forget schmoozing on the golf course; women organize forums and attend seminars. They do lunch and go to lectures. They conference, they associate, they exchange advice as well as hugs. Like any minority or disenfranchised group, women know that if they don't help themselves, no one else will.

Many women build careers around assisting other businesswomen, and one of them, Leslie Grossman, helps them build financially success-ful businesses. As a cofounder of the Women's Leadership Exchange based in New York City, Leslie, fifty-four, teaches women entrepreneurs the basics of finance, a mission she embraced when her own marketing company, CMA, fell apart in the midst of the dot-com bust. In building CMA, Leslie focused on the fun stuff—marketing and client work—but relied too much on her accountant and lawyer to manage the company itself. As a result, she lacked the requisite understanding of basic finan-cial management, and when her business started to collapse in 2000 under the weight of the ailing economy, Leslie did not know where or how to cut spending to offset declining revenue. The problem was not exclusive to Leslie. She looked around at other women and realized that many had let the financial piece of the success puzzle—in both their businesses and their personal lives—go missing. To fill that gap, she and two colleagues began the Women's Leadership Exchange.

Women have come a long way, but the money piece is still missing. Too many women don't pay attention to the financial management of their own businesses, and as a result the business loses money or is not as profitable as it could be. Maybe there is a fear of math that stems from when women were young, and by the time they operate a small business they're too busy to go back and learn about finance. So, like me, they hand it off to someone else. I also think there is a fear of money, a perception that wanting a lot of money is looked upon as being greedy, and greed does not fit with more stereotypical female characteristics, like nurturing. Women rarely get together and talk about money issues, about cash flow and how to finance growth. I want to teach other women what I wish I had known myself.

The goal of the Leadership Exchange is to give women the financial tools and knowledge to drive growth. In the beginning we wanted to have a full-day seminar focused on nothing but financial management, but deep down we knew women wouldn't come. Now we hold five one-day seminars around the country and spend one-third of the day focused on nothing but finance. It's important that we invite only women because, we've noticed, women prefer not to learn finance in the company of men. Women are afraid they will look stupid, and so the Women's Leadership

Exchange gives them freedom to ask any question. The truth, of course, is that men don't have all the answers, either. They just think they do.

After I closed down most of my business (I still run a company called B2Women, that helps organizations market to women), I realized it was very important to create more female leaders in the world, and for me the way to do that was to help female entrepreneurs create profitable businesses. Successful women-led companies lead to more respect and recognition. They also help abolish the glass ceiling. When you grow your own company, you can grow yourself as big as you want!

There are many ways to make a difference in women's lives, and Leslie identified an overlooked niche. And, like many Sisters—as well as Heroines and Healers—Leslie's motivation stems from personal experience. There's a career lesson here: If you're searching for a cause to champion, look inward. Your past may already hold the keys to a future job you'll love.

They sell good sex.

Perhaps you've had a lifetime of fantastic, mind-blowing sex. (Or perhaps you blushed reading that last sentence.) If you consider yourself among the there-must-be-more-to-this variety when it comes to sex, you are hardly alone in the female dissatisfaction department. What you need, sister, in addition to a loving, sensitive partner, is a clean, well-lighted sex shop. You want a store without screaming neon and offensive magazines, but with cozy couches and soothing music. You want a shop with salespeople who don't make you mortified to ask, "Excuse me, *sir*, can you recommend a really good sex toy?" You want sales*women* as familiar and friendly as your best friend but who know more about orgasms—and ways to induce them—than your best friend ever will (or at least cares to share over Sunday brunch). Let's face it, not all of us have *Sex and the City* gal pals, and many of us could use some friendly advice.

Kari Kupcinet Kriser, thirty-two, and Cheryl Sloane, forty-three, had women in mind when they conceived of their store G Boutique in 2002, an erotica and lingerie shop in Chicago. Trimmed in hot pink, leopard, and wood accents, the bright, 2,000-square-foot store is playful and comfy. G is sexy chic. There are oodles of panties and bras, racks of classic and trendy lingerie (custom-made corsets, nice and naughty nighties, even hip bras for nursing moms). There are also a variety of vibrators, pornographic videos, and lots of lubricant. But, most important, there are G's owners, Kari and Cheryl. These two friends and former theater professionals—a soap opera actress and a producer, respectively—have made it their job to sell good sex. And they're having a blast in the process.

Cheryl: Retail is very much like theater—with sets, lighting, actors, and props—and I grew up onstage. My mom was a theater producer and used to convince the plays' directors to cast me in the kids' roles. That doesn't mean I was always comfortable talking openly about sex. When Kari and I thought up the idea for the boutique, we giggled constantly for the first three months as we researched sex toys on the Internet. It's okay to be nervous about all this, and we make sure our customers feel okay with their discomfort. "Go ahead and giggle," we tell them, we did.

My favorite part of this job is helping women. A lot of our customers say we are a community service. [Laughs.] They won't even walk into other erotica stores, but ours is friendly. They come into our store and we educate them and they go out happy. There is something to be said for demystifying sex and not making it feel raunchy, that it's okay to buy a vibrator with your pretty lingerie. A lot of women buy their first vibrator from us. Women come in and talk about problems they have with the men in their lives, and men come in and talk about the issues they have with women. There is still such a gender communication gap. The good thing is that more and more women are learning what it means to have sexual fulfillment and being able to make that choice for themselves. We sell the toys to enhance people's lives.

Cheryl's and Kari's satisfaction is not limited to sex. One of G's most memorable customers was a cancer patient about to have a double mastectomy, and she purchased an elegant, sheer nightgown. A week later the woman returned to the store, grateful. "Wearing that nightgown was the sexiest I've felt since I got sick," she said. "My husband loved it, and so did I." G also assists postmenopausal women in search of toys and lubricant to make their sex lives better (and their husband's jobs a little easier). "Even if women are aging or sick, or if their husbands have passed away, they still have sex lives," says Cheryl.

Kari: This may sound crazy, but it's wonderful to have average women come into the store and tell us they've never had an orgasm. We just talk to them like girlfriends, sell them their first toy, and so many come back and say how it helped their sex life. I especially love doing the buying. It's just so exciting to be able to select what we think people will like and then watch customers find something they want. Some come in just for bras, others head straight for erotica. My husband thinks my job is so much fun. [Laughs.] I'll come home with some new videos and say, "Honey, we have to check out the new merchandise."

What's refreshing about Kari and Cheryl is their familiar, almost girl-next-door spirit. They are not intimidating sex divas, erotic extremists, or on the fringe of good taste. In fact, they have an excellent eye for lingerie, which they travel to Paris to purchase. They also respect their own personal boundaries, and while they refrain from judging others, they also refuse to carry certain products. "If it makes us go 'eeew,' we won't stock it," says Kari. Adds Cheryl, "Someone wanted an electrical prodding device, but if we don't understand it, we don't buy it."

Sex, like work, is relative: What satisfies one woman might not satisfy another.

Her many nursing lives

As mentioned at the beginning of this chapter, Cherry Ames was a character in a fictional book series published from the 1940s through the 1960s that tracked a young nurse in her various jobs: *Cherry Ames: Army Nurse; Cherry Ames: Veterans' Nurse; Cherry Ames: Mountaineer Nurse.* You get the gist. When Jan Pickett read the Cherry Ames books as a young girl in Midland, Texas, nursing and traveling became her fantasy future, and eventually her reality. At fifty-five, Jan is a breast cancer clinical nurse who follows women through all phases of treatment. She works in the small town of Temple, Texas, 165 miles northwest of Houston, population less than 60,000.

Like the fictional Cherry, Jan's most recent nursing incarnation—Jan Pickett: Rural Nurse—was preceded by many others. In the early days of her career she was Jan Pickett: ICU Nurse, tending to cardiovascular patients recovering from open-heart surgery. That was back in the 1970s, when "nurses wore white caps, white skirts, and were much less empowered," recalls Jan. Instead of proactively treating patients with their minds, most nurses simply followed doctors' orders. Fourteen years later, at New York University, she became Jan Pickett: Graduate Student Nurse, studying emerging theories about multicausal care and pain management. While working at St. Vincent hospital in New York's West Village in the 1980s, she was Jan Pickett: Union Nurse, lobbying for nurses' rights, as well as Jan Pickett: AIDS Nurse, treating AIDS patients before the autoimmune deficiency disease even had a formal name.

In 1984, Jan and her husband moved back to Austin, Texas, where she taught at the University of Texas (Jan Pickett: Teaching Nurse) and eventually took a management position at a hospital (Jan Pickett: Nurse Administrator) helping other nurses pursue continuing education courses.

It was a real emotional struggle to return to Texas after living and working in New York, where I came into myself as a woman and a professional. The gender hierarchy in Texas and the way female nurses were treated by male doctors hit me in the face like a cold, dead fish! I could not just accept the unfair stereotypes, and because there were no unions in Texas, I dealt with it the best way I could: I expressed my irreverence for the organizational structure in my dress and attitude. I became known as "that eccentric nurse from New York." I worked in nursing education administration at the Scott and White Hospital and Clinic for four years and really learned my way around the administrative structure. I did HIV, oncology, and pain management education, developed curriculum, planned nurse conferences, and arranged speakers, but I began to feel that I was no longer a nurse. I missed the clinical part of the job. Working one-on-one with women was always where I got the greatest satisfaction.

In the mid-1990s Jan returned to hands-on nursing as a hematology and oncology clinical nurse specialist at Scott and White Hospital. Today she's a member of a multidisciplinary medical team that follows breast cancer patients from diagnosis to recovery, or until they pass away. Phases of treatment include biopsy, surgery, counseling, financial administration, pain management, and getting to know other cancer patients.

I see about eleven patients a day, that's about all I can handle emotionally, and my role is to think about the real world, how their disease and treatment is affecting their whole psychological, spiritual, and physical being. A breast cancer diagnosis is extremely sobering for a woman. There is no time for superficiality, and I continue to be amazed at the grace and courage by which most women face adversity. I am passionate about helping them understand the side effects and rationale behind treatment. Because I work in a rural area, it's common to have indigent patients with no educational background who can't understand what's happening to them, so I try to explain it. There are also tremendous sexual issues that arise because the disease and treatments diminish a woman's body image and her desire or ability to have an orgasm, and that's a damn big deal! (One of the pharmacologists calls me Libido Girl because I am always thinking about how different drugs will affect a woman's sex drive.) In addition to emotional support, I see patients for pain issues. Many times nerve endings are damaged during surgery and radiation, and sometimes women face a slow death, but there is so much that can be done to deal with the pain, both physical and emotional. People do not have to die in agony, or distanced from their families, or not having made peace with the world. All those things are achievable, and it is a tremendous bang for the buck in terms of how I spend my time and energy.

Women who walk down my hallway are either afraid of dying, or they are dying. I face that every day. The only thing that makes me feel bad is when the system fails them: when the clerical staff does not know what they're doing, or a patient's lab reports are missing, or the computers don't work. I still ask myself if I am emotionally up to this job. Yes, I cry easily. I cry with nurses and with my patients and with families. But I don't view sadness as negative. I know that the care I'm able to provide impacts lives of many patients at a critical time. All of the other nursing experiences I've had over the years have prepared me for this role.

While this may not be Jan's last nursing job, there is no doubt what phase she has achieved: Jan Pickett: Happy Nurse!

Heroic, Healing, and Sisterly work need not be conducted bedside. It can be done in a lab, in a store, behind a desk, in a garage, in a classroom, in court, and via film, song, and fund-raising. Sometimes, the cause is clear but the role is not, and purpose alone does not lead to happiness at work. As Molly Barker learned, you must also be skilled at a job's primary tasks. It took Molly a while to realize that just because she founded Girls on the Run she did not have to run it, and eventually Molly passed the administrative reins to someone who actually loved holding them. If you're unhappy working at an organization whose mission you feel good about, perhaps the answer is not to change employers but to change roles. For what department or for whom would you rather work? Which colleagues do you imagine have the most fun? To whom do you gravitate? On the other hand, you may take pleasure in conducting your current job's tasks but at the end of the day feel emotionally empty. Perhaps it's time to use your skills to further a cause in which you believe. Every charity and foundation needs talented accountants, salespeople, negotiators, writers, and Thinkers and Determinators. Of course, you can always strike out on your own, like Julie Ratner or Leslie Grossman, and reel in a partner or volunteers who pick up the slack in areas where you lack skills.

However you choose to champion a cause, just get moving. Procrastinating won't get you any closer to workplace happiness. Take a cue from the women you just met: Worker, heal *thyself!*

Chapter Five

The Surviving Artists

Muralist, software specialist, gallery owner, writer/marketer, gym owner/aerobics instructor, actor, theatrical producer, and circus performer

The figure of the struggling artist is a deceptively romantic one, conjuring visions of painters, writers, or performers who sacrifice money and comfort for their craft as they toil away in pursuit of recognition, fame, and, oh yes, next month's rent. Consider the drunken bohemians of Giacomo Puccini's opera *La Bohême:* The creative clan had poetry but, alas, no heat. How devoted this breed has been portrayed. And how happy, right? Not necessarily. After all, Puccini's Mimi literally dies living the starving artist's lifestyle.

Few struggling artists would admit they actually enjoy the struggling. It's perhaps novel at first, but wearisome and, as former New York City painter Leslie Tonkonow admits, it can be very lonely. When Nancy Holson began producing theater, she specifically set out not to be a starving artist. And why should she? Why should writers, painters, and performers have to sacrifice a stable lifestyle for their art? Why should happiness come at the cost of, well, their happiness?

Leslie, Nancy, and others who found alternatives to struggling are what I call *Surviving* Artists: Women who know that money, art, and integrity need not be mutually exclusive. These Happy 100 members built working lives around their core artistic needs while also bringing in steady—and generally predictable—paychecks. Each isolated the creative process or purpose that originally attracted her to a life in art, then looked carefully for—and found—a unique career that satisfied her core instinct. It is not easy, the road to becoming a Surviving Artist, and each woman tackled internal demons and external obstacles until she arrived at her happiness. In many cases, these women still face daily hurdles. And while most Surviving Artists are not filthy rich, they are by no means holed up in dank apartments wanting for daily necessities. Most of the women in this chapter earn between $50,000 and $100,000 a year, although a few do make more. Half have neither husband nor partner and are thus solely responsible for supporting themselves.

Balancing commerce and creativity is the artist's challenge as she constantly asks herself, "How much freedom must I sacrifice to practice my craft full-time?" The sacrifice need not be dramatic, as the following women illustrate. Their job titles may surprise you, but their job descriptions will enlighten you to alternative ways to live an artistic life, for there is more than one way to work—and be happy—as an artist. Some opportunities are more obvious than others, but almost every industry, every company, has a role for artists.

Perhaps most important, these Happy 100 women are not just surviving in the financial sense, but in the spiritual and emotional sense as well. In short, they're happy—and they have heat.

Her practical painting

Tracy Lee Stum knows that oil on canvas is not the only medium in which painters can express themselves. At forty-two, this residential and commercial muralist gets paid to decorate other people's walls, from living rooms to entryways and even walls in malls and ceilings in casinos. Her hand-painted interiors—many of which have Greco-Roman influences—sell for from $5,000 to $75,000 and can be found in wealthy residences throughout the West. As a muralist-for-hire at the helm of Tracy Lee Stum Fine Art, Tracy has found an ideal business that both supports her financially and allows her to express her signature warm, Italianate style. What's more, she spends her days engulfed in the creative process she first discovered as a child.

I pretty much came into this world knowing what I wanted to do. My earliest memory is drawing on paper. That's all I wanted to do. Draw. Eventually my mom realized it was not a passing fancy and signed me up for art classes. I excelled and was doing pastel drawings at age seven or eight. I just went for it. I had nothing in my life that I loved as much.

In sixth grade I went through a phase where I actually wrote down a list of all the things I could do as an artist: architect, fashion designer, illustrator, painter. I listed things I had heard of or that just popped into my head. It was not a how-can-I-make-a-living list, but jobs I thought would be fun and satisfying. I was also thinking practically. I didn't imagine I would be a renowned sculptor prominently featured in museums.

When I attended college at the Tyler School of Art near Philadelphia, a lot of people tried to discourage me from the profession. While my mom continued to be supportive, my dad didn't think I could make a living as an artist. He wasn't alone. A lot of students majored in graphic design because it was considered practical, but I majored in painting and drawing.

When Tracy graduated, her journey took an ironic twist. Unlike most artists who crave freedom, Tracy was uncomfortable with too much autonomy and avoided the solo artist's lifestyle. Instead, she took commercial jobs with built-in boundaries. Back then if you told Tracy the sky was the limit, it paralyzed her. She needed rules, and commercial work—specifically visual merchandising—provided just that. Her first few jobs were for retail stores like Gimbels and Urban Outfitters, where she built window displays, followed by a job painting the interior of a 20,000-square-foot New York City boutique. Recalls Tracy, "That store was like a giant blank canvas waiting for someone to come in and add color." So she did, painting her own version of Sandro Botticelli's fifteenth-century masterpiece *The Birth of Venus* on a prominent wall; on other walls she plastered giant collages. It was grueling, enjoyable, collaborative work that kept her busy for three years, although too busy to pursue her own painting. Eventually Tracy grew restless and sensed she'd contributed as much as she could to the hip little retailer. It was time to go out on her own, to explore a life with slightly less structure and, as she puts it, "to do the things artists do."

The move to complete independence took time. Searching for something but not quite sure what, Tracy packed her bags and moved to Los Angeles and took a job painting props and backdrops for a movie studio. But the lack of creativity discouraged her, and she briefly returned to doing window displays.

Meanwhile, Tracy serendipitously hooked up with two restaurateurs building a chain of Cuban-Mexican restaurants that needed décor. The assignment proved a nice blend of freedom and structure. Because the entire restaurant was her canvas, Tracy had more room to express herself. Still, her work had to fit the restaurant's commercial context, and the owners wanted a playful, Latin flavor. Beyond that, Tracy was free to create. She hired a staff and educated herself in interior design, lighting, construction regulations, and flooring. For the next five years she created funky restaurant interiors, working on and off for the chain as it expanded. There were months when she was booked every day, and periods where she had nothing to do.

"Even though I tried to be true to myself in every job, my first eight to ten years out of art school were a struggle. I was barely able to support myself and had come to accept that financial uncertainty was a part of my life." In her free time, Tracy visited museums where she could indulge her love of Italian art. For extra money she took jobs painting residential interiors—children's bedrooms and dining rooms.

Her big break arrived in 1999. Working with an agent who matched painters with customers, Tracy landed her largest project at the time: designing 11,000 square feet of casino ceilings and wall murals for the opulent Venetian Resort Hotel Casino in Las Vegas. Not coincidentally, Tracy's Greco-Roman style was a perfect fit for the resort, which required re-creating ornate Italian artwork and landscapes. To meet the almost impossible four-week deadline, Tracy teamed with an agent and together they hired twenty-five artists to work with her. The intense project helped Tracy further discover her own artistic style.

"After doing the casino I relaxed into historical decorative art," says Tracy. And no longer did Tracy work for just one boss: she began the life of a full-fledged freelance muralist, for a while taking on more residential painting projects for additional income. "I have a strange ability to interpret decorative elements in a way that is harmonious for people and brings calm to their lives. It comes out of me; it just kind of happens." The only problem with residential work: It required travel and took Tracy out of her studio. "I didn't feel settled working in so many locations," she says.

These days, Tracy has returned to commercial work, most recently designing more casino interiors in Las Vegas and Atlantic City, as well as a project for a Walt Disney resort in Hong Kong. Because she, and often a small staff, do all the painting in Tracy's 2,000-square-foot studio, Tracy rarely travels. The commercial work is both lucrative and creatively satisfying: clients tend to have large budgets, and Tracy says she has built up a reputation, so "people let me design and do what I need to do without getting in the way or dictating too much. I feel very free creatively. Plus, I like large projects that take a while to research, projects I can sink my teeth into."

As Tracy describes her work, notice how primal her sensation is, and how comfortable she has become expressing herself, even when it's on behalf of others.

I love what I do because it comes from the unseen part of life. When I'm making artwork I'm in an actualized state. I don't think about anything else; I'm in the moment. It's pure bliss to be in that state continually. And I love to collaborate with the clients and figure out how to translate their desires into a visual format. They feed me information, I filter it, and when it comes out it seems to satisfy everyone. I am fortunate enough to have many clients who just let me do my thing.

As an artist, Tracy found an unexpected home for her unique style in large-scale commercial work. The public spaces also give this artist's work a public stage. Adds Tracy, "If I can inspire and influence more than a few people, that is really exciting for me."

The computer is her canvas.

Freedom may be some artists' idea of happiness, but on a tiny farm in Muskego, Wisconsin, Sandra (Sam) Racine's work-related happiness stems from just the opposite: structure. In fact, the thirty-six-year-old has deliberately sought out greater rules and boundaries for her art.

"I need to create things in response to a task," says Sam. "An illustrator stares at a blank sheet of paper and must build everything on her own. As a young artist, that was exhausting for me, and I could not imagine trying to make a living at it." Sam needed art with purpose, and a single, nagging issue spurred her journey. She desperately wanted to be able to articulate why one design was better, or more useful, than another. For Sam, "better" meant art that prompted a desired action, but for years she struggled with how to achieve it. Her journey took her to an unexpected end.

Today, Sam is a senior usability architect for computer services company Unisys. Translation: She helps design the way software programs look and feel so they are easy for people to use. The more effectively designed and intuitive software looks to a user, the easier the program is to understand. "It's funny. I've been doing the same thing since I was six years old," says Sam from her home office on her farm, which also houses two shaggy white dogs, a horse, some goats, and several chickens.

It's hard to believe that a little girl growing up in the manufacturing town of New London, Wisconsin, predicted a future in software. But consider that as a child Sam was always a practical artist. She worked on the school yearbook, designed newsletters for her church, and made posters for band concerts. Her artwork was always about communication, and with every creation there was purpose: to get people to act—for example, to donate money or attend an event. Having concrete goals made Sam feel productive.

Sam also yearned for a life outside the meat-packing plant where every member of her family had worked. Sam's parents expected her to join them at the factory, but for Sam, success meant wearing high heels and suits to an office, not bundling up in layers of clothes to stay warm in a cold warehouse. With prodding from teachers and friends as well as her family's blessing, the small-town girl escaped and attended the University of Wisconsin in Madison, where she majored in art and graphic design.

After graduation, Sam's obsession with purposeful design continued, and she took a job doing desktop publishing and illustrations for a hardware company that sold seemingly unsexy tools like hammers, nails, and chain saws. But Sam *loved* the tools. She loved their hard angles and their well-defined shapes. And she loved that they had a purpose in and of themselves.

Sam went on to design marketing materials for industrial companies in Chicago, indulging her fascination with what made design successful. Meanwhile, she began writing her own software programs to do the so-called drudge work of graphic design—like formatting headlines—so she could focus on the more creative aspects. It ruffled her intellect when people based design decisions on emotions or gut feelings, and Sam recalls heated discussions with colleagues when it came time to select a look for, say, an invoice or a product's packaging. Still, Sam didn't yet have the knowledge or language to explain why she felt one design was better than another. To ease that frustration, she attended graduate school in technical communications and went on to earn a Ph.D. with a concentration in human behavior.

"I am most interested in the visual cues that get people to behave a certain way. If I see two buttons, I'll ask why someone would choose to push one over the other. I love the theory," says Sam, who has been at Unisys for two and a half years, in a job where purpose, theory, and art finally converge.

I design computer interfaces, the part of a computer program that people see. Users don't understand what is going on behind the screen, so the screen view must communicate it to them. I interview people who use our software, so I can understand their needs and the information they require to do their jobs. Then, we go on to create visual metaphors of sorts. Much of my work is for the transportation industry and companies that move cargo. You would not believe the amount of work and information required to move a single package.

Usability is about building things that people want to use. You have to make them want to go to the band concert, buy a certain piece of hardware, or input information to move a package. I started out in paper and now I've completely moved to the Web. I'm still drawing pictures and making spaces; the technology has just changed.

As for the suits and high heels she so desired as a child, Sam got over that. Her home-office uniform consists of thick wool socks, sweatpants, and an oversized sweatshirt. Without a time-consuming commute and workplace dress codes, Sam can focus on work that puts her in that same state of mind as more traditional artists.

She's a better business owner.

Struggling artists, as they churn out poetry, fiction, or paintings, can find themselves questioning their purpose and at the very least feeling lonely. Back in the late 1970s in New York City, then-artist Leslie Tonkonow worked alone in her own studio, experiencing the ups and downs of the struggling artist's life.

When I first got to New York after graduate school I started doing art in various mediums, from video to two-dimensional work using unconventional materials like floor tiles and contact paper. I always needed other jobs to support myself, but for a young woman there were limited opportunities to make a decent amount of money on the side. The male artists I knew could do construction and make good cash quickly. I did administration for galleries. I did temp work. I was even the personal secretary for violinist Isaac Stern. I worked a lot, and by the end of the day I was so tired that I couldn't make the mental adjustment to go into my studio and paint.

Worse, I didn't like the isolation of working in a studio. Being an artist is very up and down, and for me it was mostly down. When my work was going well I was extremely happy—there was no better high. But too often my work didn't go well, which made me very unhappy.

Then, just as I was starting to exhibit my work, I was randomly contacted by a guy who knew someone who owned a building and wanted to put a gallery in the building's empty space. I called a bunch of friends who were all artists and said there was an opportunity for us to put a show together, and we did. I kind of led the effort but had no intention or interest in becoming an art dealer, let alone quit being an artist. But as a result of the positive reaction to the exhibition I thought we should try to keep it going, and I thought some of my artist buddies would join me . . . but they didn't. So I was the only one who had the tenacity and determination to show up every day and open the door. Eventually the space evolved into a real gallery, and I discovered I really enjoyed being there, talking with other artists and meeting the public. I liked that even more than I enjoyed working on my own.

This was an epiphany for the struggling artist: Art dealing was a way to enjoy art without the loneliness she encountered while creating it. Slowly, Leslie embraced the business of art and wove it into her own artistic endeavors. She and her husband, a curator and a critic, both accepted part-time jobs as curators in Connecticut. Around the time she grew tired of commuting from the city, Leslie was coincidentally offered a job as director for a prestigious, established gallery in Manhattan, where she went on to work for six years. It was during that time Leslie realized she was perfectly happy to stop doing her own artistic work and, instead, work full time as a dealer.

I felt, and still feel, strongly that you can't be an artist and a dealer and be successful at both. It takes 100 percent of your effort to be a good artist, and 100 percent to be a good dealer. Both are 24/7 jobs. I chose dealing over art because it was very intellectually stimulating; I had always been interested in writing and history. Besides, I had been lonely in my studio and never figured out a way to make a living. Today there are more opportunities for young artists, but thirty years ago it was a different world.

After a brief stint working at another gallery, Leslie, now fifty-one, again opened her own gallery in 1997, in a small space. She kept overhead costs to a bare minimum so she could make as large a profit as possible. For the first year Leslie's husband paid their household expenses, and positive publicity helped the gallery take off relatively quickly. After three years Leslie moved to a larger space—and took on even greater expenses.

Today, Leslie Tonkonow Artworks + Projects resides in a 1,700-square-foot space in the hub of one of New York City's gallery districts. She represents twelve international contemporary artists, who range from twenty-nine to sixty-seven years old, and she has also handled art from Picasso, Roy Lichtenstein, Richard Serra, and Jean Dubuffet. If inspired, collectors spend anywhere from $2,500 to half a million dollars on a piece in Leslie's gallery.

For Leslie, running a small business provided an even greater outlet for her creativity without sacrificing her connection to the artistic world. Operating the gallery was an alternative way to express herself, and while running a business does not replace the sensation of painting, it satisfies her in other ways, providing an even greater sense of accomplishment.

The truth is that I'm better at being a business owner than an artist. I organize exhibitions and write about art, which I find incredibly stimulating. I've grown the gallery myself, with the emotional support of my husband, and it was an immense challenge. It's very competitive and costly to run a gallery, and there's a lot of administrative work: tons of bookkeeping, tracking paintings, and designing promotional campaigns. I also deal with museums and other galleries, collectors, and the press.

How did I learn it all? Most of it is just plain logic—I never took any classes—but I also worked for other galleries before opening my own. And as an artist you also gain experience making and showing your own work, which makes me very different from other gallery owners. It's funny . . . as an artist I hardly sold anything, but the artists I represent sell very well. I do not look at my work as living vicariously through them. Rather, I approach my relationship with artists as a partnership: It is their job to make art and it is my job to send it out into the world and be its advocate. In order for us to succeed we have to work in concert.

Still, so much of the business is out of my control. Because customers are buying real art for their home, you never know if they'll choose the avant-garde pieces that I have in my gallery. It's brave for people to spend huge amounts of money on unproven things.

It's also a brave gesture for an artist to break away from her craft and take an unproven career path. But as Leslie's story proves, nontraditional roads can yield even greater happiness—and tap hidden skills.

Her writing life

In Chicago, writer and public relations practitioner Lois Padovani, forty-two, has dramatically shifted her career once and then further tweaked her second profession to accommodate new priorities. In the mid-

1990s, Lois left a coveted career at *BusinessWeek* magazine to work in public relations. Such a leap is tough for many writers, who consider transitioning from a profession that informs to one that sells a sell-out. But Lois disagrees. Many journalists, she says, are snobs and don't realize that a better writing life may await them in other fields; there are lots of ways to apply one's writing.

At one point, Lois was guilty of snobbery herself. For years, journalism was the only career option that interested her; she wanted to be a reporter. The college journalism major was strongly influenced by the events of Watergate and the movie *All the President's Men* (1976); she believed that because journalists, at least theoretically, served the public good, they had a more noble purpose than other professionals.

Lois's quest for *what* to write about as a journalist was resolved when an internship on the business desk of *The Washington Post* further introduced her to the intellectual rigor of financial reporting. That was in the early 1980s, when the country was climbing out of a recession. It was the age of leveraged buyouts and colorful, unpredictable characters—Michael Milken, Lee Iacocca—who were fun to write about. For Lois, business was also a meaty topic that kept her challenged. With each new story came a new industry and company to learn about: finance, aerospace, retail, technology, consumer goods.

After school, Lois took a position as a young writer at *BusinessWeek* and eventually moved to the magazine's Chicago bureau. Her experience holds a valuable lesson for anyone struggling to excel in any profession.

BusinessWeek was an incredible experience and I loved it, but it was very competitive and I was essentially on my own. No one taught me how to cultivate sources, how to interview. Unlike other professions that provide formal, on-the-job training, you're given very little direction in journalism, and it's really up to you to figure it out for yourself. No one ever talked about how a story could be developed, and if you asked, you risked looking like you didn't know what you were doing.

In Chicago I had a bit of a career crisis. Several editors in New York said my articles were thin and that I failed to get the inside story. I was tremendously upset that I was not excelling, and I called my sister, who gave me the best career advice I've ever received. She suggested I go to the main

*BusinessWeek office in New York and talk to everyone. Bureau reporters
don't get as much face time with senior editors, so I flew to New York and
met a variety of people, asked them what they thought was wrong with my
work and how I could improve in the future. They were very honest and
helpful and appreciated that I approached them with my questions. The
visit alone helped solve two-thirds of the problem right away because it
cleared the air and convinced my editors that I wanted to do good work.*

Lois applied her editors' advice when she returned to Chicago. For example, she further questioned what executives told her, and she increased her pool of sources, often calling employees at home at night to
get the inside scoop about their companies. Future articles received
positive feedback and Lois would go on to write three cover stories, including in-depth articles about Motorola and McDonald's. As it turned
out, going to New York and meeting with her superiors made Lois a better, happier journalist.

As the years rolled on, Lois outgrew her own success. To be promoted
she would have to move, but Lois was not interested in leaving Chicago.
What's more, she felt "done with journalism." The problem, however,
was that since the age of thirteen she had never thought of herself as
anything but a journalist.

The artist's dilemma had finally caught up with Lois: How else could
she apply her writing craft? The answer came with a phone call from
a public relations executive Lois admired who asked her to join his
media relations staff at technology services firm Andersen Consulting,
now called Accenture. The job would boost her annual salary by about
$30,000, but, more important, it provided a fresh intellectual challenge.

In many ways, the practice of public relations turned out to be a similar intellectual exercise to journalism. Both involved the gathering and
packaging of information. "Journalism and PR are both like putting together a puzzle. It's challenging to figure out how to position a company,
make the best of its situation, and get reporters to want to write about
it," she says. Lois also embraced a new purpose. In journalism, she says,
she wrote to help sell a magazine and report stories that no one else had.
In marketing, she helped influence an entire business's direction and
success. Life at a large company was not without frustration. It was very

political, and Lois worked long hours that gave her little free time for friends or her husband.

Although Lois had found a new purpose for which she could ply her craft, lifestyle issues eventually got in her way. It's another common dilemma: Just when women have satisfied one previously unmet need, another pops up. So, with enough money in the bank and several years of corporate public relations experience behind her, Lois broke free and went out on her own as a public relations consultant, taking Accenture as her first client. Today, her firm, Padovani Communications, charges $160 an hour, and her clients include a hospital system, a financial services company, and the consulting firm. "My journalism background and corporate experience make me a better public relations practitioner," she says. "I know what story ideas are going to sell and what's not going to sell."

Lois's journey as a writer has been a process of satisfying one desire at a time, keeping writing as the focal point. Identifying writing as her craft was easy. She then found a topic of interest—business—and once journalism bored her, public relations provided a fresh purpose that stimulated her mind just as much. When corporate life wore her out, Lois found balance as an independent consultant and today has time enough for her two toddlers. "What I love about writing is that you can do it anywhere, and not just in journalism. Every kind of company has departments that need writers: communications, community affairs, Web site work, not-for-profit areas. Writing is such a basic skill and so few people are good at it. My advice to writers is, first, go work somewhere and learn the craft. Let someone pay you to learn it before you go out and do it on your own." And being on her own allows Lois to keep doing the work she loves in a manner that also works for her family.

Her kinesthetic connection

Of course, not all artists are painters or writers. They are also performers. But aside from acting, singing, or dancing for stage, television, or film, it seems jobs requiring raw performance skills are limited. For those who find happiness in the spotlight, it's a difficult sensation to replicate in other professions.

Former dancer Lori Lowell, who works in Woodbridge, Virginia, grew up performing onstage, and as she got older she found an unexpected outlet in the health and fitness business. Talking with Lori, who is forty-three, feels a bit like a workout. The five-foot, five-inch, 118-pound Lori, clad in black pants and a black Gold's Gym T-shirt, talks fast, punctuating each word as if she's punching the air during a kickboxing routine. Lori's road was fraught not so much with struggle as triumph, considering that few dancers can extend performance into their forties. Yet Lori has. And while many performers are driven by fame—and feel traumatized when it's lost or elusive—Lori discovered an aspect of performing that was more gratifying than stardom.

A natural performer, Lori began singing and dancing onstage—and in the family kitchen—with her mother, an internationally recognized Sephardic folk musician. After graduating from the University of South Florida, Lori joined several modern dance companies in Washington, D.C. One problem: The pay was lousy or nonexistent. To make money, Lori took a job with Nike helping to lobby Congress for international trade. It was the early 1980s, and aerobics—with all its related music and fashion paraphernalia—was coming into vogue. For extra cash she taught aerobics classes, and, slowly, Lori's interest in dance morphed into a fascination with the fitness business. As Nike grew from a sneaker manufacturer into a fitness company, Lori grew with it, hawking Nike gear to aerobics instructors and trainers so they would flash the brand in their gyms.

For six years, Lori was a fitness professional by day and a dancer by night. It proved an exhausting balancing act. Despite Lori's energy, the pace wore her down, forcing her to give up dancing in the early 1990s. She did not, however, abandon performing and continued to teach and choreograph aerobics classes.

In 1996, a fluke business deal made Lori and her husband, a dentist, 25 percent owners of the Gold's Gym where she worked. Two years later, they completely bought out their partner. Lori was now a business owner. And by then she was a specialist in the fitness industry, one of the few gym operators trained in health and body issues as well as proficient at managing the business. "My dance background gives me the kinesthetic connection that, I think, fitness teachers and club owners need to be able to explain workouts to their customers," she says. "Dance allowed me to understand where the body needs to be and how it moves through space. As a dancer, I got to see how the power of my own movement affects other people." Today, Lori and her husband own two Gold's Gyms that, she says, cater to the suburban community with a variety of classes and programs, including hip-hop dance, body sculpting, and yoga as well as children's fitness. And because she still teaches, this artist has not abandoned dance. Her art just has a different purpose.

I just love changing people's lives. It's so gratifying, and I have story after story about how I have helped clients. They tell me they're not depressed anymore; women tell me they no longer have PMS and feel so much better about themselves. These days my only job is to give my members results. As for me, at the end of the day I have everything I want: I exercise, I entertain, I make a difference in people's lives. It just makes me feel good.

Lori no longer refers to herself as a dancer, but she is no less of a performer than when she was onstage. In addition to running her clubs and teaching, she competes in sport aerobic competitions and lectures at fitness industry conferences. And with 4,000 club members, she has a large, paying audience. "I am passionate about fitness. It's in the fabric of who I am, it's in my soul. I live, eat, and breathe this industry." Sentiments of a happy—and fit—woman.

In her own words

Stockard Channing, 60
Actor
NBC's *The West Wing*
Los Angeles, California

Stockard plays Abigail Bartlet, a doctor and the First Lady of the United States, on *The West Wing*. She has been acting in movies and television and onstage for thirty years and has received Emmys for her work on *The West Wing* and in *The Matthew Shepard Story*, as well as Academy Award and Golden Globe nominations for the movie *Six Degrees of Separation*.

Among Stockard's more than 100 theater and film credits are *Grease; Practical Magic; The First Wives Club; The Business of Strangers; Le Divorce; Where the Heart Is; The Lion in Winter;* and *A Day in the Death of Joe Egg,* for which she won a Tony Award. Stockard has survived as an artist for so many years because, quite simply, she loves her craft.

For me, the process of acting is about listening. It is about reacting, and creating with another actor a reality that a third person, the viewer, is sucked into. I don't always succeed at that, but I try. I've been doing this a very long time, and I try not to make too many decisions before I am in front of the camera. I don't know what the light is going to be like, what the room is going to look like, and I don't know how I'm going to move around the room. It's best to live in the moment as much as possible, and over time you develop a technique . . . but acting is a mysterious process. I used to prepare for parts by doing a lot of backstory work, but sometimes that type of preparation is not really germane. In the right circumstances it's an interesting thing to do—for example, when I played a poor woman from Oklahoma and had to get out of myself and learn an accent, figure out the wardrobe. But there was no backstory for my role on West Wing, which grew out of a little germ in writer Aaron Sorkin's mind. Abbey's relationship to the other actors emerged over time, like a path in the snow. Martin [Sheen] and I never sat down and talked about the backstory between the president and his wife. In fact, the first day we met was right before we shot a scene. I was wearing this gown and walking with Martin down a staircase. Right before the camera rolled I said to him, "So how long have we been married?" [Laughs.] We got along great from the beginning, and viewers had a great response to the character of Abbey; they wrote in saying they wanted to see her in more episodes. Over the next four years the character of Abbey took hold, and I am very proud of the impact she has on people, on women, and on young women. The only time acting really counts is when an audience is moved, to laughter, to tears . . .

I grew up on Park Avenue in New York, and my father was a prosperous businessman. My mother was born in 1910, so that should give you some indication of the world I was raised in regarding what women were expected to do for a living. There was tremendous emphasis on etiquette, and I was going to get a good education and get married and raise children. But I also used to draw when I was a kid, and I wanted to be a painter and a dress designer. I was also a bit of a performer. I always told stories and was the one who got out of doing chores by telling a story about something I'd seen. [Laughs.] I'd act out parts and was the clown in my little family unit. I did pretty well in school, but basically I was supposed to marry a man who made a couple of bucks. There was a lot of expectation, but not a tremendous sense of reality.

My father got cancer when I was fourteen, and with his illness came tremendous fear and drama; it's horrendous to have a life-threatening illness in a family. He died a year and a half later. It was a massive influence on my life. Meanwhile, I essentially left home when I went to boarding school, and in many ways I raised myself. My life away from home became very separate from how I was raised. For college I went to Harvard and met a truly wonderful man, who was irreverent and funny, and from the world I had been born into. The marriage broke down because I got into acting. I was also a product of the sixties, definitely someone who sniffed the air and smelled something that she had never experienced when she was a kid. I've thought about this a lot and it's really interesting. I think the rebellion I found inside myself paralleled, or at least resonated with, the outside world. It's difficult to explain to people who did not grow up in that era what a watershed it was. It could take you in many different directions. The path was quite narrow as presented to me as a child, but in college everything was possible, the world was wide open . . . I don't know if I would have become an actor if I did not grow up during that time.

The real galvanizing element for me occurred when I was in dress rehearsal for a production of The Threepenny Opera at Harvard. I will never forget it . . . the lights, the people in the audience. I was playing a prostitute in a brothel, Jenny Diver, and singing the song "Pirate Jenny," which is about this prostitute's fantasy of bloody revenge. It's heartbreaking because this woman is so fucked up! I was all of twenty years old, and here I had tears pouring out of my face and was dressed like a Victorian hooker in black lace undies. It must have been very eerie to see this baby-face undergraduate singing such a sexual song. But I remember that scene as if it happened just now. You could hear a pin drop in the theater. I even asked myself, How did I know how to make it work, *even musically,* because I never had any formal acting training? But have you ever experienced something when your unconscious brain and your emotions and your creativity and your ego all combine in one moment? It's extraordinary. Out of context it probably sounds insane, but once I had that experience singing "Pirate Jenny," I could not give up acting.

Still, I was not commercially successful for years. I was very bad at auditioning and did not understand the business of acting. For about ten years I would go back to New York and then back to Boston and work on Broadway and this and that . . . nobody told me I had no talent (well, no—one agent did tell me that). I just needed a break. Pursuing acting was like feeling a wall and trying to find a crack in it, something that would give. It was a really creepy time, because there is something about the tedium of failure. I had this degree from Harvard and was approaching thirty. People looked at me like I was out of my mind. I felt like an unbelievable failure. But I did not have any other skills. I had some income from a trust fund from my father, so I had enough money that I did not have to wait tables, but I was treading water. And when you don't have any money, you can't do anything. You can't just take off somewhere to forget your circumstance. You are forced to confront your reality.

At the lowest part of my life I was stuck in the chorus of Two Gentleman of Verona. So I asked to audition for the understudy part, and I got it. And then I was a standby, and then I went on to the national company, and I went to Los Angeles, and that is when things started to move. To sum it up, I was almost thirty when I had my first sort of break. I was cast in my first movie, The Fortune, directed by Mike Nichols and starring Warren Beatty and Jack Nicholson. It was a wonderful experience, but it was not a successful film. I did a few other movies and then was cast in Grease, which drove me crazy when it first came out. It was sort of looked upon as a low-rent project, and I didn't make any money from it or get any work from it. Its financial success was amazing, but it did not earn critical acclaim. Ironically, in those days a box office hit did not have the impact on one's career as it would now, but Grease certainly lives on in tape and DVDs.

But the early 1980s were a difficult time for me. A lousy time. My TV show was canceled, my marriage broke up, and I was not making any money. That's when I wrote letters to three directors, telling them I wanted to get back into stage work. It is very hard to ask for what you want, especially when the stakes are incredibly high. But one of the directors, Arvin Brown, responded and asked if I would consider being in his production of Joe Egg, with Richard Dreyfuss, in Williamstown. Being in that play was one of the best experiences of my life.

I believe no one should be an actor if they want to be famous. Fame is a double-edged sword. You're much better off if you really like to act, just like you should not be a painter unless you really like to paint. But in our society, people associate acting with fame and fortune. Success for me has evolved over the years. A long time ago I had a friend, an actress, whose mother was beyond famous and I could never figure out why she did not want that kind of fame for herself. But now I am glad I don't really have that. It is very claustrophobic. Obviously, I feel successful when people admire what I do and give me kudos—let's face it, I'm not some hermit in a cave; I'm not writing things and then burying them in the ground for people to see once I'm long gone. [Laughs.] We live in the world, where other people evaluate a lot of what we do, and what I have chosen to do for a career is about entertaining, about communicating to other people, stimulating them, telling stories. For me, still being here and functioning as an actor, doing my job well, is an achievement. I have a lot of respect for it. Being successful is about people coming up to me, thanking me, and saying, "I love what you do." At least then I know I'm giving them something.

Her show must go on.

Nancy Holson is a comedy writer and producer for The News in Revue, a political satire theater company that performs during summers in the Berkshires of Massachusetts as well as other venues around the country. At the time of our interview, Nancy's script was rife with jokes about President George W. Bush and the upcoming Democratic primary elections. About the uninspiring pack of Democratic candidates, Nancy had just written a song-and-dance number titled "We're Forgettable," set to the tune of Nat King Cole's classic "Unforgettable." A skit about "disaster preparedness" in times of terrorism was set to the tune of "The

Hokey Pokey": "You got duct tape, ma'am. Got your own supply. Tape your face between your legs so you can kiss your ass good-bye." Another skit had the still-in-hiding Osama bin Laden working at a Starbucks.

You can't analyze why something is funny and how you get there. You either have it in you or you don't. As far as writing songs, I have always just known where to put the punch line. I usually know whether I want a big number with lots of choreography, or a short-and-sweet solo. I sit by myself to write a skit before I bring it back to my musical director and codirector and other colleagues to stage it. We can sit for hours, and it takes a great deal of work to get it right. Although my lows have been low, the highs have been amazing. I love my job because what starts in my head ends up onstage, interpreted by singers and actors, and I can see my ideas fully realized. When an audience convulses with laughter, I'm elated!

Nancy—a witty, gregarious married mother of two who lives in Connecticut—quite literally decided to put on a show back in 1991, when her youngest child began kindergarten. Although her husband owned a retail store that supported the family, Nancy wanted to turn writing into a business, not just a hobby. Her story is an example of perseverance, lessons learned, and a true love of comedic art.

I knew I did not want to be a starving artist, and so I had to think of comedy as a business. I meet so many amazing, talented people in theater who just can't succeed financially. They live a very different life than I live in Connecticut, and it does not bother them. But I don't want what they have. I wanted to get paid well for what I did and be able to live in the area where I grew up.

Nancy, forty-eight, may have entered musical theater with a practical eye toward finance, but the money did not flow easily or quickly, and she learned the hard way that the big league and bright lights of Broadway are not the only—or best—way to succeed in theater.

Nancy's first step in bringing her grandiose idea to fruition was to try out her brash political parodies during open-mike night at a comedy club near her home. As the evening wore on, the crowd got drunker and drunker, the jokes sicker and dirtier, and Nancy chickened out and went home before she went onstage. "And you know what?" she asks with a laugh. "It was one of the best decisions of my life. I was already vulnerable when it came to showing people my work, and the reception would have been so bad that night, my career would have ended before it began!" She changed tactics. A few days later, the local Jewish Community Center (JCC), a not-for-profit organization, invited Nancy to use its JCC auditorium for her show, *The News in Revue*. Nancy created the songs herself—mostly rewriting popular tunes with lyrics based on current events—and auditioned actors, hired a pianist, and built a stage. Her parents invested the first of many dollars, and Nancy pulled from her own savings. *The News in Revue* ran in the suburbs during the 1991 presidential primary season, and Nancy's jokes about candidates Mario Cuomo and Paul Tsongas went over well. Feeling pressure to grow the tiny little venture, she made ambitious plans to open the show in New York City.

A domino effect of mistakes ensued. Nancy overloaded her operations payroll with too many employees, and when she tried to unionize them, tensions erupted. She hired a director who did not read newspapers or know much about politics, which threw off the show. A run-through the day before opening night was catastrophic to the point that on a white paper tablecloth one of the audience members doodled a gravestone inscribed with "*The News in Revue:* R.I.P."

We knew it was going to be a disaster if we opened the next night, so we pushed back the date. It was clear I needed to codirect the show, and when I offered to do it, my director resigned. That was it—even I was ready to leave! I remember us all meeting at my parents' house—my husband, my sister, my children, my mom and dad—and everyone was so worried about me because I had put so much into the production. But that night, when my husband and I got home, he put in a video of the show I did at the JCC and said, "Get on the phone to Steve," my old musical director. I did, and we decided to redirect the whole show. When we finally opened in 1992, we had good reviews and ran in New York for four months. Still, the show lost a ton of money.

With no profits, *The News in Revue* shuttered, leaving Nancy in a quandary: What to do with her popular but unprofitable product? Rather than quit and chalk it up to a nice try, Nancy turned to her family for ideas and, in a twist of repackaging, sold the show to corporate meeting planners as an employee event, with content tailored to conservative corporate audiences at the likes of IBM and Hitachi. In addition to the corporate gigs, Nancy continued to put on shows in several states and in the Berkshires. *The News in Revue* even snagged a series of television specials on PBS, for which it won five Emmy awards. Perfect, right? Wrong. Nancy was still losing money because expenses for the corporate shows often exceeded revenue. In a last-ditch effort, Nancy even sold the show at one point, only to buy it back when the actors threatened to quit. Her family's savings were almost depleted, and profitability was the only option, especially with two children headed to college.

At yet another crossroads—quit or stick with it—Nancy attended a weekend career seminar in New York, the Carole Hyatt Leadership Forum, which helped her pinpoint her priorities and network with entertainment professionals. They told her to get rid of the dead wood. So Nancy refused to do corporate gigs for anything less than $10,000, and she stopped the weekly, money-losing shows in Connecticut. But she kept the Berkshires shows, which at forty dollars a ticket were the most profitable venue. Today, they are *The News in Revue*'s main source of income. Her days consist of "producing chores, writing chores, and directing chores": staging new sketches; arranging songs with her codirector; planning costumes and props; auditioning actors; marketing the show to boost ticket sales; and general business administration. Nancy may dub these activities "chores," but they are all labors of love in the name of keeping her art alive—and profitable.

Comedy, it turns out, is serious business, and many women would have given up at any one of Nancy's crossroads. Nancy stuck with it because, she says, she simply imagined the worst-case scenario: Her family could always sell their waterside Connecticut home, move to Greece, and buy a cheap house. "Once I realized that the worst-case scenario really wasn't all that bad, it made it easier for me to commit to my path." The comedian is only half joking.

She can "jazz it up" for a living.

Her office is a 1.5 million-gallon swimming pool. Her work attire: a blue, lizard-skin bodysuit with white, red, and yellow makeup and cascading orange hair. Her hours: five P.M. to 12:30 A.M. Wednesdays through Saturdays.

No, Ana Cukic is not a lawyer.

Ana is a synchronized swimmer and one of eighty-five performers in Cirque du Soleil's dreamlike, decadent show *O* at Las Vegas's Bellagio Hotel and Casino. Twice a night in a cavernous auditorium, an enormous red curtain parts to reveal ninety minutes of mind-blowing choreography with dancers, acrobats, divers, clowns, contortionists, and swimmers engaged in precision-timed stunts and inventive staging. It's an eye-popping circus, a surrealist painting come to life. And for twenty-eight-year-old Ana, performing is not so much the realization of a lifelong ambition but an alternative to competition, which was all she had known before joining the circus.

I was born in Yugoslavia, but my parents moved to Toronto when I was one, and I got into synchronized swimming when my mother accidentally signed me up for lessons at a professional club instead of a recreational pool. I was eleven or twelve, and people thought I had a natural talent in the water and encouraged me to try out for the club. I just stayed with it but never really thought about it as a career. People want you to get to a certain point, and they push you and push you. The sport was amazing for me, but it kind of retards your growth because it leaves little time for a life outside of the pool. You also come to rely so much—too much—on other people's opinions. I've struggled with my own confidence, and learned to stop worrying so much about other people's opinions.

After the Nazi-like regime of six-hour daily practices for seven years, I went to college on a full athletic scholarship at Ohio State University, where the sport was still rigorous but took a backseat to school. College gave me time to grow into my own person, and I just loved being part of the school's athletic energy and spirit. When I graduated summa cum laude with a major in criminology and sociology, I didn't have a plan, which was very worrisome to me.

Ana struggled with whether to continue swimming. Although her parents urged her to try out for the Olympic team, Ana didn't feel the competitive itch like other swimmers. "If I had an off-day in the pool I'd be, like, 'Whatever' but when other people didn't do a technical element right, they took it to heart. I wanted more than to just be good at synchronized swimming." But she did not want to abandon it. In lieu of competing, Ana wanted to perform. It was not a far-fetched notion. As a competitor, Ana was always being told to "tone it down" when she tried to "jazz it up." Jazzing it up was her natural instinct. So in 2000, Ana applied to one of the only organizations that hired swimmers, the French-Canadian theatrical and acrobatic troupe Cirque du Soleil. While she waited to hear if she would be granted an audition, Ana lived at home, took an office job, and put the circus out of her mind until 2001, when she was finally invited to try out in Montreal.

I didn't know what to expect at the audition, and it turned out to be less swimming and more land activity. They were looking for charisma and personality and stage presence. This is where I excelled. They gave me scenarios to act out—"You're meeting your boyfriend at an abandoned church to run off and get married, but he never shows up. Act out all the emotions"—and they had me do headstands, climb rope, and even sing. When they called me at home and said I'd been accepted to the four-month training camp, I knew I'd do it. I was shaking on the phone because I knew it was right for me. I have always struggled with my self-worth, and I was learning to face my fears and take risks that felt uncomfortable.

I was one of only two synchronized swimmers at the camp, and there were people from all over the world, mostly Russia and Europe, and we all lived in dorms. Everyone was from a sports background and was used to rigid physical movements, and the camp tried to loosen us up so we could find our personal flair. We had movement and drama classes, swimming and voice. We were even given a stipend. Still, there was no guarantee we'd get picked for a show when camp was all over. Up until a week before it ended I didn't have a job; then the other swimmer and I were called into the office and given temporary contracts for O in Las Vegas. I flipped out! I think that was the turning point for me, when I knew, without a doubt, that this was what I wanted to do.

Ana moved to Las Vegas, where she watched O from the audience ten times before she began to practice. Ana was overwhelmed at first, the director slowly integrated Ana into the complex performance. For her first role, all she had to do was walk across the stage and stand still. "I felt like all eyes were on me, and I was so nervous. But the more I let go of that feeling, of the Ana part of me, and tried to get into character, the more I became a performer." Today, Ana is one of eighteen synchronized swimmers who spend the majority of O kicking, twirling, spinning, and dancing in the water.

They call the synchronized swimmers the workhorses of the show because we're in eleven acts, the majority of the show. We also have the highest injury rate (but not the most serious ones) because we get sick and have a lot of overuse injuries. I'm recovering from a back injury and usually show up at work an hour early to do exercises and Pilates. It's hard to do the show ten times a week, but you feel the energy of the crowd. You can sense their appreciation for what you're doing. The show kind of takes them away from their lives for an hour and a half, and from the stage I can see people's faces. Usually they're in awe, but occasionally you see people sleeping, and on nights when the audience is not enthusiastic, I go internally and find the energy within myself. I love to ham it up, and while we have to stay in character onstage, I always try to keep it fun and light backstage. I love that my friends and I have fun every day behind the scenes. And I love that I can be myself without fear of judgment, learn from others, and explore new avenues of self-expression.

After two years of appearing in O—in more than 900 performances—Ana says there are nights when it's easy to get in a groove, go through the motions, and forget how grand the show is. But by the end of each evening, as she bows with the cast in front of 1,800 applauding people, she is reminded that her job is quite rare. "I plan to do this until it's no longer fun. I don't know what the future holds, but I am just trying to live in the moment right now. It's a once-in-a-lifetime experience, and I try to enjoy every day for what it is. This is the perfect place to find out who I am."

. . . .

Artistic passion and talent need not be relegated to weekends or, worse, completely abandoned and left in childhood. The Surviving Artists each discovered, through various routes, that there's more than one way to indulge art as life's work.

These Happy 100 women survive as artists mainly because they are fulfilling core needs that their craft originally satisfied, and the compromises have thus become incidental. Tracy is creating original paintings even though her murals exist on commercial walls, not in galleries or museums. Sam still uses art to induce action, even though her canvases are computer screens. Leslie remains a voice for art, even though it's no longer her own. Lois is still writing about business, albeit through a marketing lens. Lori continues to perform, but on the stage of a company she owns and operates. Stockard relives, in performances, the indescribable wave of emotion that flowed over her in her first college production. Nancy is learning there is more than one way to put on a show, and former competitive swimmer Ana took a chance and discovered that the circus let loose her inner devil while utilizing her skills.

True, these women's needs changed over time, and they will change again. We have met them at a place where they can declare, to themselves and others, that, yes, they are truly happy with their working lives. Ana may eventually tire of the same synchronized swimming routine five nights a week, but that's okay. She'll find another niche as long as she constantly listens to herself and explores her options. Self-examination got many of these women where they are today, and it's critical that we never stop listening to our own feelings and thoughts as we react to our work.

Surviving Artists succeed because they exert control over their situations. To constantly move beyond your comfort zone, like Tracy; to reinvent your business model, like Nancy; to confront and learn from critics, like Lois; to reach out to people who are in a position to give you a chance, like Stockard; and to follow one's instincts into previously unconsidered territory, like Leslie and Lori, then, as an artist, it is hoped you may arrive at your happy place sooner—and recognize it when you get there.

Crafting a career is no less creative than crafting a painting, a sculpture, or a show. Happiness is, indeed, a work of art.

Chapter Six

The Faithful

Acupuncturist, public relations practitioner, foundation administrator, and bookstore owner

In the history of the human heart, one of the most traditional frameworks for thinking about happiness has been religion. But when it comes to thinking about labor, religion in its traditional sense has little to offer most people pondering the meaning of happiness. Yet faith, religion's close cousin, does.

I christen the women in this chapter the Faithful not because they are religious or spiritual in the more conventional sense, but because they found a framework in which their faith—or rather, their belief in a value system greater than themselves—grounds their happiness in what they do, even if what they do seems eccentric (acupuncture), mundane (public relations for a state highway), horrifying (reliving the Holocaust), or routine (selling books).

To have faith is to believe in somebody, something, or a set of principles, and it's from such devotion that the Faithful extract a large degree of happiness in their work. Our happy acupuncturist has faith in the system of Chinese medicine. The marketer has faith that her firm's Christian values foster effective, moral marketing campaigns and a supportive, almost spiritual workspace. The foundation administrator has faith that educating others about the atrocities of the Holocaust will help overcome worldwide suffering. And the entrepreneur has faith that honoring God will smooth her professional path.

As you read the following profiles, you'll notice that these Happy 100 women also have strong faith in themselves.

She believes in Qi.

The 5,000-year-old practice of acupuncture is based on a theory that an energy source known as Qi (pronounced *chee*) runs through the human body. Those who believe that health is a balance of the spiritual, mental, physical, and emotional aspects of life also believe that when the flow of Qi is interrupted, health declines. To redistribute that energy, acupuncturists insert needles at strategic points on the human body.

For Chicago acupuncturist Nicole Settle, creating harmony between body and mind is a philosophy she applies not only to her patients' well-being, but to her own as well. Nicole practices traditional Chinese medicine. "That differentiates me from Western medical doctors who practice acupuncture but don't subscribe to Chinese theories and diagnostic tools," says Nicole. For Nicole, happiness and health, the professional and personal, are closely intertwined. To practice Chinese medicine is to live it. "One reason I love my job is that it helped me find a spiritual connection and to understand my own beliefs," says the former premed student. "The more intertwined my work and life are, the more helpful I am to my patients." For three days a week, Nicole works at Pulling Down the Moon Center for Holistic Fertility, a dimly lit, loftlike space with lots of windows, candles, and comfy couches. She spends the other two days a week at a more clinical medical facility.

Nicole was first exposed to acupuncture in college at the suggestion of a family friend when doctor-prescribed antibiotics were not curing a urinary tract infection. The treatment not only improved Nicole's condition but radically recast her belief system, and thus her career track. "Acupuncture was such a positive experience for me that I had to seek out more of it," says Nicole. She quit her medical studies and refocused on childhood and family development studies; after college Nicole pursued a master's degree in Chinese medicine. In addition to three and a half years of graduate school, Nicole worked at the Zen Health Center in London, where she studied under a Chinese herbalist and acupuncturist. "The herbalist not only taught me about the medical part of Chinese medicine, but about Chinese culture and lifestyle and how it integrates into everyday life." As a certified yoga teacher, Nicole found most appealing in her studies the tenets of Buddhism: honesty, truth, and helping others. "I don't necessarily think in terms of Buddha or God, but a higher energy power that can be reached through meditation and yoga." This newly adopted belief system is quite different from the one Nicole grew up with.

I was raised as a Methodist in the Midwest, although we weren't brought up very religious. When I began to study traditional Chinese medicine it was difficult to leave behind everything I'd grown up with, and when I told friends and family that I was not going to be a doctor and instead study Chinese medicine, my parents tried to talk me out of it. But I told them to trust me because I really believed in it, and that nontraditional medicine was going to be a huge part of the medical world in a few years. It helped that my parents visited me when I was working in London. We went to dinner with the Chinese doctor I worked with, and my parents also saw how Europeans can just walk into a chemist's and get natural medicines, very different from here in the U.S. My mom was also treated for her diabetes with herbal medicine. It gave them a whole different view of alternative medical practices. Now when I go to family functions, they say, "Did you bring your needles?" [Laughs.]

I always treat the mind and the body together. People may disagree with me, but if you look hard enough you'll find they are connected. The Qi of one organ system can create an imbalance in our overall system and then other symptoms arise. Our society is so go-go-go and I think many people don't realize how much stress impacts their body. I tell patients that I help them connect the dots, make a connection between the mind and body so that, even if I am out of the picture, they can use it. Maybe I teach them how to use breathing to relax, or diet as a preventative technique to stave off disease. I spend a lot of time with patients and draw diagrams to explain how the Chinese believe the body works. My goal is to educate people on what alternative medicines can do, and then let them draw their own conclusions. Many say I change their life, and they become more open-minded. The other night at the center there was a prenatal class where I saw two women who, when they couldn't get pregnant, came to me for acupuncture and Chinese medicine. Seeing each woman almost six or seven months pregnant made me burst into tears!

Nicole, who at twenty-seven makes less than $50,000 a year at her job, says that just hearing she made a difference in someone else's life is worth any of the money she gave up to practice alternative medicine. While Nicole and her husband may not travel as much as they'd like— "and I may not have Jimmy Choo shoes"—no amount of money can replace the faith that she has in Chinese medicine, both personally and professionally. Adds Nicole, "It's not just a job, it's a way of life."

In her own words

Lori Rodney, 25
Senior Account Executive
Sonshine Communications
Miami, Florida

One of twenty-two people at this Christian-based public relations communications firm, Lori designs and executes marketing campaigns for a variety of clients. The company's name, Sonshine, refers to the Son of God, and its logo is a stylized olive branch and dove. The company's motto: "Strive to bless, edify, share, and touch every component of effective public relations every day."

Our president and CEO is a Christian who was helping members of her church with public relations activities when she started her company ten years ago. We had God on our side and we grew, and we are the largest black-owned public relations, advertising, and marketing firm in the southeastern region. Christian values permeate our work, and we incorporate Godly principles into everything we do. Religion is expressed through our values, and the values are part of the activities we do every day. It's about doing work with the honest-to-goodness goal of helping people and upholding high standards. Those values help us see a clear line between good and bad, and that line is not so fine when you're driven by doing the right thing: making a contribution to the world. It's not that religion is pushed or forced on people, or even something we speak of all the time. It's just something people here know.

Most of our clients are cause-related, like the American Legacy Foundation and the Florida Department of Health. We do not take on any clients just for the money—we would never do work with a pro-tobacco-related company, for example—and we look for clients with good hearts and good intentions. The office, which has a waterfall in the lobby, has such a sense of peace; I have to say I think it is God. I hope it is God. The spiritual environment affects how we sell our clients' messages. For example, for our antismoking campaign, we don't just communicate how smoking can kill you, but we also encourage people to help others quit.

I started here as an intern my senior year in college, and over the years my role has grown. Today, my job involves a combination of tasks. We assess clients to see what they need. For example, maybe an organization wants to increase awareness or change consumer behavior. Then we develop a strategic plan based on their goals. Maybe it includes adver-tising, PR, or sponsoring an event. I develop the plans and work with a team of graphic designers, media buyers, and writers to execute it. For two clients, the Miami-Dade Expressway Authority and the National Highway Traffic Safety Administration, we help make sure the public knows about changes in highway construction, new tolls, to buckle up, and avoid drinking and driving. I always get excited when planning a new ad campaign, when I can work with the creative team to do a new television or radio spot. Advertising is where my heart is, even though I also do a lot of public relations.

I love Mondays because that's when we have a team meeting, and everyone gets together to talk about what we're doing. Some business-people just do what they need to do to get by, and so many people just hate their jobs, but I love what we do and the people I work with. I rarely feel the same sense of peace when I visit other agencies. If and when I ever leave here, I'll definitely take the skills and the ethics that Sonshine taught me. I didn't just learn about PR here, I learned how to be an honest and ethical businessperson—which can be hard to find in this day and age.

She has faith in others.

Happy working women do not necessarily make or distribute feel-good, happy products. Kim Simon, thirty-three, has spent the past ten years thinking and talking about what is perhaps the most horrific tragedy of the twentieth century, if not human history: the Holocaust, the mass murder and extermination of 6 million Jews and an estimated 5 million others during World War II. Kim works for the Survivors of the Shoah Visual History Foundation, a not-for-profit organization founded by film director Steven Spielberg in 1994 after the director made the movie *Schindler's List* (1993). Since its inception, the Shoah Foundation has videotaped, cataloged, indexed, and is now distributing personal narratives from more than 52,000 Holocaust survivors and other eyewitnesses to the war, both Jews and non-Jews alike, from fifty-six countries and in thirty-two languages. In these testimonies, each Holocaust survivor recalls, often through tears, the details of his or her ordeal during the war. Each testimony has the power to convey history in a personal way that more academic approaches cannot.

As the Shoah Foundation's vice president for partnerships and international programs, Kim is further connected to her own Jewish heritage, a connection that sparked when Kim trekked to Prague in search of her roots back in 1992.

I'm a Jewish American, and I honestly don't know where my interest in the Holocaust comes from. No one in my immediate family was killed. Maybe it is an existential thing, maybe it is an identity thing, but it was never a religious thing. I think I am one of those people who struggled for a while with what it means to be Jewish. I had my own brand of that struggle: I was intensely interested in others'.

After college I bought a one-way ticket to Prague to research my roots and get involved in the city's Jewish community. My grandfather wrote about Prague and how he loved it, and although I never knew him, we had the same birthday. There was nothing specific I was searching for in

Prague, it was just a feeling. The concept of going to Prague was so comforting, almost instinctual. Back then I didn't know any of the language of the Holocaust, or how to talk about it, but I was interested in people who had lived in the Czech Republic after the war, people who not only survived the Holocaust but who lived under Communism for a period of time. I wondered what their lives were like and I immersed myself in the Jewish community. For money, I managed a nightclub, and, because I spoke both English and Czech, I was hired to help on the film set of a movie that was being made in Prague. That's how I got into film production.

After I had been in Prague for two years, my mother called to tell me Steven Spielberg was starting a project back in the States that seemed up my alley. It was after his movie Schindler's List *had come out, and he was filming Holocaust survivors as they told their stories. But getting a job like that sounded crazy to me! I didn't even know Steven Spielberg, and I couldn't even contemplate how I would get to work for an organization he founded. So I let it go.*

I came home to the U.S. in July 1994, and a friend happened to know someone who worked for the Shoah Foundation. His father put in a good word for me, and I got an interview. They weren't hiring at the time, but I said, "Listen, I can't afford to volunteer, but I have to work here." I just had such a feeling that this was the right place for me, and I was the perfect candidate because of my personal interest in Holocaust survivors and the fact that I had worked in film production. We kept in touch, and, about four months later, the foundation called and hired me.

Sometimes I think going to Prague was not about finding my roots but about finding my future, because the whole trip set my life in motion.

Kim's first job at the foundation was working behind the scenes, hiring professional interviewers to speak with survivors as they were video-taped. She traveled to communities throughout Europe in search of witnesses to testify to their painful war experiences. By 2004, with thousands of testimonies cataloged, the foundation's mission shifted from documentation to education and outreach, by sharing the filmed testimonies with students and others around the world in schools, museums, and government organizations. Ultimately, the Shoah Foundation's goal is not only about the Holocaust or the Jewish experience; it is more universal and definitely grandiose: to overcome the suffering caused by prejudice, intolerance, and bigotry. "When you have such an enormous mission, you have to take one step at a time," says Kim, whose specific job is to contact organizations in other countries and establish relationships so they can use the Shoah Foundation's visual material in culturally appropriate ways. Kim says her work is really about bridging cultures, building trust, finding common interests, and making things happen. "I am very process oriented, and my job here has always been very administrative, mostly program management, which sounds boring, but there is nothing boring about administration on behalf of something you love."

It is hard to imagine how anyone can immerse herself in stories of death and loss and not become depressed, let alone enjoy her job. When I asked Kim about that, she replied that the job was intense at first and the content so mind-blowing that for many years she simply could not speak about it, only listen. She even had nightmares. But Kim's constitution "had a lot of space" to house the intensity, one reason she's lasted for so many years. "You can't always be crying, or you won't get your work done." Kim has also desensitized herself to a degree and tries to be conscious of the need for boundaries between work and home life.

As for her own beliefs, Kim did not grow up very religious but today considers herself an observant Jew. She and her husband (who was raised as an observant Jew) maintain a kosher home and regularly attend temple. But her work, she says, is less about the Jewish faith than having faith in humanity. "I used to say, 'It's not like we're making paper clips here,' which was a mistake because someone who makes paper clips may feel just as strongly about her mission." That's true, but at least someone who makes paper clips has a tangible product as proof that her work paid off. It's much more difficult for someone like Kim to know for certain whether prejudice, hatred, and bigotry are being eradicated. So Kim takes solace from—and has faith in—the process and the Shoah Foundation's method: "There is something about watching a survivor's testimony that is so powerful, no matter who you are: black or white; Jewish or Christian; young or old. When a person reveals their life to another human being, empathy occurs and affects you on a very deep level.

We may not erase hatred from the world, but at least I have a tool and can chip away at Mt. Everest."

She is salt and light.

Annie Bauman's faith in God may be absolute, but it was not always so. Intense and ambitious, Annie describes herself as a lapsed Catholic who, throughout her twenties, focused on vague professional goals of "ruling the world." But a series of unfulfilling corporate jobs left Annie dispirited: The design services she sold during the 1990s Internet boom held no special meaning for her, and the financial waste she witnessed at one prestigious company left her disenchanted with corporate America. Thought Annie, *If this huge company can make such poor choices, I might as well make mistakes all by myself.* In search of a product she could sell herself, as well as "cherish and never question the validity of," Annie settled on books. Not necessarily a Lover of books, she did fall in love with a cozy community bookstore outside Boston, where she lived. About the same time she began plans to open her own bookstore, the eldest of Annie's three sisters, Kara, was diagnosed with late-stage breast cancer at age thirty-two. Kara was also five months pregnant.

Kara was ill the entire time I pursued the bookstore. It was so hard for my family, but it was also clear that we could not just stop living and sit around and look at her—we had to continue to live our own lives because there would be a time when Kara would no longer be with us, and we'd all need our own lives to go back to. So there I was, picking out vendors and hiring contractors and my sister was undergoing invasive testing and treatments. Despite her own health crisis, Kara was always an enthusiastic supporter of the bookstore. I remember thinking, If she can face cancer and premature death, I can certainly pull this off. *In a way, her illness provided me with a sense of perspective and fearlessness.*

That was not all Kara passed on to her sister. A Christian, Kara often quoted the Bible when she was with Annie, who found that talking about faith was a way to connect with her dying sister, even though Annie did not share Kara's particular beliefs. Slowly, though, Annie's perspective began to change. Says Annie, "Kara was able to read scripture in ways that were completely relevant." When Annie turned twenty-nine, Kara gave her a Bible and highlighted her favorite passages. And when Annie's bookstore opened in May 2002, Kara wrote a blessing for it: "Lord. We pray that in each step, decision, and trial that Annie would follow your word and claim your promises. You tell us to be salt and light, and we ask that Annie be that salt and light in this neighborhood and to all who know her that she would be a blessing." Touched by her sister's faith, Annie eventually joined a church and began living a life that, she says, "God intended for me." I asked Annie how her religious transformation affected her practical view of business and career.

It used to be all about establishing and proving myself, but now that I have established a relationship with God, the role of the bookstore in my life is not about me. I don't know that God wanted Annie Bauman to open Village Books. Annie Bauman wanted it for herself. But that does not mean that good can't come of the bookstore. Now that I answer to God as opposed to myself, I have a responsibility that is greater than ensuring, for example, every single best-seller is in stock. My spirituality has also brought a certain level of peace, and I am more confident with my business decisions.

But just because you are a Christian and believe God is in control does not mean you are a doormat. We still have free will, and there is a difference between having faith in God and making good business decisions. Before I opened the bookstore I wrote a thirty-page business plan and ran financial spreadsheets that were very conservative in their sales estimates. My husband and I took out equity from our home to get a loan but made sure we could still pay the bank on my husband's salary if the store flopped. I also did a lot of research: I worked in two other bookstores to learn the business, and I joined the American Booksellers Association, a group that educates and encourages independent store owners. When I hire people to work for me, I check at least four references.

I do not sit and talk about my faith with my employees, I do not run a Christian bookstore, and I sell books whose content does not coincide with my faith. Still, selling books is not like selling soap or clothes. I can't tell you how many customers are searching for something in their lives, and they buy books about Buddhism or the Dalai Lama or spirituality. People want meaning in their life, and it takes a lot for me not to say, "Have you heard about Jesus Christ?" I respect that. Christianity has definitely made me more appreciative of people.

I am no bibliophile. What gets me excited is connecting with others. There is nothing like having a customer come in and say she liked a book I recommended. Recently I hosted children's author and illustrator Jane Dyer, and the store was packed. When she read Time for Bed, *kids started reading along with her. It was like a rock concert for toddlers! I thought one of the parents might start waving a lighter. That was a great day.*

Despite the family's prayers for a miracle, Annie's sister Kara died in 2003. Village Books lives on and has sales that exceed Annie's original estimates. As for Annie, her love of work is directly tied to her love of God. "For today, running Village Books is God's will," says Annie. This Happy 100 member's happiness stems from doing God's work.

Faith alone does not yield happiness at work, and the women in this chapter are also appropriately skilled at their chosen professions. In other words, while purpose is a primary factor in the work satisfaction of the Faithful, process is also crucial. Karma and candles alone don't endow Nicole with medical expertise, and she calls upon her more formal medical knowledge all the time. Lori's prayers do not change consumer behavior, and she excels when it comes to applying secular marketing techniques. Kim's innate love of detail makes her an ideal person to handle the Shoah Foundation's more administrative, less emotional and content-driven tasks. And Annie knows that God alone will not sell books, so she educated herself in the book-selling business and continues to operate her store with discipline.

Just as happiness is not relegated to weekends and time away from the office, faith is not exclusive to church, houses of worship, or our personal lives. As these women show, both faith and happiness can be found on the job.

Chapter Seven

The Builders

**Brand developer, chief executive officer,
Hollywood producer, sneaker factory manager,
magazine publisher, business professor, screwdriver
manufacturer, airport-tram engineer, inventor, costume
designer, and construction site manager**

When toy manufacturer Mattel wanted to invent a new product, its researchers observed both boys and girls playing with toys such as blocks and Legos. Their conclusions, while not scientific, revealed what Mattel researcher Dr. Michael Shore believes are telling truths about gender differences.

Boys, says Shore, enjoy playing with pieces that stack or snap together because they can quickly create things they can enjoy. For example, using Legos a boy can easily construct a rudimentary car, a plane, a fort, even a gun. This is not the case for girls. Of course, girls *can* make cars or weapons, but they don't usually *want* to. According to Mattel's researchers, girls want to build relationships, not just toys, and thus they construct objects or environments that facilitate relationships. Rather than build a fort to withstand an attack, a girl is more likely to build a castle with many rooms where characters can interact. Girls also construct settings where stories can unfold, such as a garden, or useful items that they can share with friends and family, like jewelry or a picture frame. Explains Shore, "What's satisfying for a boy is not necessarily satisfying for a girl. The products that girls build are more about relationships between their imaginary characters, themselves, or their friends." Mattel concluded that because girls want to create fundamentally different things than boys want to create, girls build differently from boys.

In essence, females tend to build communities, environments, or objects that facilitate relationships.

When I first spoke to Dr. Shore about Mattel's research, I had already interviewed dozens of women and identified many as Builders, which I defined as women who love their work because they are building, developing, or creating something, such as a company, a magazine, a sneaker, a skyscraper, or a movie. When I went back and reread each Builder's interview, I noticed a common theme: Many of these women were actually creating communities or environments, the same pattern Dr. Shore observed in girls. For example, the magazine publisher is not just binding pages of articles and advertisements but creating a niche readership community. The Nike factory manager doesn't care much about sneakers, but she does care about helping her factory's employees work well together. Both retail executives in this chapter are driven to build inspiring corporate cultures, and the movie producer feels happiest when the film crews she amasses come together on a set for the first time.

Builders who don't necessarily develop communities tend to build objects that facilitate relationships or have a specific, useful purpose: The costume designer's clothing helps actors relate to their characters and in turn helps her relate to actors; the construction manager's buildings will house future companies; the engineer constructs airport trams that carry people from terminal to terminal.

Finally, as you read the following profiles, consider not just what each woman is actually building, but also how she built her career. Look for lessons in their past as well as their present.

She jump-starts imagination.

Over the years, Ivy Ross has worked for many well-known brands: Liz Claiborne, Calvin Klein, Avon, Coach, even Barbie. Her latest task is to enhance Old Navy's existing products and expand the stores' "fun, inclusive" image to a wider variety of clothing and other items, such as accessories and gifts. When I first met Ivy, she was in her sixth year at toy-maker Mattel, where she was responsible for a division that invented new toys for girls. Even though Ivy changed jobs in the course of our interviews, she remains a member of The Happy 100 because she is an example of a Builder whose love of work is not dependent on the company for which she works. Her forte, be it at Mattel or Old Navy, is building brands by nurturing creativity in the people who work for her. Says Ivy, "It's my job to jump-start the imagination of my creative staff." To that end, Ivy is fascinated with, and somewhat of an expert on, how to elicit innovative ideas from employees. In effect, she is a Builder of creative corporate environments.

Ivy, who looks more artist than executive with her wavy black hair and colorful silk attire, grew up the daughter of an accomplished car designer who taught her to look beyond the obvious for inspiration. While Ivy began her career making jewelry, she eventually gravitated to corporate life. "People bring me in as a turn-around artist," she says. Artist, perhaps, but Ivy tempers her creative tendencies with a practical, appropriate diplomacy that helps her flourish in strict corporate cultures. Still, if Ivy feels too stifled, her work will suffer.

I came close to quitting only a few months after I arrived at Mattel. When the company hired me, I was told creativity had gone away and that I might have to get rid of a few toy designers. That wasn't the problem. The problem was that there was no trust because some people in upper management were too controlling. When top management comes to every single design meeting and must approve every single thing, creative people stop putting their best foot forward because they assume their decisions will be reversed. Instead, they just wait until they're told what to do. I was not happy under the regime, and it was destroying me emotionally to see creative people so stifled.

After a new management team was in place, I was determined to create a new methodology that would help Mattel explore fresh ideas. You can't expect output from employees unless you give them input, sort of like a computer. Creativity is a way of seeing the world through your own filter and spitting it back to create something new. To see the world, to get input, you have to give people time to explore, to graze, to cleanse their palates. But companies rarely do that for their employees, they just keep asking for more output.

To stimulate creativity at Mattel, Ivy had to construct a more creative physical environment. She took over an empty warehouse on Mattel's corporate campus in El Segundo, California, and outfitted it with over-sized blocks, whiteboards, beanbags, toys, magazines, cool books, and a welcoming, bright red door. For three months at a time, a group of twelve Mattel employees would leave their regular jobs in marketing, de-sign, packaging, copywriting, or engineering and come together in the very unbusinesslike space. Their objective: Invent a new toy that would yield at least $50 million in revenue within three years. To help, Ivy in-undated them with an unorthodox mix of improvisational theater, story-telling, sociology, psychology, and chaos theory. She brought in speakers like architects who taught principles of shape; Jungian analysts who discussed pattern recognition; and living-systems experts who taught collaboration. The three-month experience, which Ivy called Project Platypus, was designed to spark collaborative creativity. And it did.

For Ivy, building the actual Platypus program allowed her to ponder the very process of collaborative innovation. She built a place where adults could indulge their imagination in the same manner that children can while playing with toys.

As toy designers, our goal was to jump-start a child's imagination. I remember playing with my Barbie as a girl and making up stories. But kids today want the stories written for them because they're lazy. If kids don't grow up exercising that part of their brain—if they're always handed story lines—then it will hurt them in the long run. Most of the people I work with still have a little bit of kid in them—and that's just what Project Platypus tried to retain, a community that brings out that kid.

Although Ivy left Mattel in early 2004, Platypus lives on and Ivy herself hopes it continues to grow. But in order for Ivy to continue growing pro-fessionally, she often has to leave one company for another. And with Old Navy, Ivy saw an opportunity to expand her brand-building skills.

"While it's my job to inspire others, I must also continue to be inspired. Someone needs to feed me! And that means I must constantly be learning." By working for a retailer—as opposed to a manufacturer like Mattel that sells to retailers—Ivy can be closer to customers while still leveraging her core skills. "I've always loved the psychology of understanding consumer behavior, but I still see myself playing a fairly similar role at Old Navy: inspiring teams."

Ivy is an example of a happy working woman whose satisfaction is product independent. As long as she is engaged in the process of building brands and boosting others' creativity, she too is engaged. Moving from one project to another, or one company to another, is actually inherent to the Builder mindset. Indeed, no one can build the same thing forever. Says Ivy, "Whenever I go from one job to another, I take me with me. And as long as the company allows me to do what I do best, it does not necessarily matter where I am."

Rebel with her cause

Even in jeans, chunky black boots, and a black zipper sweater, Hot Topic's chief executive officer, Betsy McLaughlin, is overdressed for work. Most of the employees at the company's California headquarters show up in any combination of T-shirts and baggy pants, off-the-shoulder tops and flip-flops, nose rings and tattoos, black nail polish and pink (or red or white or multicolored) hair. That's standard attire at this retailer, whose 600 mall-based stores sell music-inspired clothes and accessories aimed at teenagers with punk, rock, and gothic tastes. We're talking spiked rubber bracelets, bloodred eye shadow, and black T-shirts emblazoned with skulls or phrases like I'M IGNORING YOU.

Chief executive Betsy, however, isn't ignoring anyone. Rather, she's built a company culture that reflects Hot Topic's edgy customers and, at the same time, upholds professional operating standards. Her approach has helped the retailer more than double its sales, to $550 million, since she was named president and chief in 2000. While Betsy won't take credit for building Hot Topic, she will share credit for creating its unique culture, which, she says, entails hiring the right people and giving them a creative, fun, open environment in which to work. Like Old Navy's Ivy Ross, Betsy loves her work because she is able to build a culture that, in turn, builds a company.

In many ways, Hot Topic's schizophrenic environment—edgy yet practical—personifies Betsy, who has always been part rebel, part play-by-the-rules pleaser. As a young girl she listened to Led Zeppelin as well as Donny Osmond. She admired her father's sales and marketing job but rebelled against her parents' very strict control of the household. In high school, Betsy was popular "in an intellectual, not cheerleader" sort of way. And at forty-three, the woman who makes a living building a brand shuns brands for herself, going so far as to try and scrape the Dolce & Gabbana logo off her gunmetal-rimmed glasses. And although proud of Hot Topic's rank as one of *Forbes* magazine's 200 best small companies, Betsy cringes at the framed *Forbes* article featuring her picture, which hangs in Hot Topic's otherwise gothic-inspired lobby. Finally, the red-haired and freckled CEO is at once socially and financially savvy: She walks the office chatting easily with everyone from warehouse managers to merchandisers but at the end of each day sits at her desk to analyze customer comment cards from hundreds of stores.

Says Betsy, "The investment community and even our young customers have an image of a CEO that I don't fit. Everyone expects a male dressed in a suit, like Warren Buffett or Michael Eisner. I get letters from customers addressed 'Dear Sir' or 'Dear Mr. CEO' all the time," she says. Not only do Betsy's looks defy the stereotype, so does her management philosophy. "Many male CEOs have a different view of what motivates people," she says. "Their conventional wisdom is that it's money." In contrast, Betsy believes autonomy and appreciation drive performance. "We recently did an employee survey and I was thrilled with the results. People said they felt they could make their own decisions and that they felt recognized for what they uniquely contributed to the company," she says. "I think people perform better when the environment offers mutual respect, along with open, honest, and frequent feedback."

Over the years, Betsy has built Hot Topic's hip yet disciplined culture with a combination of tools. And a sample of her tactics follows. First, the office décor. It reflects customer and employee tastes: music videos play nonstop from multiple television screens; posters of bands decorate the walls; and the reception area has a towering replica of a gothic church facade, a red velvet couch, and lit candles replete with gothic sconces.

Orientation for new employees is all about culture, including having employees share their own customer service experiences as well as learn about the history of music. To make sure stores always stock the latest trends, Hot Topic employees are reimbursed for concert tickets if they author a "fashion report" highlighting new product ideas. And at company-wide meetings, Betsy asks employees to stand up and recognize a coworker's achievements. Each year, she personally hands all employees their bonus checks and thanks them for their unique contributions to the success of the business. Betsy also remains accessible by answering customer and employee e-mails herself. Says Betsy, "Any Hot Topic associate knows that they can pick up the phone and speak to any of us at headquarters, including me."

Not everyone fits into the culture she has created, and Betsy admits she has made some poor hiring decisions over the years. She must also counsel executives who come from more staid corporate environments to "change the way they are used to interacting" when they speak to others.

To reach this point in her career, Betsy has climbed the corporate ladder since college, when she made $2.65 an hour as a department store salesperson. After she graduated from college in 1982 with plans to go into business, Betsy was offered a job in the finance department of the department store where she worked for $22,000 a year.

They moved me around a lot, which was important because I eventually wanted to be in a senior position and knew I needed well-rounded experience. After two and a half years I was promoted to manager of planning and budgeting. I loved it because I could interact with all of the different parts of the company, helping the merchandising and operations executives plan and analyze their budgets. It was creative and social, as well as financial.

Then I received a call from a company called Millers Outpost, which recruited me as director of planning and analysis. The best part of that job was working with an organizational psychologist who observed me for a year and told me I was one of the few people with both deductive and creative thinking skills. He said that if I ever wanted to be a CEO I should look at other successful retail chiefs and figure out what experiences they had that I needed. I followed his advice and eventually realized I needed to get out of finance and work in other parts of the company. I moved into store operations for several years, then asked for a shot at merchandising. Most merchandise managers move up the buying ranks, so it was a very untraditional request. But the company agreed. Why? I guess because I asked. Also, I had a track record for good performance.

Here's what happened next at Millers: I was the director of merchandising for accessories, footwear, and seasonal sportswear when a new CEO came on board and told me that I would never make it as a retailer. I don't know why—maybe he did not like the way I looked—but despite the business results that my team had produced, he just declared that I had no talent. At first I thought maybe he was right, and I went through an emotional three or four months distraught, thinking my career was over. But I talked it over with friends, I saw a therapist, and I finally got over the emotion. Then the core part of me kicked in and said, "Fine, you asshole. Just watch me."

Betsy did not actually say *that* to the CEO, but her actions did: She quit Millers and accepted an offer from Hot Topic in 1993. At that time, the clothing chain had only fifteen stores and was run by its founder.

I came on board and worked seven days a week for the first couple of years. I traveled a lot. We were young, and I had a lot of autonomy and could finally put my beliefs into action: I always thought people did their best work when they loved their environment and felt respected, that they were making a contribution. It's a magic combination. I put together Hot Topic's first human resources policies and its training and recognition programs.

After starting as vice president of operations, Betsy moved on to general merchandising manager in 1995 and head of merchandising in 1997 and was named president in 2000.

Yes, Betsy is a rebel, but not the same ilk as Hot Topic's more outlandish teenage customers. Betsy is a rebel with a cause: to build a company culture that lets people thrive and grow while building profit. In doing so, Betsy challenges widely held management beliefs that money is the only motivator that matters. But if Hot Topic's rising sales amid other retailers' losses are any proof, then giving employees autonomy and positive feedback has a lot to do with growing a company—and a happy career.

Her favorite scenes

Hollywood movie producer Jennifer Todd, thirty-three, spent the evening of one of her biggest movie premieres in, of all places, a diner eating soup. Even though the New York City screening of her movie *Boiler Room* was replete with red carpet, media flashbulbs, and stars like Ben Affleck and Giovanni Ribisi, all Jennifer recalls was that she and her co-producer (and sister) slipped out of the theater and retreated to a nearby delicatessen. Says Jennifer, "My sister said, 'Look how glamorous we are: It's the night of our big premiere and we're eating soup in a deli.' " For Jennifer, the crews at work behind the scenes are much more interesting than celebrities in the spotlight.

I don't really get starstruck. And while I know a lot of famous people, it's usually in the context of a work relationship. I can't and don't want to try and be a celebrity's new best friend; and I would never cross a room to talk to someone famous who I didn't know, unless I was working with them. I've never had a need to go up to someone and tell her I was a fan. Personally, I don't understand the appeal of fame. I think most people like the idea before they experience it. You give up so much of your life. As nice as it might be to always get a good seat at a restaurant, you're also in line at a Starbucks and someone comments on your bad sweatpants. [Laughs.]

Jennifer's instinct for life behind the scenes goes back to childhood growing up in Los Angeles, when a friend's parents hired Jennifer to be an extra in a television movie. "Once I was on the set I remember seeing some big creative discussion going on behind the camera," recalls Jennifer. "I didn't even know who the people were or what they were talking about, but I thought whatever they were saying seemed much more interesting than what was going on in front of the camera."

Jennifer followed her sister to film school, only to drop out her sophomore year for a job assisting a producer who made action films such as *Lethal Weapon* 2 (1989) and *Hudson Hawk* (1991). For three years the two Todds worked with the producer, after which Jennifer went to Miramax, then worked for Bruce Willis at Columbia Pictures, and later joined Demi Moore's production company. Not long after that, comic actor Mike Myers gave Jennifer and her sister the script for his movie *Austin Powers,* and the two Todds "shopped" it to studios, eventually selling it to New Line Cinema. In 1997, the pair formed their own production company, Team Todd. In what's known as a housekeeping agreement, Revolution Studios gets the first peek at movies Jennifer and her sister want to produce.

Most important, the sisters have each other, and the Todds are one of the few, if not the only, sister-producer teams in Hollywood. "I'm so lucky to have a partner I both love and trust, and who is always on my side," says Jennifer, who knows that's no small feat, especially in Hollywood.

There is a lot of ugly behavior in the movie business, and you get told "no" a lot, so you have to be okay with the fact that nothing is guaranteed. I've really come to appreciate the miracle of just getting a movie made. An actress can change her mind. A studio can fail to come through with the money. It will rain when you planned to shoot a scene in the sun . . . a million things can go wrong on any given day. Right now we're producing a movie that fell apart last year and we thought it was dead, but then Sandra Bullock read the script and really liked it, and so did Meryl Streep. The two decided to do the movie together, and soon we start filming in New York. I'll live in Manhattan for four months—two months for preproduction work and two months of filming—then return to L.A. for editing and postproduction.

Producing is a hard job to define. Ultimately, a producer simultaneously tries to protect an artist's vision and protect the studio's financial investment. Some of it requires having good taste in material and knowing which stories are both well written and commercial. But a lot of the job is about relationships. Not personal relationships in the sense that you only help out friends, but in the ability to read people and understand what they want. The job requires good communications skills, problem solving, and peacekeeping. In that way I think producing is very female.

Essentially, a producer is the one person who oversees a picture's economic and creative machinery; at the end of the day I'm a project manager, overseeing everything beyond the germ of the idea. If we get a script we like, we have to find and convince a studio to pay to develop it. Sometimes we read a script and just know how to make it better. Sometimes we don't and have to go out and find writers. Once a project gets the green light, it's our job to hire the crew and oversee day-to-day production. Those are my favorite days, even when I have to get out of bed at the crack of dawn . . . it's just so exciting to see your movie happening! I get this sense that these people are all here working because we got it done!

On the set I'm like the firefighter: Every problem comes to me. Actors are also very temperamental and there's a lot of ego involved, so a big part of a producer's job is reading the social and political climate. So much throughout the moviemaking process is out of my control. When actress Kate Hudson got pregnant and pulled out of her movie, all I could think of was, "Oh, the poor producers!"

I need to see every movie that's out, to know all the current talent, know good creative people, who is a good cinematographer, and read all of the incoming scripts quickly while still working on our own ideas. I could do my job twenty-four hours a day, seven days a week, and still be behind. But I think I love it because I am just crazy devoted to it. People become producers for so many reasons, maybe it's money or power or prestige. I'm in it because I love movies and the act of making them, therefore I feel my heart is in the right place. This may sound corny, but I often think, Am I making a movie that I will be proud to see my name on when I switch on the TV at three A.M. one morning? Am I making a movie that my friends would like? *When I read the script for* Boiler Room, *I thought my friends would enjoy the morality tale. When I read Austin Powers, it made me laugh, and I could envision six-year-old kids quoting lines from it. The entire time I was making the movie* Memento *I had no idea it would break out like it did. I just knew my friends would like it.*

Still, you have to love the process, so I just come in every day and try to push my rock up the mountain.

Jennifer proves you can love work despite daily obstacles and frustrations. The key is to enjoy the nature of the problems and believe they're worth solving. And, as she decided as a young girl, life on camera may be more glamorous, but it's not nearly as absorbing as the community that exists offscreen—and building that behind-the-scenes community is where Jennifer's true happiness lies.

In her own words

Marjorie Koch, 46
Industrial Engineer, Nike
St. Louis, Missouri

Marjorie oversees the efficiency of 250 people in a 220,000-square-foot "plastic extrusion" plant that manufactures material for tiny airbags used in the soles of some Nike sneakers. Marjorie's job is to analyze and improve factory processes and continually improve output. Think of Marjorie as a coach of sorts, trying to build an efficient team of factory workers.

Industrial engineers essentially observe people working, and I just have a knack for figuring out better ways to do things. I once reduced a forty-hour work week to twenty hours. We break job elements into codes and assign them time values and create standard data for every movement so that, eventually, we can calculate the work time without even watching the workers. I am always seeking out new ways to improve business processes, and the best way to do that is to understand how each process works, know who performs it, why the process exists, and what it accomplishes. All of these questions require me to be curious and ask questions for the same reason that a young child asks questions: so she can learn.

I also love that I have an opportunity to work with people. Even if a machine is involved in a production process, there's always a human element, whether plant or office personnel. Industrial engineers like me must apply their judgment and decide, "Is this person working 100 percent efficiently? If not, how much above or below is she working?" It's fascinating to watch how an organization behaves and to see the effect that process improvement has in people's lives, on the factory community. When you work with such a variety of people, from sales to shipping, it's always interesting to watch as they get a sense of the big picture and realize how what they do affects others' work. Because factory work can be so physical, I love it when I can show people easier, less stressful ways to move around on the factory floor, or can eliminate unnecessary actions. A lot of the time I get what I call the "wow factor," when people say, "No wonder I felt so tired at the end of the day!"

I think most people don't always feel like they have the ability or the authority to question the way things are done, and as a result too many bad behaviors are kept in place. Workers continue to do things only because that's the way they've always done them, but really they just haven't had the opportunity to look for a better process. I bring that piece of the puzzle into it, and I know I've done a good job when my workers look happy; when things aren't going well, they definitely don't.

Her community

A tall, imposing presence, Michela O'Connor Abrams, forty-five, has left a slew of high-powered magazine sales jobs in her wake. In Michela's current role, she's the president and publisher of *Dwell*, an upscale, niche magazine that helps modern architects, designers, and homeowners construct some seriously hip living spaces. While its readers are industrious upscale decorators, Michela is not one of them and not a typical *Dwell* reader. "You don't have to be the reader to build a magazine," she says from her small, exposed-brick office that overlooks a thin slice of the San Francisco Bay Bridge. "You just have to understand and be a champion of the reader." In other words, you don't have to *be* what you *build*. Michela is a saleswoman first and, at *Dwell*, a design aficionado by necessity. Her career history demonstrates that building is often less about content—or the actual *thing* one creates—than about the act of construction.

I've always been drawn to sales and marketing. My mother would tell you that I wanted to convince people of things very early, whether I was selling Girl Scout cookies or my grandparents' canned goods. When I was seven my grandma gave me a fake cardboard storefront and I took it very seriously; I put it in the driveway, took food out of the cupboard, and sold avocados for fifty cents—a pretty high markup. [Laughs.] I had quite the

*little business until my grandparents realized I was selling their groceries.
In college I was drawn to content—English classes, debate, newspaper—
and I majored in journalism until I found out what journalists make!
Forget it! I decided to use my writing skills in sales and marketing.*

Anecdotes from Michela's early ascent in publishing hold lessons for
women trying to build a career in any industry. Mainly, ask for what you
want—and take advantage of unexpected circumstances.

One day, back when Michela was working as a mere intern, she found
herself listening to magazine salespeople trying to convince colleagues
to buy ad space. Something clicked in Michela's mind, and she realized
she would rather *sell* than *buy* ad space. After the sales presentation,
Michela waltzed up to the most articulate of the bunch, a saleswoman
for *TV Guide,* and boldly asked to be her assistant. A few days later,
Michela had the job. She did well and within a few years landed another job working as an assistant to the Los Angeles sales manager for
another publication. While most young women in her position wore
jeans to the office, Michela was convinced she would not be taken seriously if she dressed casually, and one day, while clad in her suit, she
found herself in the elevator with the president of the publishing company.

"What do you do here?" he asked Michela as the elevator climbed.
She told him she was a sales assistant. "Is that what you want to do?" he
asked again. "No," she told him, "I want to build my ability to sell." A
week later, the president had Michela promoted to the sales staff of a
new in-flight airline magazine, where she worked for three years. It was
a promotion, yes, but Michela did not receive special treatment. "I
was young and given accounts no one else wanted: fur and restaurants.
Here it was, seventy degrees in L.A., and I had to sell ad space to furri-
ers!" The young Michela was not discouraged. "My goal was to communicate whatever I was selling better than anyone on the planet. I wanted
my clients to love me, and my colleagues to respect me."

Michela's sales reputation grew, and recruiters came calling. One offered her a sales job at *PCjr.* magazine, which Michela accepted despite
having no technological background. But she learned the business
quickly and spent the next ten years selling ad space at technology pub-

lications, eventually becoming the publisher of *LAN Times* and *UNIX World* and later the chief executive of *Computerworld*. Michela held her most high-profile job in the late 1990s as publisher of *Business 2.0*, a consumer magazine hatched during the Internet boom. *Business 2.0* focused on helping entrepreneurs build companies, and Michela reflects on the art of building a magazine in good times and in bad.

It was both easier and harder to build Business 2.0 *during the Internet boom compared to building* Dwell *now, during an economic downturn. At* Business 2.0 *sales came so easy, and we were profitable after eighteen months, when most magazines take at least five years. It was too easy. We knew the bubble was going to burst, we just didn't know when. So even when money flew in the door, I was nervous. I told our sales staff that, yes, it was a phenomenal time; yes, our business is growing at 100 pages an issue, but please know that unless you are doing your job the same way you would do it in a different economy, we'll eventually be out of business. The staff looked at me like I was out of my mind: "We're at the richest time in history and she is talking about building relationships with clients? Who needs relationships during a feeding frenzy, right?" Wrong! I just knew that if our salespeople were not embedded with our clients, we would be in trouble. Sure as hell, when the economy started to sink, our biggest problem was that we had green salespeople and lousy relationships with advertisers. These days it's harder to build a magazine because you scrape for every penny to make sure you're profitable. There's more pride in what we accomplish today because we really earn every ounce. It was harder to say that at* Business 2.0.

I build things that focus on community, and I'm fascinated by content that speaks to different groups of people, like computer users or interior designers, not the mass market. Content has such power when targeted at the right group. Dwell's *150,000 readers are about forty-three years old, with household incomes above $122,000, and are a cross between professional designers and architects and regular homeowners. Yet they don't want just decorating ideas, so our editorial is more rigorous than that. We must speak informatively to both the consumer and the professional, in language that is intelligent enough to appeal to an expert but not in lingo that excludes a hobbyist.*

For me, the most exciting part of building a magazine is identifying
that psychographic, a community with a very specific mindset, and then
building a brand across different media.

In addition to *Dwell* magazine, there is a *Dwell* Web site and a *Dwell* television show. With such different channels to develop, Michela is essentially building a brand and a company, much like the Oprah or ESPN franchises. That means the *Dwell* community can only grow—which should keep this Builder quite happy.

She's an improvement junkie.

The late 1990s was a surreal time in which to build a company. Success was not about how much revenue or earnings a company made, but how much money investors anted up and how the market valued its stock. Companies racked up enormous valuations based on little more than business plans and forecasts, in lieu of real, tangible growth.

Among the many people who prospered financially but were left morally broke by the Internet boom was Fiona Wilson. Ambitious and articulate, Fiona, thirty-seven, has since gone from a builder of businesses to a builder of the business community. Her current role, as you'll see, is one she never imagined having during the tech heyday, but which successfully balances her dual nature: Fiona has an ambitious streak tempered by an overwhelming need to "feel good about" her work. In other words, for Fiona, it took a while for purpose to catch up with process.

Born in England, Fiona left behind her country as well as an unfulfilling advertising career—"Did I really feel great about selling Guinness beer and Ford trucks? No."—and moved to Barcelona while her husband attended business school. The couple eventually relocated to Boston, where Fiona enrolled at Simmons School of Management in Cambridge, Massachusetts, for a master's in business administration. In 1998, Fiona graduated and joined the tech fray until the economy—and her health—forced her to slow down.

I worked for CMGI, a big company that owned or invested in about
seventy-five small Internet companies. As vice president of marketing I

was responsible for building our brand and building really strong relationships between CMGI and each of the companies it owned. The first two and a half years were truly magical, exhilarating, and exhausting. My team and I were the marketing glue for all the companies in which CMGI owned a majority stake; I felt like I was making a real contribution. I was promoted in nine months. We really exploded during that time, and while I did make some money, it was not why I was there. I truly believed that the Internet was the next big platform, and when I believe in something, I throw myself into it.

This might sound crazy, but we worked so hard that some days we didn't even have time to go pee, let alone make an appointment to go see a doctor and have a checkup. I kind of knew something was wrong with me, but I just didn't prioritize a doctor's visit. When I finally did go, the doctor found some massive ovarian cysts. They were benign, but I had to have them removed. It was very scary.

Recuperating gave me a rare opportunity to really think about my work. It was amazing what four weeks in bed allowed me to dwell on, and I realized that the market was changing and CMGI's people did not have the focus to shift with it. They had lost their passion. When one of my employees visited me at home, she looked really tired, and I asked her how work was going. "Awful. Things have just deteriorated since you've been gone," she said. I asked her why she was still there. "The team is there because of you. It would be disloyal of us to leave." I had built a high-performing, talented marketing team who were staying because of me? I could not ask them to work at a company that I didn't even believe in anymore. Only if I left would I be giving them permission to leave. A few days after I was supposed to go back to work, I quit but agreed to do some consulting for another start-up. But four months later, another cyst ruptured, and when it did I thought I was dying. It came so quickly, like indigestion, and within two hours I couldn't even walk. Once I was back in the hospital, I said, "That's it. This time I'm really taking six months off." I was thirty-four.

Fiona and her husband took advantage of their savings and spent six months living in a cottage in Maine. They kayaked, sailed, took long walks, and refused all calls from headhunters. Wisely, Fiona wanted to assess her desires and skills rather than haphazardly jump to a similar job. Building a company no longer interested Fiona. Her values had changed. Yet she was still a Builder.

"So many people hang on to the past because it's safe or easy. But what we chose to do at twenty-one or twenty-two is not necessarily the thing we are cut out to do for the rest of our lives. I was lucky that I had the confidence to say, 'Hey, I've changed. The things I valued ten years ago aren't what I value now.'" While the nonprofit world had always seemed like a "meaningful" pursuit to Fiona, she still believed in corporate marketing. The tug of war between building a professionally fulfilling career and creating a more physically and ethically sustainable lifestyle continued until her mother-in-law and a friend both independently asked if Fiona had considered teaching as a career.

The seed had been planted.

Fiona had been a guest lecturer before and thoroughly enjoyed it. The more she thought about academia, the more it intrigued her, so rather than just think about it, she went out and talked to people who knew. She even called the dean of Simmons, where she had earned an MBA, for insight and advice. "You'd make a great teacher," the dean told her immediately. "Business schools need people with real-world experience, and we would be happy to support you . . . and by the way, can you teach a class for us next month?" Coincidentally, Simmons needed a teacher for an already scheduled class, and within weeks Fiona had a full-time faculty position. Because Fiona had listened closely to advice from friends who knew her, she recognized teaching was a natural fit. So when an opportunity to teach arose, she took advantage of it.

I loved building companies, brands, and people, and the latter— building people—is what I do now by teaching marketing to MBA students. I work with smart, focused, ambitious women as they develop new skills and start the next phase of their careers. I love helping them realize their dreams. I've come to believe that I am an improvement junkie, not a classic entrepreneur. I don't have great ideas for new businesses, but I love taking things and making them better. Plus, I have to build something that lasts.

I see teaching as my future, so I'm pursuing a doctorate in business. I've become fascinated with how business schools train future leaders, and I like being part of that process. I care deeply about the school's mission to prepare women for powerful leadership positions. We're the only MBA program in the world designed specifically for women. Fifty percent of middle managers today are women, yet more than 90 percent of the highest-ranking positions are still held by men. We need women's skills and talents shaping business today more than ever, and I love helping the school build its reputation. What I do every day interests me so deeply and has lasting value, I feel like I am creating something for the future.

Fiona eventually accepted a job whose day-to-day activities—mainly teaching and research—she excels at and which fulfill her desire to build a sustainable product: future communities of businesswomen. Because teaching marketing instead of practicing it holds more meaning for Fiona, the psychic paycheck helps make up for the six-figure income she left behind.

She is not a woman in a man's world.

Women not only love building communities and environments, they also find satisfaction creating tangible objects—things that can be held, touched, and ultimately used for a purpose—even if that purpose is nothing to write home about. Lauralee (Lee) Cromarty has spent her career helping to manufacture and distribute some terrifically boring items: filing cabinets, office cubicles, pantyhose, and, most recently, screwdrivers. Yet Lee—who describes her job at Pratt-Read Corp., in Bridgeport, Connecticut, as "dynamic"—proves that one does not have to make toys, movies, or magazines to have a ball.

Raised by entrepreneurial parents—her father's company erected neon signs and her mother baked wedding cakes—Lee attended Georgia Tech and majored in industrial management. Unlike her parents, Lee would never build her own company, but she did find a niche as a worker bee by participating in all aspects of manufacturing operations. Over the span of six jobs, Lee became adept at industrial engineering, labor relations, construction oversight, finance, factory design, process efficiency, and safety on factory floors. While working at consumer product company Hanes, she traveled around the country studying how long it took workers to restock L'eggs pantyhose racks in stores. At grocery chain Finast, she conducted "time studies," tracking, for example, how long it took to butcher a piece of meat and documenting how store managers spent their day. For a company that manufactured explosives used to clear mines and blow up buildings, Lee spent eight years helping manage its chemical manufacturing processes: She designed a new factory, studying worker processes to come up with more efficient, safer procedures.

While traveling on a plane in 1997, Lee sat next to the vice president of a wholesale office furniture outfit, and the two spent the entire trip talking about the latest "lean" manufacturing trends. "He was very excited," says Lee, who didn't even recall giving the gentleman from HON Company her business card. A few days later she received a call from HON's human resources department, and within weeks she moved to Iowa to become general manager of HON's distribution, coordinating orders for thousands of filing cabinets, desks, chairs, and office-cubicle walls to wholesalers' and retailers' warehouses.

"By now I had grossly departed from Dad's entrepreneurial spirit," recalls Lee. "I was not a person who dreamt things up; my expertise was making things happen. I am a doer who likes to take roadblocks out of the way for other people and then watch them succeed." By 1998, Lee's mother had died and her father was ill, and to be closer to him she returned to Connecticut, where, via a referral from her company's former president, she landed a job at a small, $30 million company named Pratt-Read. The former piano manufacturer had transitioned to screwdrivers and needed an expert to help grow manufacturing and fulfillment. Today, Lee is vice president of the company's Bridgeport-based blade and assembly operations and spends her days improving how some twenty workers make, package, and deliver screwdrivers to keep up with an influx of orders from new customers, such as Sears. Says Lee, "Making screwdrivers is a very simple process," but screw it up and the small, growing company will be out of business.

It's not as if Lee is fascinated by screwdrivers. As in her former jobs, her work happiness is product-neutral. Pratt-Read could just as easily be making party favors—or explosives or cabinets or pantyhose. Just like Michela O'Connor Abrams and Ivy Ross, building for Lee is not merely about the product. "Bottom line, it's the people I enjoy most," says Lee.

And in her line of manufacturing, the people are usually men.

Currently, Lee is the only woman among five management-level employees, a situation that neither intimidates nor impresses her. Having grown up female in a predominantly male industry, Lee holds her own by not thinking of herself as a woman among men, but a worker among colleagues. "A lot of women assume there will be problems just because they're female, but I never had that in my head. Because I look at it that way, I think it helped me succeed." Once, when asked to create an award for women industrial engineers, Lee refused. "I would not want to win an award because I was a woman who happens to be an industrial engineer. I'd want to win an award because I am a damn good industrial engineer."

While Lee does not cry foul at the mere hint of flirting, her work life has not been without incident. Back in the pre-discrimination-law 1980s, a supervisor routinely brought up inappropriate topics at the cafeteria lunch table. "He'd talk about the porn movie *Deep Throat* or ask the guys, 'Hey, did you get any last night?' and then look at me for my reaction," says Lee. On the advice of her father, Lee kept a journal of the man's comments and maintained a photocopy of the journal in a file marked CONFIDENTIAL. "I didn't know exactly what I was going to do with the notes," says Lee, but one day the offending supervisor actually rifled through Lee's desk and found the file. Knowing Lee had a copy of her journal, the man curtailed his sex-laced conversation, and Lee never complained to senior management. Not long after, the man was accused of other harassing behavior and, unapologetic, was let go. That incident aside, gender has been a nonissue for Lee. "It's not about forgetting you're a woman in business; just don't throw it out there. My message to other women is not to worry that you're a woman in the working world, but whether or not you're a good working person."

In her own words

Laura Espinoza
Project Engineer, Airport Automated People Mover
Lea+Elliott, Inc., Consulting Engineers
Houston, Texas

Since 1997, Laura has been a consulting engineer for a company that specializes in automated people movers—the electronic trains that transport people and their luggage around airports. For the past several years, Laura has been supervising the construction of a fifty-foot-high outdoor tram system at George Bush Intercontinental Airport in Houston. Laura and her colleagues designed the physical and technical structure, and now she oversees contractors executing their plans.

When I was maybe six I built a two-story dollhouse out of cardboard for my Barbies. Each floor had three rooms with furniture, and I played with it all the time. I don't remember how the house got destroyed, but I'm sure my brothers had something to do with it. [Laughs.]

When I was twelve my parents moved our family from Durango, Mexico, to Houston. My mother is an accountant, and my father is a mechanic, and I always thought I would be a social worker. But when I told that to my high school guidance counselor, she looked at my math and science grades and said I should consider engineering because I could make more money. I started as a chemical engineer but switched to industrial engineering because it's not as technical; there's more project management involved and more interaction with people, which I like.

This was my first job out of college. Building an Automated People Mover [APM] requires a very specific body of knowledge, and when this job is done I will probably move to another city to work on another people mover. The APM at this airport is very much like the ones at Orlando's airport, or on the Las Vegas strip. When it's complete it will have ten trains and about two miles of track shaped in a pinched loop. We have a schedule and know where we want to be week by week, and I always look forward to our status meetings. Most of the time we come up with more work to do, but it makes me happy when things get completed, and of course it's always nice hearing from my boss that we're doing a good job. I really enjoy the people I work with; they're very supportive, and I learn new things from them daily. Sometimes being younger than everyone else is harder than being one of the only women in the room, which I'm used to, because engineering school was about 90 percent men.

Unexpected things come up every day. Just when I've solved a major issue, another one pops up. We're building a new maintenance facility for the trains, and the other day we got a call telling us the fans in the building were too loud, so now we have to find a way to make the fans quieter so the workers can hear their two-way radios while they work. These are the types of things that come up, and there's no time to get bored. In school, everything is theoretical, and if there's a problem, there's always an answer. In real life there are thousands of ways to find the answer, and sometimes you just have to say, "This is good enough, it's what we have the budget for and it's what the client wants."

I mostly focus on the big picture, and I think about when the system will be complete. The day-to-day problems are just something we do to get to the end of a project, and I look forward to coming to the office every morning to see how many issues can be put to rest that day. I get a great sense of accomplishment when things are resolved. These days we are starting to test the trains for everything that could possibly go wrong. We even put our hands and sticks in the trains' doors as they close to make sure they won't close on passengers. We check the traffic signals and make sure signage is easy to understand, we test the new software, and we time and adjust how fast the trains travel, down to the second. Soon we'll have to work odd hours and test the trains at night, when the airport is less crowded.

After we completed the tram, the first phase of the project, that runs between terminals B and C, I rode the train with the public, a really great experience. Most people take the train for granted; they just want to get on it and get where they are going. But I have all the knowledge that it took to build it.

She mines consumers' minds.

Remember when you were young, and there was always one girl who wrote skits, choreographed dances, and personalized popular songs?

She'd take the theme from *Laverne & Shirley* or Don McLean's "American Pie" and substitute lyrics for a friend's birthday, the last night of camp, or sorority rush. Betty Jagoda Murphy was that girl, and at age fifty-five is still developing fresh concepts out of material that already exists. But Betty is not in the entertainment business, and her creations may not be glamorous, but they are, more important, useful. Instead of lyrics, Betty invents new laundry products. In lieu of shows, Betty comes up with newfangled hairstyling devices. And rather than choreograph dances, she creates skin care treatments. This domestic diva has made millions of dollars from at least one of her household inventions. What's more, she's had thirty years of career satisfaction.

As the president and cofounder of ReGenesis LLC, in Montclair, New Jersey, Betty and her business partner, Jim Smith, invent "consumer and drug delivery products." The pair met in the 1970s when they worked for companies that invented products such as Mop & Glo and Wet Ones. Betty did consumer research, and Jim was a chemist who also managed new product programs. Together they worked on the likes of Carpet Fresh and AirWick. "To say we had chemistry was to put it lightly," says Betty, referring to her and Jim's professional relationship. Both were married and still are, but they shared an entrepreneurial spirit that refused to be fenced in by corporate bureaucracy. So in 1979 they started a company called Creative Products Resource to develop and license their own product ideas as well as consult with companies who were developing their own.

Jim and I kept coming up with product ideas that did not fit our employers' agenda. We both kept pencils by our respective beds, and we would constantly call each other at three o'clock in the morning with new ideas. Together we were like a fountain! He's a very creative chemist and would say, "You know, I've got this polymer I'm using in a floor wax, but I think it would be great for something in the hair." And sure enough we'd run with it. You can't do that in a big company, where the floor wax chemist works only on floor wax.

Like many inventions, many of Betty's and Jim's ideas stem from the needs of mundane daily life. Example: Betty religiously applies various gels and conditioners to straighten her curly hair, and once, when she and Jim were traveling for business, Betty came down to breakfast with a piece of toilet paper impaled over the bristles of her brush and told Jim she wanted to be able to apply hair product to her head via the brush. Sure enough, Jim developed a thin, hydrophilic foam polymer sheet that holds conditioners, shampoos, and proteins and fits onto any plastic brush to style, rejuvenate, and color hair. ReGenesis patented the product and is currently negotiating licensing deals. Jim's and Betty's most successful and lucrative product to date has been Custom Cleaner, a home dry-cleaning kit that lets consumers get the benefits of dry cleaning without the cost—or the trip to the dry cleaners. Betty and Jim spent three years developing the product and recently sold it to a large consumer products joint venture.

The story behind Custom Cleaner's evolution illustrates how the inventing process unfolds. Betty's main job is to come up with and refine ideas by interviewing consumers about their lives. Such interviews are the building blocks of invention, and Betty listens carefully to how consumers talk about household chores and personal hygiene. In essence, she is mining consumers' minds for ideas to improve upon existing products. As she travels to different cities interviewing people, she has faith that new product ideas are buried in people's frustrations and desires. To tap them, Betty just has to interview one person at a time.

Every person I interview is a jewel rich with information. When I show them a new product description or demonstration, I want to know what each person thinks, what is bad, and what is good, what they remember about the concept. Sometimes people don't even know what they want, they just know something is missing. Once you weave research results together, it is like reading a novel!

While being interviewed for a disposable fabric softener Betty and Jim were developing, one woman said to Betty, "Couldn't you make a sheet to dry-clean clothes? I am so sick of taking clothes to the dry cleaner when they are not really dirty." Betty excused herself from the interview and went behind the one-way mirror into a room where Jim was watching and she said to him, "Forget fabric softener. We're going to invent a dry-cleaning sheet." Within two weeks Betty wrote a new-product concept, and Jim and his staff of chemists, with Betty by their side, spent three years testing hundreds of chemical formulations. Eventually they patented and manufactured Custom Cleaner. They sold it on the QVC home shopping channel, where 2,400 boxes sold for $24 each in only six minutes! Eventually, they raised $11 million to fund manufacturing, distribution, and marketing, and the kits were sold through supermarkets, drugstores, and mass merchandisers. When a large consumer products company offered to buy the product for millions of dollars, Betty and Jim sold it and returned to the business of inventing. ReGenesis currently has forty-five patents and is negotiating licensing deals for several new skin care products, including pads that automatically release acne or psoriasis medicine when applied to wet skin.

Betty insists that she and Jim invent for the thrill of coming up with something new that makes practical sense—not the potential windfall. If they do their job right, dollars follow. Sure, there were months in the beginning when Betty did not collect a salary, and her husband's income helped fill the gap. But these days, revenues from licensing royalties— up to 5 percent of sales—flow in regularly. "We think we're doing pretty well," says Betty.

Inventing is a form of building that requires vision and patience. The people who enjoy Betty's inventions probably have no clue that behind each product is a woman who is very happy to make their daily lives a little easier—and make a living in the process.

She builds character.

Not all creations are built to last, and Andrea Varga's masterpieces usually disappear in a matter of months. A freelance costume designer, Andrea practices a craft that is an exercise in minute detail and requires a broad understanding of art and history, as well as the patience of a saint. Andrea, thirty, was born with the latter but acquired the former by getting a B.S. in history, a B.F.A. in theater, and a master's in costume design. She earns her $25,000 salary working as an assistant for a more experienced designer, buying his fabric, researching costumes, and bookkeeping. Lately, Andrea's been landing her own freelance gigs, which is a good thing because one day she hopes to be on her own. While she lives in New York City (population 8 million), her current assignment has her temporarily stationed in Logan, Utah (population 45,000), designing costumes for a local opera's summer production of *Fiddler on the Roof*.

For every show, Andrea's challenge is to separate her ego from the outfits she designs and visually portray each character in a manner the play's director, playwright, and actors envision, even if she disagrees. Herewith, Andrea's thoughts about how to build character, both personally and professionally.

First I read a show's script and then spend a lot of time thinking about each character and meeting with the director. For Fiddler, I first met the director about six months ago, and I spent the early winter researching the characters and doing sketches. I have to think about every single piece of clothing, every shoe, every earring, every hair accessory. All these little things come together to create the whole look of the person and the show.

When I got to Utah a few weeks ago, the forty-four cast members hadn't even been chosen. When they finally arrived, I spent a lot of time fitting them, a part of my job I just love. The actors and I chat during the fittings and I always meet the most interesting people. Each actor brings something special to the character, and I try to reflect that in the costume, plus make sure they're comfortable in the clothes. I've had disasters, like an actor refusing to go onstage during dress rehearsal because she thought the costume made her look fat.

A lot can change from my first design to what appears onstage. Take Tzeitel, one of Tevye's daughters in Fiddler on the Roof*. I saw her as a very romantic woman and created a dress that softened her hardworking peasant lifestyle. The blue, untucked blouse had raspberry trim and a little ruffle, and there was a curve to the collar. I imagined that Tzeitel would wear her hair down, and flowing. When I showed my sketch to the director she disagreed with my ideas because she didn't think Tzeitel was so romantic, but a more practical, salt-of-the-earth personality. So I calmly set my drawing aside and drew a plainer outfit, with more textured fabric in creams and yellows. I used stripes instead of paisley and wooden instead of pearl buttons. I kept the shirt blue because I had that color stuck in my head and I just felt it was right.*

I've come to expect changes like that, especially early in the process. I

*no longer get too attached to my ideas. One time a director cut a costume
I really liked after it was already made. The play took place at the turn of
the century and I'd made a beautiful Gibson-designed dress, but the
playwright was not happy with the character and changed her from being
upper- to lower-middle class. The beautiful gown I made was useless,
and I had to hunt through storage for a dowdier blouse and skirt that
would work. At times like that I have to try and be less emotional about
things. I take a step back and try to remember that it's about the show, not
about me.*

Despite the occasional creative conundrum, Andrea weaves her signature into every character she helps dress. Her ideas and unique touch
are woven into every outfit. Meanwhile, her identity as an artist—and a
Builder—is taking shape.

They assume she knows nothing—because she's female.

Considering only 10 percent of the country's some 9 million construction workers are women, a thirty-two-year-old petite blonde in a hard hat
is one of the last people you expect to see on a noisy New York City construction site. But that's exactly where Bonnie Andersen is. And it's
where she's happiest.

Conscientious and confident, Bonnie "absolutely loves" her job overseeing construction projects. As an owner's representative, she represents a building owner's interests—and its money—on commercial or
institutional construction sites, managing a building's budget, monitor-
ing schedules, and asking dozens of questions every day, like whether it's
too cold to pour concrete, or what to do when construction crews en-
counter underground obstacles, such as a stream or old pipes.

Construction is familiar territory to Bonnie, whose father's company
cuts and fabricates stone. After college Bonnie studied architecture but
envisioned a bleak future drafting plans on a computer for someone else
to build. She wanted to have a hand in the whole process, the big picture, and in 1997, Bonnie graduated with a master's degree in civil engineering and construction management.

I've always felt good about succeeding in what is more or less a man's industry. In my first job I worked for a construction company and was truly on the front lines, watching plumbers and electricians doing their work. They were very open to my questions. I'm young, and the truth of the matter is that many of them probably preferred working with me as opposed to some cranky sixty-year-old guy. There's an advantage to being a woman in construction, and sometimes I believe I might actually be more respected. Sometimes I walk into a room and everyone assumes I know nothing because I'm female. But they assume a man knows what he's talking about—until he screws up. I can only impress! But I also know my limits and have no problem admitting when I don't know something. I don't try to B.S. my way through. Asking questions was difficult at first, but it helps me in the long run.

At her current job with Levien & Co., which she's held since 1999, Bonnie earns six figures a year. A recent client, Columbia University, had a 170,000-square-foot facility built on Manhattan's residential Upper West Side, where Bonnie spent most of her time.

As the liaison for Columbia, I stop by the job site for two or three hours a day to see what's going on. I'll probably get stuck at the field office for a couple of hours chatting with the site superintendent about miscellaneous issues and problems. Maybe there's a piece of steel that doesn't fit as intended and they want to know if they should spend the time and money to find the perfect piece. I have to weigh the facts—and figure out if I am actually getting the right story—against the budget and decide whether to spend the money. I also deal with a lot of different groups of people: my clients, people in the neighborhood, the architect. I have to listen carefully to everyone. In one recent situation the architect thought it was important to have stainless doors, but the construction manager disagreed. While they fought about it, I scrambled to make sure the schedule and budget were okay. Finally we opted to get rid of the stainless steel because it would take too much time. It is unexpected issues like these that take up a lot of my day.

There is never a dull moment, and I have to be a good communicator, be very organized, technically adept, and able to handle a whirlwind of issues. I have to have a lot of energy—especially when the elevators aren't yet up and running in the building! It's all very rewarding. I can look at something that I am part of constructing and it's tangible. I walk into a building and think, I'm actually helping to create this. *I'm part of every little step. Some of my friends have jobs where things are always on paper, but for me it's cool to see something physical come out of my work.*

Like the little girls they once were, Builders are, in some form or another, creating communities or functional, useful products. At Old Navy, Ivy builds environments that stimulate creativity. In Hollywood, Jennifer assembles crews that make movies. In San Francisco, Michela builds a magazine's readership. In Boston, Fiona is educating future businesswomen. In St. Louis, Marjorie helps factory employees work together to create a more effective workforce. Lee manufactures screwdrivers, Laura engineers trains, Betty invents household products, Andrea designs costumes, and Bonnie builds buildings.

While the tools Builders use vary—from sales savvy to math skills, advanced education to intuition—there is a universal tool all of them need to succeed: relationships. Relationships with colleagues, clients, bosses, and staff help Builders successfully produce their products. Without such alliances, none of these women could do her job. They could not sell, lead, or get people to return their phone calls. Most Builders operate as team members, not solo artists. Unlike, say, a sculptor, a Builder rarely works alone and must effectively interact with others to achieve the greater goal. Having healthy relationships does not mean everyone likes a Builder, but it does mean she builds relationships that engender respect and communicates clearly so that others support and follow her.

Women's ability to nurture such relationships calls to mind another observation from Mattel's consumer researchers. Dr. Shore says that boys who played with superhero dolls, such as Batman or Spider-Man, tended to identify a good guy and a bad guy and usually had the good character destroy the evil one. In a different approach, girls who played with superheroes also identified opposing characters of good and evil, but the outcome was different: Rather than vanquish the bad guy, girls transformed him into an ally—and had the one-time enemies become friends.

Chapter Eight

The Counselors

**Social worker, pharmaceutical sales manager,
park ranger, residential real estate broker,
restaurant owner, and teen-magazine editor**

Writer and business consultant Nance Guilmartin administers what she calls "communications first aid." The author of *Healing Conversations: What to Say When You Don't Know What to Say,* Guilmartin tells people to get past blame, assumption, and emotion in everyday discourse and, instead, step into other people's shoes, be curious, and connect in ways that go beyond the business at hand and instead foster goodwill and strong relationships. In short, she teaches people to live and work better by listening with open, nonjudgmental minds. Says Guilmartin, "Everyone has their own version of the truth."

The ability to channel others' truths into productive business-related activities defines the work of Counselors, women whose job happiness is based on listening and advising.

Counselors are not limited to stereotypical roles of therapist, social worker, or psychologist. As you'll see, they are executives and entrepreneurs, blue-collar workers, and real estate brokers. Whatever their industry, Counselors share a common skill: They use communication to bridge worlds and solve problems. But unlike The Happy 100's more quantitative Thinkers, Counselors solve problems that are more psychological in nature. A pharmaceutical sales manager guides her sales reps

230 / Joanne Gordon

away from burnout and toward success. A real estate agent helps house hunters turn intangible dreams into brick-and-mortar reality. To bring people closer to nature, a park ranger teaches the public to enjoy and respect the outdoors. A restaurant owner helps her teenage waitresses navigate the day-to-day traumas of youth, while the editor in chief of a teen girl magazine uses articles to empower millions of young women.

Listening is more art than science. And it's exhausting work, not something everyone can muster or master. Those who do it well, however, can find it useful in any number of professions. Just listen carefully to the stories that follow.

Disease is her friend.

This chapter begins with a traditional social worker who followed a not-so-traditional career path. Gloria Gaev was fifty years old, single, and living in Manhattan when, after a lengthy career in fashion, she returned to school to earn a master's degree in social work. Today, instead of making $80,000 a year and working in Manhattan's fashion district, Gloria lives off school loans and spends her days in New York's middle- to low-income high-rise apartments visiting the elderly. Having shifted from selling Calvin Klein to counseling widow Klein, Gloria is overjoyed with her career change. Not only does she believe that social work is one of the few jobs that will support her for the rest of her life, but assisting the elderly is a natural extension of who she truly is.

Still, Gloria's reinvention has not been easy: "I'm no overnight success story. My search lasted a long time."

There is something light and playful about Gloria. From the puffy silver parka and pink fuzzy hat she wears in winter, to her sassy blond hair and easy smile, this is a woman to whom you can tell your life story over coffee. As for Gloria's own life story, her father, a doctor, died of heart failure when she was only six years old, and in addition to dealing with his death, Gloria grew up with diabetes and undiagnosed dyslexia. The former forced her to take control of her life with daily insulin injections, while the latter sapped her confidence and hopes of ever holding a so-called professional job.

For about eighteen years after college, Gloria worked in the jewelry business with her mother, Adelle, designing and selling semiprecious necklaces and earrings through their company, Aloria. When her mom retired in the 1980s, Gloria looked for other outlets in the fashion trade and went on to hold a string of jobs that each left her, through no fault of her own, unemployed. She was vice president for an outfit that licensed Andy Warhol's art for accessories until the company lost its license. She sold close-out designer merchandise for three businessmen, who eventually shut down their business. And she was merchandise director for a large company's Internet division, which eventually went under. Each job loss left Gloria more discouraged. "You start to think a lot in between jobs," and what Gloria thought about was how fashion had lost its dazzle for her and was a young person's business. She worried whether age would work against her, and that was a risk the single, self-supporting woman could not afford.

In search of answers, Gloria went to a career adviser who, she says, told her nothing new. So, on her own, Gloria explored options outside fashion. The idea of working with the elderly bubbled up in the course of her search, and then a stint volunteering with seniors, taking them to and from doctors' appointments, confirmed her suspicion that she would enjoy such a field. Practically speaking, the country's aging baby boom population promised a never-ending customer base for social workers. But there was also something emotional in Gloria's past that allowed her to empathize with the aged. As a lifelong diabetic, Gloria understood how difficult it was to take control of one's own health. "You can either make a disease your friend or your enemy," she says, and as a social worker specializing in gerontology, Gloria could help others accept their ailing bodies and take charge of their lives in much the way she took charge of her own.

A friend suggested that a social work degree (as opposed to just a counseling certificate) would boost Gloria's chances of employment, so at age fifty she took a deep breath, applied for student loans, and went back to school, a move that, given her dyslexia and aversion to writing, posed other hurdles for Gloria to attack head-on. She was up front with teachers about her condition and signed up for school-provided tutors to assist with writing assignments.

To pay for school, Gloria used some of her savings and took out an equity line of credit on her apartment. As for accommodating her significantly reduced income, the urban fashionista revamped her Manhattan lifestyle. No more trendy clothes or pricey salon visits; rather than pay full price, Gloria has beauty school students cut and color her hair. She started taking subways and buses, canceled her cable subscription, and now when she does eat out, the self-described Leftover Queen brings half the meal home for her next day's lunch.

When I first interviewed Gloria a year before she graduated, she'd already begun working part-time for the Jewish Association for Services for the Aged (JASA), a not-for-profit organization that assists the elderly throughout the New York area with their day-to-day needs, from meals and Medicaid to counseling and transportation.

JASA is often the first line of defense in assessing a senior's well-being and quality of life. A lot of older people feel fine when they retire, but then they get sick or their spouses die. Even if they put money away for a rainy day, it eventually rains and folks use up their savings. One woman I work with, Marsha, is a widow going blind, who lives by herself and needs an escort to get her to and from doctors' appointments and to run errands. Marsha was just learning how to maneuver the system, and she became anxious when I told her I was going away for a few days. I took her hand and said, "Marsha, I won't let you down and will arrange for an escort while I'm away." I explained to her how to leave a message for me at the agency I worked for. It's easy to forget that a lot of elderly don't even know how to use voice mail, so I told Marsha how to speak into the phone and what numbers to push. She was so appreciative that someone just took the time to walk her through it!

Another woman, I'll call her Ruth, was living with her cousin and really wanted to live in Co-Op City but could not afford it on her income. By simply chatting with Ruth I learned that she'd been married and separated years ago, and her former husband had died. I set up an appointment for us with the Social Security office and got Ruth survivor benefits, which increased her income enough so that she could afford to rent her own apartment. Ruth's life was changed for the better. Then there was an elderly man whose face was severely deformed from a childhood stroke. After his ill wife died he lost his purpose for living, so I signed the gentleman up to lead weekly senior groups, where people gathered to just talk about issues bothering them. He was a good speaker who I knew would be helpful to others in a situation where people could look beyond his appearance. Leading the groups gave the man a purpose. Whereas before he was extremely depressed, he now has a place to go and people who talk to him. It really changed his life. "I'm so happy," he told me. "People thank me for running the group so well."

The elderly are a window into my own future, and I learn so much from them. They've been through the Depression, through war, through the death of a spouse. And they are able to understand me, whereas children may not. I am not saying that all elderly are loving, considerate, warm, friendly people—a lot of them want to take advantage of the system to get what they think they are entitled to. But on the whole they are appreciative of kindness and don't take things for granted. I help make their lives easier and can see the difference on their faces from when I arrive to when I say good-bye. One day I will be their age. Should I be on my own and alone, I hope I meet kind and loving people.

I am still in school, living on almost zero income, and the most I will probably make after I graduate is $40,000. But I feel totally different at the end of the day now than I did at the end of my fashion career. When I come home at night I may be tired and emotionally spent, but it's a different feeling from closing a business deal. I feel extremely appreciated. My life is meaningful now, no longer a numbers game.

I asked Gloria if, ten or twenty years ago, she imagined herself going back to school and becoming a social worker. She shakes her head. "No way." But midlife has a way of making women reflect on past accomplishments and redefine their futures. By helping the elderly find new purpose, Gloria renewed her own.

She's more mom than manager.

In Houston, Texas, Donna Lindsay and her sales team sell pharmaceuticals to hospitals and doctors, but it's her management style that makes her staff feel so good. Donna, forty-four, is a regional sales director for pharmaceutical company AstraZeneca. She's responsible for eight dis-

trict sales managers across the country and another seventy sales representatives who all work for the company's Gastroenterology and Cardiovascular Medical Center team. When Donna took the post in 2002, the
group was in disarray, morale sagged, and her department was tiny compared with other divisions. Donna laughs as she remembers how, at one
company gathering, the meeting's organizers even forgot to set up a table
for her sales reps.

Although Donna has grown her department over the years, she
doesn't reel off a litany of financial achievements when asked why she
loves her work. Instead, Donna speaks of the day-to-day business of
tending to others. "The reason I truly love the pharmaceutical business
is because I know I'm helping people," she says, referring to her sales
staff. To help her sales reps maneuver the pace, pressures, and complexities inherent to the pharmaceutical sales business, Donna addresses them as people with lives—emotions, personal goals, and private
problems—outside of work.

*The job can be very draining, so I encourage folks to recharge their
batteries. My district sales managers travel a lot and get burned out, so I
have to keep them motivated. To do that I get out in the field and work
directly with reps to learn their concerns and what they're up against.
Sometimes I feel more like a mom or a counselor than a manager. I have
very good communication skills, and being a good listener is important
because sometimes people just want to be heard. Listening—really
hearing people—is key to being a good manager. I think people feel very
comfortable with me and trust me enough to talk about their personal
issues, whether at home or on the job. I have an open-door policy, so
anyone can come in and talk to me at any time. My managers also know
that they can call me at home, or on my cell phone if it's an emergency.*

*One of my managers recently called me, devastated about the death of
her mother. Two weeks later she and her father were in a car accident and
he had a heart attack. My manager was also a single mom with two
children and felt guilty about not being a good boss and supporting her
people. I told her to step back, take a couple of weeks off, see a counselor,
and think about things. Life is bigger than this job. She came back to
work and is a new person now. It makes me feel good to have reached out*

and helped. And when you treat people like human beings and truly care about them, they want to do whatever they can to make sure you are successful.

Donna could use her counseling abilities as a manager in a variety of industries, but pharmaceutical sales fulfills other criteria intrinsic to her happiness. The job has her on the go 80 percent of the time visiting customers, perfect for a woman who hates sitting all day. Donna is also a natural saleswoman who was bred not to take no for an answer. Her parents both hold Ph.D.s and pushed Donna to excel. She also grew up a bit of an activist, taking part in African-American organizations in high school and college. As one of the few African-American women at her level at AstraZeneca, or for that matter in the pharmaceutical business, Donna takes great pride in being a role model women look to for advice.

People sometimes ask me, "Donna, how did you come so far?" First, I came from a very educated family and had a wonderfully supportive upbringing. I also think that a lot of one's success has to do with the company you work for, and AstraZeneca has been very supportive. The company allows me time to teach and speak publicly about being an African-American in corporate America, and last year I was the company's first national diversity champion, an official position that helps recruit and promote minorities. That brought me a lot of satisfaction, and it also increased my loyalty to the company.

That loyalty was tested in 2004 when, several months after I first interviewed Donna, she was diagnosed with breast cancer and had a double mastectomy, followed by reconstructive breast surgery. I did not think it was possible for Donna to be happier with her work, especially after battling cancer, but amazingly she was in high spirits and insisted the disease was "the best thing that ever happened" to her. Although she is physically cancer free as of this writing, cancer still plays a major role in her career. After Donna recovered, she decided it was time to throttle back the hectic schedule she'd supported for years. Her body needed the rest, and her newly adopted daughter needed her time. So Donna approached her bosses and told them she wanted to demote herself from regional sales manager to district manager for a division that sells on-cology drugs. She also told them she wanted to earn the same salary she had made before and to work out of her house. To its credit, AstraZeneca delivered—proof that when valuable women ask for what they want, they often get it. (Indeed, 91 percent of Happy 100 women who asked for a raise at some point in their careers got one.)

Instead of traveling the country managing seventy reps, Donna now oversees eight in Texas. "As long as I can give encouragement, hope, and understanding to people and point out possibilities rather than limita-tions, then I am giving something back," says Counselor Donna. She also plans to extend her counseling skills and newfound cancer expertise to the African-American community, where she says the prevailing no-tion among women is that cancer cannot be prevented. "Black women feel that if something is meant to be, then it will be," says Donna, who will hit the speaking circuit, using herself as a prime example of the good that comes from preventative care.

Donna's story is a reminder of the power women have not just over their health, but over their careers as well. Either can change at a mo-ment's notice.

Counseling is her nature.

When folks see park ranger Jennifer Stowe approach them in her green and tan uniform, gold badge, and brunette braid tucked into a Smokey Bear hat, "All eyes immediately go to the belt," she says. The first thing everyone wants to know is whether Jennifer is packing heat. "That phe-nomena both interests me and makes me nervous," says Jennifer, who carries only a small cutting knife. It interests Jennifer because she is a people-watcher who finds the consistent belt-eyeing behavior fascinat-ing. It makes her nervous because, at thirty-two, she works alone, and it's quite possible that whomever she approaches may actually be involved in criminal activity that warrants a gun's authoritative presence. Indeed, a large part of Jennifer's job as a ranger for the Department of Conserva-tion and Recreation in Massachusetts is to enforce the law, from parking restrictions to illegal trash dumping. That said, Jennifer never needs a weapon to do her job. Her communication skills work just fine.

My primary goal is to help preserve natural resources. I've seen everything from kids dropping soda bottles on the ground to men who dump VCRs and TVs in a river. Just this morning I found a ratty old orange couch in the woods! While it infuriates me to see people harm our natural resources, I don't let it get to me. I see people break the rules all the time, and when I try to educate them, I often get yelled at. Some people are very disrespectful. They think it's their park because they pay taxes and who am I to come up and tell them what to do. But I am trained to deal with the public, so I'm very good at sizing up a situation and determining whether I can handle it myself. If it's a large, out-of-control party, I'll get police backup. I actually think, being a woman, I am not as intimidating as a male park ranger. And I make sure that no matter who the person is, even if it's a homeless person living in a campground, I never put them down and always treat them with respect. I think that's why I have such success. Instead of coming in yelling, like some officers, I calmly tell people their options. One time I had to kick a homeless man out of the park, and he actually thanked me! He said he understood I had to do this to everyone. As long as you are respectful, people listen. Most people who break the rules just don't know what they are doing is illegal. Others simply don't care. That's why my priority is to educate before I enforce. I explain what the rule is and why we have it.

Jennifer spends many workdays at her office reviewing reports about injuries or illegal offenses from more than twenty parks under her oversight. Sometimes she patrols the woods in her dark green Chevy Silverado with her golden retriever, a trained search and rescue dog, in the passenger seat. Occasionally, Jennifer is summoned on an emergency to help find a lost hiker or a missing person. These days, the most common lost-person reports are for elderly Alzheimer's patients who wander away from their home or nursing facility and, possibly, into a state park. Finding these folks is an exercise in psychology and sensitivity. Says Jennifer, "Alzheimer's patients tend to walk a straight line, so we have to go to the place they were last seen. And because they may still remember things from their childhood, we talk to relatives to get their history. Maybe the lost person walked to her old house or a place where she once worked."

Unfortunately, there are incidents when a person is not found alive. Other times Jennifer has the joy of returning them to their families.

This ranger's primary source of pleasure, however, is not derived from the glory of locating a missing person, or from the power trip other people might derive from a career in law enforcement. Jennifer's favorite activity is talking to ordinary, rule-abiding citizens about the outdoors. She loves working at park events and speaking to kids about safety; she gets a kick out of handing out maps to hikers; and she feels good assisting injured visitors. Sometimes, Jennifer just walks the woods. "People see me coming down the trail in my uniform and they feel safe," she says. "I stop to say hello and end up spending forty-five minutes answering questions about the trails and nature. I love that about my job! People can see the excitement in my eyes."

That excitement goes back to childhood. She thought she wanted to be a firefighter or a police officer because her family lived on a busy city street, and from the porch Jennifer witnessed a weekly parade of car accidents—and the rescue crews who cleaned up after them. During her junior year in high school, an enrollment package for an environmental school in Maine "mysteriously" showed up in the mail from Unity College, which offered classes in conservation law enforcement, a program that fit Jennifer's interests to a T. When she graduated, Jennifer was the only woman in that program. (Curious side note: While attending Unity, Jennifer worked in the admissions office and realized that enrollment packages are sent only to people who request them; to this day she has no idea who requested the package be sent to her.)

It's tempting to assume Jennifer is happy as a ranger because she's a Lover of nature, but Jennifer is just as fond of people as she is of beautiful vistas. Rather than a Lover, Jennifer is a Counselor because she wields communication to improve others' relationships with the outdoors—and she doesn't need a gun to get her point across.

She sells the American Dream.

While a house is the most expensive purchase most people will ever make, it is also the most emotional. Therein lies the challenge for real estate agents. In addition to helping secure financing, realtors must talk clients into embracing a place where they will not only eat and sleep, but where they will live out their American Dream: grow old and prosper, laugh and cry, celebrate good times and mourn bad, raise children, discipline teenagers, fight with their spouse, make up, and make love. Selling homes is an intensely personal business, which is why Yola Haddad Ozturk loves it. Born in Lebanon, Yola, thirty-five, was educated in electrical engineering, received an MBA, and worked in France before settling in San Francisco, where she quickly discovered, as a broker for Hill and Company, that real estate's entrepreneurial spirit fit her more comfortably than the clubby, stifling culture of the technology companies for which she once worked. When she first switched careers, Yola considered entering the commercial real estate business—selling offices and warehouses—because of her engineering background. But the emotional element of selling homes won her over.

You have to have natural compassion and empathy for this job. Real estate is sales in its purest form, but given the amount of money that's involved, you also need to be like a psychologist to the people you work with. People want to build futures and have kids in their new houses, so I have to address the psychological component with each sale. Most agents become good friends with their clients, and you can't mind mixing personal and professional lives. I have one client who calls me from vacation to tell me about problems with his girlfriend, and I am just his real estate agent! Then there are the married couples: She wants a great kitchen, and the guy wants a great BBQ spot. It's all about trade-offs and not making either partner feel like they're compromising too much. People get very emotional, and I feel so happy when I solve someone's problem and give them the dream they were looking for.

Two of Yola's clients were looking to buy a residential building as an equal investment, and their constant bickering forced Yola to play mediator. When client A liked a building that client B did not, client A made B feel horrible for saying no. As her clients' emotions flared, Yola says her role was to soften the atmosphere. "I'd explain why one said no and help the other get over her disappointment." Whenever her clients dislike a property that requires renovation, it is Yola who helps them imagine what the future can look like: the beauty of a recaulked bathroom; the appeal of a kitchen with new appliances; the sunlight that will spill into a room with larger windows. Her quantitative skills also help ease her clients' financial jitters, and Yola runs spreadsheets to determine monthly payment options and to calculate a property's potential future value. "I participate in the most important investment decision people make," says Yola. It's her counseling skills that ultimately help clients cross the threshold into a new home, and a new life.

In her own words

Anna Pinto, 21
Restaurant Owner
Joey's Diner and The Grape Vine
Buhler, Kansas

Anna owns two restaurants in the small town where she grew up and was home-schooled. She bought Joey's Diner in 2000 from the previous owner, using money reserved for her college education. A year later, with a loan from her grandparents, Anna opened The Grape Vine, a pizza and pasta restaurant. Much more than a boss to her teenage staff of waitresses and cooks, Anna is a mentor and a role model. Although she never went to college and has no degree in counseling, Anna practices it every day.

The only reason I was going to college was so I could be a youth counselor, but when the opportunity came up to buy the diner where I worked as a waitress, I used my college money to go into business for myself. As a Christian, I really wanted to do something in service and believed this is what the Lord wanted me to do. My dad helped me with the arrangements, and my mom keeps my books. I do everything from cooking to managing the staff.

At first I thought owning a restaurant had nothing to do with counseling. But I was wrong. I have a lot of teenagers working for me, and as their boss who sees them every day I have a greater impact on their lives than I would have as a professional counselor, who would see them only when they had problems. Most of the high school kids in Buhler will graduate and go to the nearby junior college for two years. They don't know what they want to do with their lives, and moving away from Buhler is very hard for them to imagine. Most will stay here and raise families.

Buhler is a very small, traditional town. The kids are raised to be good Christians, but they are also typical teenagers who lead two separate lives: Around their peers they are totally wild, but at home and at church they are completely different people. They try to keep up the image their parents want them to be, but a lot of parents are clueless and deny that their kids would do anything wrong.

I have very good relationships with a lot of the girls who work for me, and I just like to spend time with them. Some don't have a lot of friends or aren't sixteen yet and can't drive, so they sit home on a Friday night. I host Joey's Diner events, where we'll all get together and go see a movie. I like to be able to get everyone out, doing something without alcohol or drugs. Sometimes kids just want to get out of the house with friends and be themselves.

At work, I try not to be critical of what they do wrong. I don't yell at them for innocent mistakes, and I try not to get really mad. But they know when I disapprove, and I want them to understand why so they will change their behavior. If they put too much salad on a plate for a customer, I might say, "Isn't that supposed to be smaller?" They might not change the salad right then, but they'll change it next time. If I see a bad attitude, I just look them right in the eye and say, "Hey, you need to calm down," or "Go sit in the office until you cool off." If things get really bad, we'll go talk. Usually I just listen. Sometimes they wander in when I'm taking my break and just start talking to me about how their brother is doing this or their parents are doing that. It never fails: Every time I come into the restaurant, one of them will come up to me and tell me about their life. I think that's very cool.

A year or so ago, one of the girls was having problems with a guy and he ended up raping her, but no one, not her friends or her parents, believed her. I knew she was telling the truth, but she was so scared because everyone thought she was lying. The boy threatened her, and she came to work with bruises on her face. She eventually changed her story and said she had made it up and was grounded for lying and ostracized at *school. Being in the restaurant was the only time she could be true to herself and did not have to lie. She could talk to me about it so her feelings were not bottled up. One of the things that most upset her was that no one believed her. So my belief in her meant a lot. That was a very humbling experience because I didn't feel like I was doing anything except listening. I could not fix her problem, but sometimes it's not about doing something, it is about just being there. It also made me think about how many other girls have to live lies because no one believes them. Everything I went through with that one girl made me realize that I was meant to be in her life. If I didn't own this restaurant, then she never would have had me to talk to. I have a heart for counseling, and I believe there is something bigger in this world for me.*

People say to me, "Why don't you spend time with people your own age?" But I see my time better spent with the girls, and their lives outside the diner bring variety into my own life. I always try to keep my mind bigger than the small town we live in.

Her girl power

While Anna Pinto counsels one teenage girl at a time in her Kansas restaurants, Susan Schulz counsels more than five million via the pages of *CosmoGIRL* magazine, where she is the New York–based magazine's editor in chief. If you don't have a teenage girl—or aren't one—then you've probably never picked up an issue of *CosmoGIRL,* a punchy, candy-colored publication that is the younger sister, if you will, of *Cosmopolitan.* Yes, *CosmoGIRL* runs articles about boys and fashion, but there are also feature pieces about careers, successful businesswomen, and financial education. Susan, the magazine's second-ever editor in chief, views *CosmoGIRL* as an empowering voice for young women at the threshold of adulthood. "I want the magazine to answer all the questions I didn't even know I should ask at that age," she says.

Like *CosmoGIRL*'s readers, Susan—a slim, fair-skinned brunette— once dreamed about her future. She got good grades, was elected to student council, and had lots of friends, but was always a bit scared to stretch herself for fear of failing. Back in the eighth grade, one of her teachers actually predicted Susan would work for a teen magazine after she handed in a report about, of all adolescent afflictions, acne. But beauty, per se, was not Susan's "thing." Most comfortable in jeans, she was never a shoe-obsessed, cosmetics-hoarding fashionista. In college she studied journalism and English. Even though she excelled at math and science, no one ever encouraged her to pursue related careers.

After graduating, Susan wanted to write but had no idea what to write about, so she began at the bottom of the magazine publishing ladder when her older sister's college roommate, who worked for *Entertainment Weekly,* got her a job filing newspaper clips about celebrities. It was relatively mindless work, but Susan was a workaholic and a good-spirited team player who offered to substitute for laid-off or vacationing colleagues. Her performance helped her build a network of industry friends, and those contacts as well as Susan's skills eventually landed her a more senior job at *Redbook* magazine as an editorial assistant for a former colleague. Susan followed the same woman to *Good Housekeeping* as an assistant editor.

"I just focused on doing my job the best I could, so I don't think I can say I was very ambitious," says Susan. "I was not always looking for the next thing, but once I mastered a job, people wanted to give me another."

Yet despite her ascension to editorial positions at two national magazines, Susan was not writing for her ideal audience. At the older-women's magazines, articles on recipes, marriage, and family were not the twenty-two-year-old girl's topics of choice—but she persevered because she realized content was merely a catalyst for her education as an editor, not her identity as a writer. That philosophy paid off, and the job after *Good Housekeeping* brought Susan closer to a readership she identified with: young women. Susan joined *YM* magazine as an assistant editor charged with "the guy beat." Again, interviewing cute boys and creating dating quizzes were hardly intellectually stimulating, but Susan used the experience to hone her underdeveloped editing skills.

At the time I didn't even know if I liked editing because I was so scared of it. I just thought you assign a writer a story who took it from there. But

*the assignments that came back to me were terrible, and not at all what I
wanted. For months I'd rewrite or fix people's work until I finally realized
that being an editor is like redoing a kitchen. You don't go off and leave
the contractor, you tell him you want cherry-wood cabinets and stainless-
steel light fixtures. Writers are independent contractors just like construction workers, and an editor has to have and communicate the vision
so the writer can build accordingly. And each writer is different. You can
think you're explaining yourself clearly, and one writer will get it but
another just won't. Communication is an art, really.*

In 1997, Susan quit *YM* for a job at an Internet Web site, which closed
for lack of funding a few days before she started, forcing Susan to write
freelance to make rent, a circumstance that led her to *CosmoGIRL*.
While visiting the magazine's office to discuss a freelance story, the
then–editor in chief was interviewing for an open staff position and sat
Susan down for an impromptu meeting. Susan took an editing test and,
a few weeks later, in November 2000, was named deputy editor.

She had found a home. *CosmoGIRL's* audience and empowering
voice won over Susan's heart as well as her head. *CosmoGIRL* was all
about motivating young women to be more than girlfriends to boys and
slaves to fashion. Despite cover lines promoting dating and celebrities,
CosmoGIRL also encourages girls to run for president, save their al-
lowance, and plan their future. It runs serious articles about rape, abor-
tion, getting good grades, and getting along with parents.

When Susan was appointed editor in chief after its well-known
founding editor left to edit competitor *Seventeen* magazine, *Cosmo-
GIRL's* mission was in Susan's hands, a daunting task for someone so
young. Everyone watched—and they still do—to see how Susan would
perform. She routinely works twelve-hour days editing articles, holding
editorial meetings, reviewing layouts, and going on sales calls. When
work gets particularly stressful, Susan calms herself down by talking out
loud to herself, delivering a little pep talk under her breath. "It's easy to
get so caught up in the pressure that you can't do the work," she admits,
and slowly Susan is also learning that she can't please everyone—bosses,
staff, readers, and advertisers—all the time. When things get particularly hairy, it's the magazine's mission that keeps Susan grounded.

I want to help girls stand up for themselves. A lot of girls don't because they're told to be nice and not to rock the boat, but there is a difference between that and allowing yourself to be stepped on. I'm driven to help girls know the difference. For me, speaking up for myself is like speaking a second language because it's very hard. I have to think through what I'm going to say before I proceed. The sooner I can teach girls how to be fluent in that language, the more they'll feel comfortable using it when they get to the adult world and need to ask for a raise or explain to a guy what she wants out of a relationship.

What our readers need most is encouragement. Our girls are respectable, they have a sense of humor, they are smart, and they are cool. But our readers are also at an age when they start to edit themselves. At age eight, if you want to make a mud pie, you make a mud pie. At thirteen, if you want to start a business, you think of all the reasons why you can't. Our mission is to counteract the naysayers and show our readers others who turned ideas into reality.

So many girls I hear from want to be fashion designers, singers, and magazine editors, but they also make career choices based on what they're familiar with, the jobs they see every day, because they're scared to pursue things they don't know much about, like careers in math and science. But there are so many jobs that girls would enjoy and excel in if only they knew about them. So, as happy as I am with my job, I want to help girls understand all the options they truly have.

My goal is to make CosmoGIRL a place where girls go for opportunities. And we don't just want to tell them what to do, but show them how to do it, and actually let them do it. We recently asked readers to interview amazing women for articles. One girl who's into politics interviewed Madeleine Albright; another girl who knows a lot about technology interviewed Michael Dell; and in May a girl who volunteers for Planned Parenthood interviewed its president, Gloria Feldt. A sophomore at Columbia is our presidential campaign correspondent, and she and I traveled to the South Carolina primary together.

At this point in my career, I want to work for a teen girl magazine only because that is the population I want to help, and I feel like we're doing that. I know, because I e-mail and talk to our readers all the time, and they prop me up, too. Ever since I took over the editor in chief job, letters

*from readers have been only encouraging. Sometimes I look at war
correspondents, and while their jobs are so important, that type of
journalism just does not speak to me. I need to show people how to apply
information to their life to make it better. If I went back to school, I'd
probably be a counselor.*

How fascinating that one of Susan's goals as an editor is to prevent
teenagers from editing themselves. In the process, this Counselor is
being true to herself.

You may be surprised to find Counselors working in non-social-science
settings, and in places such as restaurants and large corporations. But on
further reflection it's actually obvious why there are so many nontraditional jobs for Counselors: Business, in its many forms, is grounded in
communication. It's about how people inform each other, motivate each
other, and share ideas.

Counselors understand that, and thus they see people they work with
not just as employees or customers, but as mothers and fathers, sons and
daughters, friends and spouses. Counselors can look beyond job titles
and address the whole individual in the course of a workday. Anna knows
that the waitresses at her diner are not mindless robots taking orders,
but girls with more on their minds than what customers want on their
salads. Donna knows her high-powered salespeople do not exist just to
help her make AstraZeneca's sales quotas but also have their own agen-
das and limitations. For editor Susan, *CosmoGIRL*'s readers are not just
consumers of clothes, a faceless demographic, or an anonymous subscriber base; each is an individual young lady with the potential to
change the world. For park ranger Jennifer, the folks who pass through
Massachusetts's public parks—from the homeless to families of four—
deserve to be treated with respect. And for real estate agent Yola, house
hunters are not just clients, but couples or families for whom a home
represents the American dream. Finally, as a social worker who visits the
elderly, Gloria understands there is much more to each client than her
small, humble apartment or failing eyesight; the aged have histories rich

with love and loss, and while they may be closer to death, they still have daily lives to lead.

Effective communication is not about "being correct"; it is not always about fixing, rescuing, or judging, writes Nance Guilmartin in *Healing Conversations*. It is about stepping into someone else's shoes and acknowledging their story. Just being willing to listen is key to good relationships and good business. For Counselors, it is key to why they love their work.

The preceding chapters focused on the primary reasons why women love their work. We met the Lovers, the Thinkers, the Determinators, the Heroines, Healers, and Sisters, as well as the Surviving Artists, the Faithful, the Builders, and the Counselors.

These final three chapters focus on Happy 100 women who fall into the aforementioned categories but whose career paths stand out in one of three ways worth separate attention. The first group, the Loyalists, have worked for the same company for an unusually long period of time and illustrate how a happy career can blossom at a single employer. The After-Achievers, after having reached the pinnacle of one career, successfully transitioned to another job they now love, showing what a happy working life can look like after one has reached the top. The Hurdlers end the book on a note of inspiration, as all have overcome significant or unusual obstacles in their career paths.

What they all share, of course, is a love of their work.

Chapter Nine

The Loyalists

**Engineer, herbal tea buyer, trade magazine editor,
college administrator, cancer foundation president,
and product marketing executive**

Remaining loyal to a single employer throughout one's career is—unfortunately—an antiquated concept. On average, U.S. employees work for nine different companies over the course of a lifetime. More specifically, most women in their late forties and fifties have been with their current employer only six to eight years, on average, according to the U.S. Bureau of Labor Statistics.

By contrast, most of the following women, the Loyalists, exceed that tenure at least twofold, having worked for the same company for anywhere between fifteen and twenty-five years. Such longevity boggles the mind. Don't these women get bored? Do they stop growing? Not the women in this chapter, whose experiences show how a dynamic career can unfold under the umbrella of a single employer.

That said, Loyalists do not love their jobs because they are loyal. Rather, they are loyal because they love their jobs. To that end, their employers have earned their allegiance in two intertwined ways: first, by being open minded and flexible in addressing each woman's changing lifestyle needs over the years; second, by providing career frameworks and experiences that foster intellectual and professional growth. These factors are both necessary if companies are to engender such long-term loyalty. Loyalists do not stick around merely because of flexible work schedules, but also because the job itself remains interesting and challenging. In turn, intellectual engagement alone does not induce loyalty unless a company can address a woman's long-term, ever-evolving personal needs.

Loyalty, as these profiles demonstrate, is very much a two-way street, and each woman gave back to her company in the form of hard, first-rate work. Quality performance usually precedes, and thus is key to winning, flexibility and responsibility. Employees must earn respect before they challenge the system.

Courage of her convictions, confidence in her abilities

Going from full-time to part-time does not mean a career must come to a screeching halt. In fact, part-time stints actually helped propel Jeanne Rosario's twenty-five-year engineering career at GE. "I am the poster child for how to manage your work and life," says Jeanne from her office in Cincinnati, Ohio. Today, as vice president and general manager of commercial engine design for reliability and services engineering, Jeanne, fifty-one, works directly with GE Transportation's CEO and manages a team that designs and tests commercial airplane engines.

I am in love with the challenge of developing and certifying new complex, high-technology products for aircraft. I am absolutely enamored with providing the customer the right solutions for his needs. And I enjoy coming to work every day because the team is great to work with. Not only are the people a great blend of technical experts, colorful personalities, and business-savvy individuals, but the organizations are flat, and boundaryless behavior is the norm. This empowers the workforce at all levels and makes the job much more satisfying.

This Loyalist's profile focuses not on the job itself but on how she raised young children and preserved her career at a time when the notion of the "family-friendly workplace" did not even exist in the nation's business lexicon.

Jeanne's challenges—and learning curve—began when her first child was born:

Part-time work wasn't really an option in the early 1980s. So when I got pregnant after my first six years at GE, I met with my boss over lunch, and when he asked what my plans were after the baby was born, I told him, point blank, I didn't want to work full-time. I had the courage of my convictions and confidence in my abilities (I had already won the company's young engineer of the year award), and I truly believed that I could come back when I wanted. I didn't even think to ask for part-time, so I essentially quit.

I was home for ten months when my boss called: "You know we'd really like you to come back on a part-time basis," he said. I didn't know anyone who had a part-time setup, but I was ready and excited to return to work. After leading such a challenging and technical career, it was a bit difficult to be home with the baby all day.

So I agreed to work twenty hours a week as an analyst, doing mostly computer work and analyzing designs for new military aircraft components. An aircraft engine has thousands of spinning parts that must all work together. It's very complex, and engineers design, test, and create one part at a time. Computer work was a good way for me to ease back into GE because it taught me a new skill. While no one gave me a hard time about working part-time, I do remember it was frustrating not to have as much responsibility as I was used to. I'd hand off my work to another manager who got the glory.

After I'd spent two years as an analyst, baby number two arrived, and again I left work. But this time I called my boss after about a year and said I was ready to come back part-time. My first goal was to get my foot in the door, and I was intent that this part-time experience would be different from the last. I didn't want to get stuck in analysis for military jets, because I knew there was little chance of promotional growth.

I wanted and needed different learning experiences.

I started out working in the military engine division just to get myself back in at GE, but I was quick to volunteer for whatever projects came up in other departments. I always went where a department was desperate for help because I figured I'd get more responsibility. I was right. I'd join a project that was in trouble or behind schedule and get in good with the manager, who just let me loose to apply my skills as they were needed. No one cared how many hours I worked or even where, as long as the work got done. I was a "telecommuter" before it was a word!

As an early example of how to successfully manage both a career and a family, Jeanne learned some valuable lessons that can assist other women seeking to go part-time. First, she did not let others pigeonhole her by reducing the level of responsibility she knew she could handle. Colleagues inevitably assign to part-timers less challenging, easier jobs. But rather than passively accepting less responsibility, says Jeanne, she just reduced the number of assignments. Second, Jeanne was proactive. She sought out work. Whenever managers told Jeanne she couldn't do what she wanted because she was "part-time," she simply knocked on someone else's door. It helped that Jeanne had established relationships with a variety of key, open-minded individuals throughout her tenure and had a reputation for professionalism and reliability. Because of her track record, Jeanne's requests were taken seriously. "If you delivered in the past, managers are more flexible and willing to negotiate. They want the best out of you, and if you tell them you'll be most valuable under the terms you set, they'll likely acquiesce," says Jeanne.

As for pay, Jeanne admits that she did not work part-time for the money. "By the time my husband and I paid for the baby-sitter, commuting costs, and work clothes, I had maybe fifty dollars left!" But Jeanne says she more than made up for the money she lost during her part-time years by the promotions she received when she returned full-time. That leads to a final lesson, says Jeanne: Do not think of part-time work as a part-time career, but simply one phase of a multiphased career. That distinction, she says, can make all the difference.

Part-time work let me gain knowledge and experience that propelled me when I was ready to return full-time. I became a manager because of the different experiences and knowledge I'd accumulated through my part-time projects. I like to think of my part- and full-time career paths visually: If a normal career path is a diagonal line always going up, then mine went up for the first six years, was flat while I worked part-time, but once I returned to work full-time the diagonal surged back up very quickly.

My part-time work was an investment in my future.

She's a seasonal gambler.

In an office on Sleepytime Drive in Boulder, Colorado, Kay Marie Wright works as the botanical purchasing director for Celestial Seasonings, a company that makes herbal tea. Each season, Kay carefully blends a variety of data in her mind before purchasing upward of 7 million pounds of raw ingredients—from spearmint leaves grown by Oregon farmers to blackberries harvested in Albania—that Celestial then blends into Raspberry Zinger, Madagascar Vanilla Red, Mint Magic, and hundreds of other teas. Each year Kay procures 7 million pounds of botanicals, 500,000 pounds of black tea, and about 400,000 pounds of fruit and flavors. It's an enormous shopping list, and she has a strict budget. To complete the overwhelming task, Kay collects and analyzes a variety of facts before making each purchase. In short, she tracks many factors—global weather conditions, economic indicators, local political climates, crop prices, currency fluctuations, her company's sales forecasts, and international import regulations—to determine when, from whom, and for how much money she will buy each ingredient or batch of fruit and flavors. While the sourcing process takes her to remote farmlands throughout the world, the novelty of global travel has long worn off for this fifty-six-year-old who has held the same job for twenty-eight years. What has not abated, however, is the intellectual challenge.

Even though I've been doing the same thing for so long, I don't get bored, because we deal with so many different types of plants in more than thirty-five countries. When you buy raw materials from all over the world, there's always something unpredictable happening with politics, the weather, harvests, or market conditions. These things all affect the price or quality of a crop. Weather plays a huge part in deciding what and when to buy. For example, a drought means farmers will lose a large percentage of their crops.

There's no substitute for showing up to inspect a crop in person. For example, each year I buy about 500 tons of hibiscus from Thailand and China, but last year, after everyone told me via phone that the crop was fine, I visited farms in Thailand and saw firsthand how sparse and dry the fields really were. I knew the farmers were not going to get their usual yield per acre, which meant fewer hibiscus for me as well as my competitors, so I immediately called my suppliers in China and ordered more than usual.

This is the kind of dicey situation that keeps my job exciting.

Other factors that go into my decision process are my company's promotional programs. Let's say our marketing department does a fall promotion for chamomile tea and we end up selling more tea than expected. I have to hurry up and buy more chamomile so we don't run out of stock, but without spending so much money that we don't make a profit. I also have to give the farmers accurate projections of what we'll buy so they plant enough, but not too much so they lose money. And I have to determine the optimal time to buy each crop so I get as much as we need for the best price possible. Sometimes I buy all at once; sometimes I choose to spread it out over time. What I do is very much like a commodities broker, and I read periodicals like spice bulletins and the Wall Street Journal to keep track of everything.

It's a continual shifting of information, and every five to seven years or so the proverbial poop hits the fan and we'll have a serious problem—something no one predicted will happen, and when it does, everyone and their uncle gets busy trading and hoarding. That's why it's good that I've been doing this job for so long. . . . I've established long-term partnerships with vendors, and those relationships often give me priority when I need something in a hurry. Still, so much is unpredictable.

Botanical purchasing director is probably not a job that college career counselors, or anyone, ever told you about. Who knew it even existed? Yet positions requiring such a unique combination of knowledge and skills—in Kay's case, quantitative analysis, agricultural expertise, international relations, logistical expediting, financial acumen—are embedded in every industry.

Kay actually found the job through a combination of instinct and serendipity. Her facility for foreign languages and her comfort with travel took root in childhood, when her family lived in Germany, England, the Philippines, and, finally, the U.S. Kay's curiosity about botanicals blossomed after college, although she did not purposely pursue a related line of work: After being let go from a job as a staff manager at a mountain lodge, a friend told her about an administrative position at a small tea company.

Celestial Seasonings hired me in 1976 to organize the company's files, and because I was naturally curious about botanicals—I even owned my own copy of Maud Grieve's A Modern Herbal—*I actually read the files I was supposed to be organizing! That's how I learned. Meanwhile, because of my childhood travels, I happened to be one of the few people in the tiny tea office who understood things like exchange rates and who could interpret many of the vendors' foreign accents. Flummoxed, people around the office just started asking me to help with orders. Once I started working with the woman in charge of expediting—dealing with customs and freight brokers—I took to the job like a duck to water.*

Today much has changed at Celestial Seasonings. The company has more than $100 million in sales and 250 employees. But much has also stayed the same: Kay is still just as intrigued by botanicals' taste, origin, and healing properties.

People play a very important role in Kay's work happiness quotient. Her sourcing trips abroad require a good dose of schmoozing, mainly chatting over interminable cups of tea with everyone from farmers to government officials. If Kay were not gregarious and friendly, that job requirement would pose a problem. And because the tea market is a relatively small community, the relationships she has established with vendors and growers are highly valued. Says Kay, "Some countries, like Thailand, won't do business with you until they get to know you personally. It's the same in Europe. They want to know you first. The business transactions are based on trust. It's all very familial, and today I do business with the sons and nephews of fathers I dealt with years ago."

Kay's own grandfather was a farmer in South Dakota, and he used to say that the quickest way to lose money is by gambling, the most fun way is wine and women, and the surest way to lose money is in agriculture.

"He was right," says Kay. "Every harvest is a real gamble." But that unpredictability is exactly what keeps Kay Marie intellectually engaged—so many variables, so much fluctuation, and so many possibilities.

In her own words

Suzanne Shelley, 39
Managing Editor
Chemical Engineering Magazine
New York, New York

Suzanne is the highest-ranking female on the editorial side and the first woman to hold the position of managing editor at this 100-year-old trade magazine. *Chemical Engineering*'s readers are engineers who work in the manufacturing, pharmaceuticals, and petroleum industries, among others. A science buff before becoming a writer, Suzanne holds a bachelor of science as well as a master's degree in geology. Her duties include writing and editing articles for monthly issues, as well as managing the magazine's staff and production. She also manages a staff of editors who produce bilingual newspapers for international industry trade shows. On a side note, it's a testament to *Chemical Engineering* that several women from its editorial and sales staff applied to be part of The Happy 100. Clearly, Suzanne is not the publication's only fulfilled female worker.

Whenever my friends joke with me about my job, I tell them Chemical Engineering *is the bible for some 200,000 chemical engineers. They look to the trade magazine to stay on top of the profession so they can do their jobs better. Our readers never throw an issue away, unlike more well-known business magazines.*

Our editorial staff is mostly engineers; I am the token geologist. I got the job when I sent a résumé to the publisher, McGraw-Hill, and interviewed with the human resources director. He liked me but did not know what to do with me, so he told me to call him every two weeks to see if something opened up. Over time I got the feeling that he was, like, "You're still calling?" But I had to swallow my pride and keep showing up. Eventually he sent my résumé to Chemical Engineering, *and I was hired as an assistant editor. Given all I had to learn, the joke was that if I was still employed in five years, I'd get an honorary degree in chemical engineering. [Laughs.]*

It's definitely challenging to be a female writing for male readers who work in male-dominated industries. Whenever I call to interview a source, I face a lot of bias, although it was worse when I was just starting out. There I was, this young woman asking men about their "pumps and valves and compressors." I still have to prove myself every single time by being knowledgeable, mature, and authoritative. At the same time, I have to admit what I don't know and ask sources to explain concepts I don't get. But acknowledging that I've reached the edge of my understanding about a particular subject helps me gain credibility.

We edit a lot of manuscripts submitted by experts who write about, for example, how to select the right valve for a job or troubleshoot a distillation system. As editors, we advocate on behalf of readers and make sure every possible question that could come up is addressed in the text. Sometimes I have to confront an author: "Correct me if I'm wrong, but I thought that when pressure goes up temperature goes down. . . ." Those are ways you establish credibility. It has not always worked out well.

One incident stands out. I was probably four or five years into the job and I'd been doing well and had great performance reviews. For one issue, a retired expert on heat transfer, a thorny technical topic, submitted a horrible manuscript. It was so convoluted and confusing because he assumed his audience knew everything that he knew. Not only did I not understand much of what he wrote, but his basic English just didn't make sense, so I edited and rearranged it. When I sent the manuscript back to him, he flipped out. "How dare you! You're a young woman and what could you possibly know!" He went over my head and called the publisher, screaming about how I had ruined his article. Clearly, he was also having an ego problem, because when I sat with the editor in chief and went through the article, he thought I did a reasonable job. At the last minute the author threatened to pull his manuscript, which would have left the magazine with no time to fill eight empty pages. Another editor took over the project, and, essentially, we ended up publishing the original version. I was humiliated that the author got his way. It was not right. I felt betrayed. I thought the editors should have had a united front. But eventually I realized that it was only a singular event, outweighed by many other contributing authors who wrote in about how great I was to work with, and I could not let my whole career boil down to that one moment.

I have continued to love the job because it never gets boring; every month I write about different technologies. Plus, my reporting and writing skills have just grown and grown and grown because I exercise them. The more confidence you have, the more I think you enjoy a job.

When I was named managing editor, it was a huge victory for me, and a validation. When the position came up they did not look outside for candidates. They said it was a no-brainer: I was a good executor and project organizer, and good with the staff.

I was also the first person to arrange a flextime schedule at my office, although I met with initial resistance. Flextime arrangements can open up a whole Pandora's box. Older male managers in particular think women are trying to get away with murder, and that they're goofing off at home, unloading the dishwasher, and not getting any work done. I worked for men whose child-rearing experience meant relegating most home chores to nonworking wives. They had no experience with women working at home. Also, our former editor in chief had a history of saying no to women who had asked for such arrangements, and many ended up quitting.

So, when I came back from maternity leave, I said, "Guess what, it's my turn to ask." They respected that I wanted to be home with my child, but they also needed me, and they knew I could manage my time and work without direct supervision—two big things you must prove before asking for a special arrangement. When I was promoted to managing editor three years ago, the publisher assumed I would give up my work-at-home arrangement. But I said, "Why? What difference does it make where I am? Most of the writers I manage live elsewhere, anyway." He was taken aback, but I was ready to defend my position. We agreed I would try it, and if it did not work, I would give it up.

Today I still work at home one or two days a week and am also raising two young daughters. I've definitely felt the split personality between magazine and motherhood, and maintaining a sane balance has been an ongoing challenge but one that, so far, is working out well.

A home for her dual desires

In a spacious, sunlit office overlooking Chicago's Lake Michigan, Margaret Sullivan gathers her mane of long gray hair into a chaotic bun and sits down to chat about why she has spent twenty-three years at her current job. At forty-eight, Margaret is a free spirit with a penchant for stability. Her employer lets her have it both ways.

When she was growing up, Margaret's family relocated so many times that she attended seven different schools by the time she reached the eighth grade. "When I thought about my future life and career, I just wanted a home base after all that moving. Plus, my father was laid off the day I graduated high school," recalls Margaret. Inevitably, such instability colored Margaret's future expectations.

When I was a social psychology major in college, I took a class in which we had to take a self-evaluation test and then write a forward-looking report identifying our ideal career lifestyle. My report said I wanted to work at an institution, such as a school or a hospital, because they were like home bases. But I also wanted creative freedom. I predicted that I would find a strong institution that would support my creative and entrepreneurial interests. At nineteen, I effectively predicted my entire future!

After graduating, Margaret was working as a freelance copywriter in Chicago when Columbia College, a private city school, invited her to speak to a class. "The dean happened to be making rounds that day, and he thought I was the instructor," says Margaret. "Later, she asked if I wanted to teach a class part-time." She did, eventually transitioning to full-time.

Columbia College had 800 students when Margaret joined as an advertising instructor. Today it has 10,000.

The school proved to be a home base from which Margaret could indulge a variety of interests. As chairperson of Columbia's marketing communications department, she oversees some fifty teachers, helps to develop the curriculum, "argues for" and manages her department's budget, and represents the school's students to their potential employers.

She has also written books, taken classes, and continued to teach. Each week is full of intellectual diversity.

On Mondays I teach a three-hour class on advertising culture. I invented the class years ago and keep it fresh by reading up on the industry. The class makes me feel like a million bucks, the most important thing I do all week.

Tuesdays I hold visiting hours for students, and there's often a waiting room full of people outside my office. I just saw a student who is lobbying to install lockers on our floor; another one put together a plan for our department's first-ever family night, which I think is a great idea. Some students are worried about their grades, and others about getting a job when they graduate.

Wednesdays, Thursdays, and Fridays I attend various committee meetings, where I help make decisions about the school's curriculum and policies. Department chairs are always fighting for the lives of their teachers and programs; there's a lot of scrutiny. Also, every Thursday I make a point to take an adjunct faculty member to lunch. They deserve attention, and it's my job to make sure they're involved in the college. I get to know them and also ask them to tell me about their full-time job, which helps me stay in touch with the marketing industry.

For as much as I dislike the bureaucracy of university life, this job gives me so much creative room to make a difference beyond the classroom. For example, last week at an all-college meeting our CFO said the college needed a new major, but one that did not require creating an entirely new department. I've already come up with a program for a major in public policy that the dean is excited about. If I weren't a chairperson, and just a faculty member, I wouldn't have gotten the administration's attention so quickly. This job gives me a lot of creative power to make my ideas real.

One year, Margaret founded a summer arts camp on Columbia's campus. The venture was a way for Margaret to exercise her entrepreneurial urge and meet Columbia's need to market itself to junior high school kids who are potential Columbia students. "The camp was like building my own little business, minus the risk. An anxiety-free project! I was given a budget, and we made the money back in future tuition," says

Margaret, who recalls how proud she was when the first camper-turned-college-student graduated from Columbia. Bonus: Her younger son is now old enough to attend the camp Margaret founded.

Academia can be either a safe haven where administrators and professors grow complacent, or a springboard to a lifetime of self-reinvention. For Margaret, it's the latter. "I found a place where I can teach in the morning, plan a budget in the afternoon, and, at the end of the day, tie-dye shirts with my son at camp." This Loyalist may have found the home base she dreamed of, but that doesn't mean she's standing still.

She's appreciated.

Not far from Margaret Sullivan, in another high-rise office in Chicago, sits Karen Carlson, a woman so dedicated to her job of sixteen years that she wishes the job would go away.

Karen is trying to cure cancer, but she is not a doctor.

Karen is the executive director of the Gynecologic Cancer Foundation, where she represents almost all the board-certified gynecologic oncologists in the country, some 950 physicians. The foundation's mission is to increase public awareness of gynecological cancer's symptoms, preventative measures, and treatment. There's a lot at stake: Between 1999 and 2003, 130,000 women died from gynecological-related cancers, and approximately 80,000 times each year, a woman in the U.S. is diagnosed. And while doctors work directly with patients, it's Karen and her staff who support doctors from the sidelines with informational materials and educational programs to reach out to women.

To achieve her goals, and in turn save lives, Karen takes a pragmatic approach to building public awareness. "Instead of amassing a huge endowment, we spend money as it comes in on educational programs," she says. Since 1991 the foundation's budget—mostly donations from pharmaceutical companies and victims' families—has grown from $10,000 to $3.3 million. Karen and her small staff work with doctors to create marketing campaigns, like newspaper supplements or television public service announcements. The foundation also hosts meetings with other cancer organizations and updates survivor groups about the latest medical developments. If someone tells Karen that patients want more information about, say, how cancer affects sexuality, she and her team raise the money to create a brochure. She also organizes annual meetings for foundation members, as well as events and courses throughout the year. There's a Web site to manage (www.wcn.org), and annual awards and grants.

In short, Karen is a Heroine who is intensely loyal not just to curing cancer, but to her constituents.

I make a difference only to the degree that our member-doctors make a difference. My job is a labor of love for the physicians, nurses, and survivors I represent, and they are so grateful for my work. I can honestly tell you that in sixteen years I don't think I have ever been yelled at or spoken to in a derogatory tone. I am their colleague, not their servant, and not all business professionals feel that way about doctors they work with. Not to sound corny, but truly not a day has passed that one of our foundation members has not inspired me in some way.

The inspiration comes from knowing what each of them has to accomplish, and that every day they have to tell a woman and her family that she has cancer and may die from it. I have seen the strain on the doctors' faces and heard it in their voices when a patient is not doing well, yet the doctors continue to speak to me and stress the importance of the foundation, and that if our work saves the life of even one woman, then everything we do is worth the effort.

Karen became involved in gynecologic cancer efforts only after she started working. Coincidentally, she also had an early brush with the disease. Recalls Karen, "My parents tended to shelter me from anything bad, and when my mother had surgery for ovarian cancer, my parents told me she was just having a hysterectomy. I don't think I realized how seriously sick she was until I started this job."

She landed the job after studying public relations in college and, in 1988, after graduation, joining a company that specialized in managing not-for-profit associations. Karen was assigned to work with the Society of Gynecologic Oncologists, which three years later formed the Gynecologic Cancer Foundation, which she runs today.

Over the years, Karen has had to alter her work situation to fit her changing lifestyle. Married and with a seven-year-old son, Karen goes into the office three days a week and works from home the other two days, an arrangement she's had for three years. While such flexibility is important to Karen's job satisfaction, she again cites the people she works with—the doctors—as even more crucial to why she has stayed at the foundation for so many years.

When I first started this job and had no experience, the heads of major cancer centers from across the country always took the time to take my calls. They were extremely gracious and patient in explaining their jobs and their goals. This is still true today. Our members are wonderfully kind and compassionate not just to their patients, but to the people who run their professional foundation. I hear over and over again from physicians that their goal is to make their own jobs obsolete—nothing would make them happier than to eradicate cancer.

I am very lucky. How many people are thanked several times a day for things that, in the bigger scheme of things, are so very minor?

In 2001, *Worth* magazine named the Gynecologic Cancer Foundation one of the 100 best charities in the country. Such praise is validating, but the biggest proof of Karen's success will come when her job disappears—along with the deadly disease.

The boss never lets her get bored.

Jill McCurdy, forty-eight, was not always ambitious, and it took a small company, Koss Stereophones, to incite her desire to excel. It's no coincidence that Jill's been at Koss since 1984.

Not particularly motivated during her school years, Jill always adequately performed whatever was expected of her. At her second post-college job at a large financial company in Milwaukee, Wisconsin, Jill would dutifully arrive at the office at 8:30 A.M. and inevitably finish assignments by noon. When she told her manager, he replied, "Shhh, don't tell anyone else or they'll think we don't need you." Content to take it easy, Jill stayed at the job. But after three years, her days lacked purpose. "I wanted to be part of something, not just show up at work to do a job."

Jill scanned the classified ads for options and interviewed for a marketing position at headphone manufacturer Koss, also in Milwaukee.

Koss's entrepreneurial environment shocked Jill's sleepy system. "At first I thought this place was a zoo. People were always hectic and running around, and I figured I'd work there for a year or so, get some good experience, and then get the heck out." But Jill was quickly captivated by the Koss family's creative and open management style, and her previously dormant ambition woke up. Koss's CEO encouraged Jill to share her ideas directly with him, which "flabbergasted" Jill after having worked for a company whose executives were "locked away on the upper floors."

I distinctly recall one day in my thirties standing in a vice president's office, talking about a new product we were launching. The whole sales staff was there, and the vice president turned to me and said, "Well, what do you think we should do about this package?" It was the first time in my life that I felt like the expert on something! And, they were ready to act on my decision. It was an amazing feeling.

Management's high expectations were contagious, and Jill adopted them herself. The trend continued over the years. The Koss family set the bar high, and Jill rose to meet it. Promotions followed. When Jill was named to her current post as vice president of product development, the chief executive charged her department to come up with a new headphone product *every week*. How many variations of headphones could there possibly be? The mandate forced Jill to push herself and her team rather than balk.

"I don't think there has been a week when we haven't thought of at least five new ideas," Jill says, holding up Koss's latest innovation: a hot-pink earpiece adorned with small rhinestone studs. "Headphones used to have limited use, but now they are integral to how we live. There's a headphone jack in virtually everything: DVDs, Walkmans, cellphones, cars. They've also become more of a fashion statement than a component, like sunglasses," says Jill, a sharp-dressed woman in head-to-toe black.

Although Jill respects the product, it's not the primary reason she's stayed at Koss for twenty years, and it's not why she loves her work. "My boss never lets me get bored," she says. "Whenever I get too comfortable with my job, he changes it." Today, she earns a six-figure salary and is one of the top twelve people at the $40 million company. She's also more ambitious than ever. "I'm happiest when things are moving really fast and I'm delivering extraordinary results."

Jill's experience is a lesson for employers: Want to keep women and keep them happy? Keep them challenged and growing.

Other than working for the same employer for more than fifteen years, the Loyalists have forged their own distinctive paths. Engineer Jeanne was one of the first mothers at GE to go part-time, which strengthened not only her own career but the careers of countless women who followed in her wake. Jeanne found a way to balance her career and her family long before pundits decided they needed to talk about it. Science writer Suzanne asked to work at home, and a once-intractable work environment bent to accommodate the talented employee. Kay Marie has done the same job at Celestial Seasonings for twenty-eight years because the complex process of buying botanicals keeps her mind active, and the people she conducts business with take her mission personally. In Chicago, Margaret pumps new life into academia by indulging an entrepreneurial nature, and not-for-profit foundation president Karen not only takes pride in helping cure cancer but remains motivated by appreciative colleagues. Finally, in Milwaukee, Jill's twenty years at a small manufacturer demonstrate that ambition can blossom in the most unlikely of places.

Ironically, some of the best advice for how to build a long-term career at a single organization came from a woman who is not a member of The Happy 100 because she left her company after twenty-one years—and five months after I first interviewed her. She was not unhappy but was presented with an opportunity at another organization that she says she simply could not turn down. Still, the Loyalists chapter closes with her own advice about how she found what she wanted from a multibillion-dollar corporation over the course of two decades:

First, know what you want and have a plan. Do you desire an advanced degree? A certain salary, or to learn a broad set of skills? Clearly articulating goals allows you to grow and develop within the same company. Your plan can change, indeed it should every couple of years, but without even a basic map to follow, you will wander aimlessly, never sure of what you've accomplished.

Second, once you know what you want, ask for it. If you're not proactive on behalf of yourself, nobody else will be. So request a raise or a promotion. Ask your company to help pay for your education, or to transfer you to another position. Approach colleagues for advice and guidance. If you don't ask, you definitely won't get. Coworkers may be jealous when you receive what you want, but they're just angry that they didn't ask for themselves.

Third, seek out variety. Working on different products and teams keeps you motivated and challenged, and it builds your skills. Which leads to the fourth lesson: Always take jobs that carry risk, jobs that push you, because they force you to grow, and a diverse skill set gives you more choices down the road.

—Former Research and Development Director

Staying at one company is not the equivalent of staying put or slowing down. Your next job, and a happier one at that, may be under the very same roof where you're now working.

Chapter Ten

The After-Achievers

Bank managing director, pro-volleyball coach,
magazine editor, writer and teacher,
and greeting card designer

Once workers retire or leave a company, they also leave the collective consciousness of those who knew them professionally, often never to be heard of again. Then there are chief executives who disappear from the headlines once they leave the public eye. Think back to colleagues you worked with or for five, ten, or fifteen years ago. Do you know what they're up to today? While television specials like VH1's voyeuristic *Where Are They Now?* seek out former celebrities after they have shed star status, what happens to stars of business, professionals who were well known in their respective industry spheres? If they continue to work, are they as fulfilled without the same level of fame, power, or attention that once tinctured their career?

In other words, what does job happiness look like after a woman has reached the pinnacle of her career?

Women who love their jobs in their post-peak incarnations are dubbed After-Achievers. The title does not mean these women are past their prime, or even that they have yet to do their best work, but rather that they have just left the job that defined them—at least in others' eyes—for years. Their stories of professional reinvention prove that power, prestige, and pay are not the main reasons even the most ambitious women love their jobs. Once those Ps fade, the three Ps—process, purpose, and people—prove to be the most lasting motivators.

Heaven where she least expected it

Since 1984, millions of viewers have watched Jan Hopkins report business news on CNN. I first met Jan when she was anchoring and reporting for CNN's nightly news show *Lou Dobbs Tonight*, and I spent a day following her around CNN's bustling, cluttered New York newsroom as she prepared stories and interviewed sources. At fifty-six, Jan was still in her element as a journalist. So a few months later, when she quit CNN to take a lower-profile job as a managing director at Citigroup Private Bank, I wondered if the woman who spent a career in front of the camera would be happy behind the scenes in corporate America.

Several months into her new job, Jan reported back to me that she did indeed love it, and the reasons why are analogous to why she had loved journalism, and a great case study in how the content of a job—what others think it's ostensibly about (in this case, journalism)—is often merely incidental when compared to its core attributes. What's more, Jan's calculated transition tactics offer lessons for anyone contemplating a career move.

Serious, intelligent, and informed, Jan had been a business reporter since the mid-1970s, holding early reporting and editing positions at ABC and CBS. "My whole reason for getting into the business was to be where things were happening," says Jan, who also loved to indulge her curiosity. The freedom to dive into complex issues—the ups and downs of the economy, the Internet boom and bust, the proliferation of corporate scandals—was a primary reason she found joy in journalism for so many years. But by 2002, the job had changed. Jan did fewer and fewer in-depth, personal interviews, and the public's appetite for business news had waned. With the end of her contract looming, Jan entertained notions that another career might be in her future, but she had no idea what it looked like. "I paid attention to the emotions that were speaking to me," says Jan, who attacked her job search with the same diligence with which she reported stories.

First, Jan consulted an expert. As a gift, a friend had given Jan an executive career coach who, over the course of a year, helped Jan "deconstruct" her skills and interests through discussions and personality tests. "The coach was great. She gave me concrete plans, deadlines, and homework," all of which made it easier for Jan to integrate the career investigation into her already hectic schedule of daily deadlines.

Second, Jan worked her sources. Not only did she consult her book group members, but she put together a formal support network of bright, insightful friends whom she hosted for dinner one evening. At Jan's instruction, the group posed questions to Jan for an hour, which helped her articulate what she wanted from her next job. Between the career coach and friends' advice, it became clear to Jan that she wanted to transfer her interviewing and moderating skills to a nontelevision job that would be as intellectually stimulating as business reporting. She also took a vacation to get perspective on her future goals, and when she returned, she conducted interviews, asking executives in nonmedia industries what role someone with her skills might hold at their company. A discussion with Citigroup paid off, and the head of its private bank created a job description that piqued Jan's interest. As head of client communications, Jan would serve as an internal correspondent speaking to the private bank's highest net worth clients—wealthy individuals for whom Citigroup managed millions of dollars.

"They saw a role for me as *me*," says Jan. "I started having dreams that I had died and gone to heaven." Who knew, after almost thirty years in broadcasting, that heaven would be a bank.

CNN was shocked but supportive when Jan announced she was leaving not for another news organization but for another career altogether. And although the purpose of her job has changed—she is now an advocate on behalf of one company and its customers as opposed to an independent watchdog on behalf of the general public—Jan's daily activities, her processes, are quite similar to those she practiced while at CNN. At Citigroup, Jan still interviews executives about timely economic, political, and financial issues. One difference, however, between reporting for Citigroup as opposed to CNN is that, prior to each interview with an executive, Jan gives them her questions to review. "That is the corporate way of doing things," she concedes.

But on the whole, intellectual rigor is alive and well in Jan's job. Once a month she helps produce and also stars in an eight-minute mini-newscast sent on DVDs to Citigroup's private banking clients. The broadcasts let clients hear from the bank's top minds, who offer insight into the economy and investment strategies. Jan may film a meeting between an investment strategist and an economist, report on a complex investment idea, or interview the bank's chief executive. She also travels to cities like San Francisco, London, and Hong Kong, moderating panels with economists and journalists. Jan says it's fascinating to be part of in-depth discussions of how world events impact people and their money, and to learn about the banking business "from the inside."

The conversations I have in this job are very different from most of the ones I had in journalism. For example, I recently attended a meeting between a Citigroup banker and her clients. I had no agenda except to get to know both of them by asking questions. I was amazed at how willing they were to talk about personal things. Journalists interview people to get answers to questions, but what you hear is what they want the world to know. This was much more intimate, more of a gift. It was very satisfying to me.

Jan's high-profile CNN career may be over, but when she watches CNN on television she doesn't catch herself pining for the national attention. "I just have a different audience now," she says. Different, yes, and much smaller. Compared to CNN's millions of viewers, Citigroup's "distribution is a bit less than I'm used to," says Jan with a laugh. But it's likely that Jan's new audience, the bank's wealthy clientele, is even more invested in what she has to report. After all, it's their money that Jan's employer is managing, not just their news.

Her evolving game plan

Recall the Lovers, women of The Happy 100 who translated childhood passions into adult careers. Most of their livelihoods can continue forever, but what of athletes who are dependent not just on brains, but on their bodies? What happens when muscles give out and age settles in and a professional athlete is physically incapable of playing her sport at the same level, and thus continuing her livelihood? Or, perhaps even trickier, what's an amateur athlete to do when the sport she loved so much—and even excelled at—throughout high school and college has few or no practical outlets after graduation?

As athlete Cartrecia DiMaggio has discovered over the past forty years, all is not lost; there are many ways to win when sport is your passion, and in a sense Chi (as she's known to friends) is an After-Achiever many times over, having consistently reinvented the role volleyball plays in her life.

As one of the first and best female volleyball players in the United States, Chi is a Lover of sport who grew up in New Orleans across the street from a playground. "In the summer, from the moment I woke up, I played every sport I could," says Chi, now forty-nine. "I was never the fastest person, I never jumped the highest, but what God gave me was an eye to read the body and the mind." Whatever the sport, Chi always hit her target and seemed to predict her opponents' next move. Because Chi is also the second cousin of baseball legend Joe DiMaggio, everyone pushed her to pursue softball. But Chi most excelled at a sport no one knew much about: volleyball. At age ten, Chi could serve a mean overhand, sending the ball thirty feet above the net. In grammar school she was named most valuable player, and in junior high, best female athlete. She played volleyball in eighth grade and went on to play at Tulane University while studying engineering. "My studies helped my sport," says Chi. "Engineering taught me to take very large projects and break them down into steps, and not to panic." More than power, the five-foot, nine-inch Chi had finesse and could always be counted on to "put the ball away."

But unlike sports such as tennis, volleyball did not have immediate professional potential. So Chi compromised, and, while living in Florida after college and working as an engineer at AT&T by day, she played beach volleyball after hours. The sport gained popularity, and in 1982 Chi joined the country's newly hatched pro-volleyball tour and for ten years traveled around the U.S. and abroad competing in beach volleyball tournaments for a "purse" of several thousand dollars. At her best, Chi ranked fourth on the pro-tour.

In 1986, after her divorce, Chi moved to New York City. The New

York area was a melting pot of international volleyball talent, and Chi played under top Russian, Japanese, Bulgarian, and Haitian coaches. Yet despite its rising popularity, volleyball still could not support Chi full-time. Rather than abandon it, Chi quit her engineering career and, instead, took on volleyball-related jobs full-time. She began coaching and refereeing high school games, which paid surprisingly well. But by 1991, cross-country travel grew tiring, so Chi left the pro-tour and joined a local, Northeastern league with weekend tournaments only a few hours' drive from her home. Meanwhile, Chi suffered a knee injury in 1996, but her Monday-through-Friday coaching career continued to grow, and by 1998, Chi was the beloved volleyball coach at the City University of New York. There, she recruited and coached players for both the men's and women's teams. One of the male players Chi recruited and coached was quickly named outstanding offensive player of the Northeastern Volleyball Conference—one of Chi's most important coaching achievements.

But in 2000, Chi was served with her toughest challenge yet: The knee injury caught up with her and officially ended her own volleyball-playing career. Says Chi, "Like most athletes, I succumbed to an injury that finally brought me down." Down, perhaps, but not out. Today, Chi lives in New Orleans to be close to her aging father, and her volleyball expertise takes many forms. She is a private volleyball coach, a college referee for the Southern Women's Athletic Conference, a volleyball pro at the Coconut Beach Sand Volleyball Complex, and a traveling instructor who gives volleyball clinics to teens across the country. All roles bring her absolute joy.

I had my glory. I had my moment. When you play sports, it's all about you—the diet, the exercise, the schedule—but when you start coaching, it can't be about you anymore. Coaching is like being a mother and a teacher and a confidant and a leader. I am very demanding and I push players to their limits, but I give players skills to help them break bad habits. When they get to a point that they understand the weapons they must bring into battle, I watch them bloom. I let them make their own mistakes because no one learns from doing things correctly.

A lot of my passion for playing volleyball has shifted into giving that passion to others, mostly juniors. I help remove roadblocks to their game, and I'm rewarded when players really understand what I taught them, when I see the light come on in their eyes showing they understand a concept and can execute a skill and can move to the next level. I also feel privileged to teach self-empowerment to female athletes, and I teach them both physical and mental skills that lead to success in sports and in life. Coaching is completely unselfish because it is all about the players; a coach does not focus on herself. I never want to be known as the best coach in history, but in developing and empowering players.

Chi, who has no children of her own, sounds very much like a parent when talking about her players. In lieu of having her own children, she nurtures her players, a purpose that resonates deeply with this former top athlete. Says Chi, "It's powerful to let others have their moment in the spotlight."

She is the perennial pussycat.

By espousing girl power at the office and sexual prowess in the bedroom, Helen Gurley Brown helped spark the sexual revolution of the 1960s. As the author of *Sex and the Single Girl* and founding editor of *Cosmopolitan* magazine, the brazen, outspoken Helen made feminism about self-confidence and careers, as well as fashion, femininity, sex, and men. Although she stepped down as *Cosmo*'s editor in the mid-1990s, the publication remains the biggest-selling women's magazine in the world.

Helen Gurley Brown began working at age eighteen, after her father died in a tragic elevator accident and she had to help support her mother and her sister, who had polio. Working as a secretary for an advertising firm, Helen wrote "entertaining letters" that were noticed and rewarded with a promotion to copywriter. In 1962, with her husband's encouragement, Helen penned the bestseller *Sex and the Single Girl,* and in 1965, the Hearst publishing company let Helen apply her girl-power philosophy to its lagging magazine, *Cosmopolitan,* by naming her editor in chief. "I didn't get to *Cosmo* until age forty-three. Before that it took me a long time to find the work I should be doing, and I spent a lot of years scrambling around," Helen told me. As *Cosmopolitan*'s subscriber base climbed into the millions, Helen became a media darling, appearing regularly on *Good Morning America* and the *Tonight* show, candidly talking about women and sexuality. She wrote several more best-selling books and in 1996 was inducted into the American Society of Magazine Editors' Hall of Fame.

So where is Helen Gurley Brown today? Financially, she does not need to work, and so she could easily have curled up into retirement and basked in her many accomplishments. But even at eighty-two, the self-described workaholic plies her trade, as both editor and icon. Although she is no longer editor in chief of *Cosmopolitan*'s flagship publication in the U.S., Helen works as editor in chief of *Cosmopolitan*'s fifty-two international editions. She shows up at her Midtown Manhattan office to critique the latest issues of *Cosmo* from Italy, France, Argentina, Russia, wherever. She even travels to other countries to help launch new editions. By April 2004, she'd already been to Bulgaria and Serbia, as well as Russia to celebrate the magazine's tenth anniversary in that country. As an icon, Helen spends time promoting her most recent book, *Dear Pussycat,* a compilation of her compulsive correspondence over the years, and she consistently appears at business and social functions in her trademark attire: a bright-red or pink Gucci suit, with black fishnet stockings and hot red lipstick. Rather than reliving the past, Helen works in the present.

The good things in life that have come to me have almost all been from working, and I get too much out of it to give it up. It brings you self-respect, and it makes other people respect you. My work always had a purpose, which is why it interests me still.

There is a specific format that works for Cosmopolitan: *It's a magazine to help young women feel better about themselves, solve their problems, reach their goals, and have a more satisfying life. If the international editions are not doing this, they must be made to do so. We have a very specific mission, and every single month, recognizing cultural differences, I pretty much keep the magazines on track as much as I can.*

Every day, Cosmopolitan *magazines from other countries cross my desk and I use my little yellow Post-it notes to go through and comment on the editorials and photos. I can't read many of the languages, like Japanese or*

Portuguese, but I can tell a lot from the photos, the layouts, and I pick up a few words. I can tell if an article is about sex or relationships, based on the photograph. If an issue has three major profiles of celebrities, I explain for the thousandth time to editors that Cosmopolitan *is not* People *magazine or the* Enquirer; *we do not need movie-star profiles. The pages should show readers what fashions they should have in their lives, and if the fashions are not easily discernible or if they are in the shadows, I make a note: "What's the point of having fashion if readers can't see it?" I tell the international editors when I can't read white type against a pink background, if there aren't enough cover blurbs, or if there isn't an article about careers that there should be. So, really I am a high-priced nanny.*

Now, I am not a complete philanthropist. Helping women helps me, and when I encourage editors to put out a better magazine, one that helps women, it's pretty much a selfish motive. If they do their job, I get to keep mine. Specifically, the work I do these days is not wildly, wonderfully exciting, but I am needed. Someone needs me to do it, and I am still paid attention to and I feel, if not beloved, at least accepted and liked. The magazine is designed to create a better life for young women—and through the years I've been able to have a better life than the one I began with. These days I work for me, not to pay rent.

As the oldest Happy 100 member, Helen Gurley Brown is living proof women don't work only for money. Career satisfaction is indeed ageless.

In her own words

Laura Pedersen, 37
Writer and Teacher; Former Wall Street Trader
New York, New York

Laura made more than $1 million trading stocks by the time she was twenty-two, and, at one point, she was the youngest person to have a seat on the American Stock Exchange. So what's an intelligent woman who bores easily, looks like Barbie, and cracks jokes like Ellen De-Generes to do after she's made her first million? Answer: anything she wants. That's because, for Laura, wealth is about not status and accumulation, but freedom.

It's important to know that I grew up in a small town near Buffalo, New York, where we get an enormous amount of snow, and as an only child, I had to shovel a lot of it, which means I had a lot of time to think, and what I thought about was, "This ain't it, kid. You better get some income so you can start delegating." I was aware that my family lived paycheck to paycheck—my dad was a court reporter and my mom a nurse—and that we had no rich relatives who were going to drop a trust fund on me. At seven I had no idea what my capacity was to make money, but I needed to test myself and establish myself as an earner in the real world. So I was entrepreneurial: I walked dogs, I cared for houses, and I took care of gardens in the summer. I was also a camp counselor and had a paper route. My mom even taught me poker, and I gambled with my family a lot. I was always cooking up some scheme so I had money in my pocket, and by the time I was eleven I had enough income to pay Social Security taxes.

Around that time a broker friend of my mom's opened up a custodial account, and I traded stocks. I liked the idea of buying something that would go up in value without my having to work (or at least without shoveling snow). At age fifteen I started taking economics classes at the University of Buffalo.

High school was boring, and I used to skip it and go to the racetrack. I'd write my own excuses to get out of school, and eventually I started writing excuses in sonnets. I'd been raised Unitarian Universalist, and my parents did not impose any rules on me. I was in charge of and responsible for my own day, and my parents never mandated that I attend school, but after a year of falsifying notes, I got suspended. It all boiled down to boredom for me. At the University of Michigan I was so bored that I went through the Yellow Pages calling New York brokerage firms to try and get a job, but you had to be at least twenty-one years old to get hired. I called the Stock Exchange from my dorm room and asked how old you had to be to work there, and in December 1983, at eighteen, I packed my bags and went to New York, naive and silly, to work as a gofer on the floor of the

Exchange. Eventually I worked for some private companies as a clerk and a specialist. Meanwhile, I was living with my grandfather on Long Island and taking night classes at New York University. I'd wake up at 3:30 A.M., commute an hour and a half, work until 4:30 P.M., go to class until 10 P.M., and commute back home. (If I tried to do that today, I think my body would revolt.)

Working on Wall Street was like being in a war; a combination rock concert, football game, and farm-equipment auction all at once. I loved it. Everyone yelled and screamed and used hand signals. I could move numbers around in my brain quickly. I'm not talking about calculus, but adding and subtracting and doing decimals. By the time someone else whipped out a calculator to decide if they should sell an option, I had already sold it, bought it back again, and sold it to someone else. Everything moved so fast, which was just what I needed. I'm an action junkie. Still, I paid a price for my success, and I didn't have a date the whole time I worked and went to school. I didn't have time to see movies or read the newspaper. I missed a lot of current events.

The year I got an $80,000 bonus I bought myself a $200 bike and my mom a condo.

Eventually I relaxed because I had proven that I could make money with just a high school education. I felt I could be functional, and so I was done trading. It was no longer fun. I was screaming fractions all day, I had lost part of my hearing, I had polyps on my throat, and computers had increased the pace to a notch I did not enjoy. By the time I left the Exchange in 1989, I'd made about $1 million.

But the day I quit I was bored by that evening. I had read an article about the new Joan Rivers show, and so I went to the New York studios and presented myself as an intern. They asked what skills I had. I said I could add fractions but didn't tell them what I'd done before, just that I was a student. I could tell they were really busy, and I had learned from the Exchange that when people are busy, they just want someone to help. I offered to work for free. "Do you think you can handle the stress?" they asked me. I just laughed. After three weeks Joan's assistant quit and I took the job. I liked it and I learned a lot working for her, but mostly what I learned is that I did not want to work in entertainment. Meanwhile, I started writing a book called Play Money, telling about the crazy behavior *on the trading floor that I'd kept track of. I'd always loved stories, and I sold the book to a publisher. When it was published I left Joan's show to do a book tour, which got me on* Oprah *and* David Letterman. *Soon people started to ask me to lecture about the stock market.*

But writing was my new thing. For ten years I wrote a humorous financial column for The New York Times *and quit when I got bored and grew tired of working with editors. Eventually I started writing books about anything I wanted, and now I write books that I hope will be made into good movies; one,* Beginner's Luck, *is! I have very mainstream tastes, and I'm confident that if I enjoy a story, others will, too. I had always loved stories that are funny and show that human beings are essentially generous of spirit. I enjoy stories where you recognize a bit of yourself in characters, or when you discover a person you want to emulate in a positive way. I also love writing because I'm not forced to compete with anyone—I've done that enough in life, especially on Wall Street. Writing is me playing against myself, to my own standards, and at my own pace.*

I also volunteer several days a week at the Booker T. Washington Learning Center in East Harlem, teaching children to read. I used to work as a camp counselor, and I'm familiar and comfortable with a group of thirty kids. They're fun and spontaneous and full of love. Yes, my kids need extra help with schoolwork if they're going to compete with their rich neighbors six blocks away who are in better schools and have tutors, but my kids also need to have fun and be exposed to theater and ice skating and pool parties. I enjoy doing all that with them, too. Recently, we all went to see the musical Beauty and the Beast, *and it was the first time most of them—all lifelong New Yorkers—had even seen a Broadway show. Who knows, maybe one of the kids will now pursue a career in theater!*

Trading was thrilling and challenging for several years, but one day it got boring and that was that. I can't imagine ever becoming bored by kids or with words. I love them both.

Her party is hardly over.

Ella Strubel's office—its green and yellow pillows, its purple rug, the floral fabric chairs—is as colorful and charming as the greeting cards Ella designs. One card features a cadre of joyous dancing animals—a lion wearing a string of pearls, a mouse in a tuxedo—and plainly reads, "Let the party begin."

As for Ella's former advertising career, it began in the early 1970s and ended in 1997, and a wall of framed magazine and newspaper articles belie her high-profile, pre–greeting card life, which culminated in a very public life as executive vice president of corporate affairs for advertising agency Leo Burnett Company. "Just the other day I realized I hadn't received my annual Who's Who form from *Crain's Chicago Business*," jokes Ella, who has frequently appeared in the local business paper's list of top executives. Since her retirement, the spotlight has dimmed. But Ella, sixty-three, has reincarnated herself as a greeting card designer, a late-in-life transition that shocked her perhaps more than anyone else.

Wearing a black pinstriped Armani pantsuit set off by a heavy gold bracelet and short, spiky hair, Ella looks every bit the Determinator she is. Her confidence springs from a tough childhood that bred her independent streak: Ella's father died when she was young, and her mother was ill for many years. After studying journalism in college, she worked at a New York television production company and did on-air news segments that aired on five local CBS stations. "I was not very good, and in those days there was very little support for women. With no one around to tell me what to do better, I had the sense to know I should get out of on-air work if I wanted to stay in broadcasting." So Ella reinvented herself for the first time and joined the station's advertising and public relations department, eventually moving to Chicago and becoming the local CBS station's first female and youngest department head. Several years later, the chairman of Chicago-based Kraft tapped Ella to head the consumer product company's corporate affairs department.

Kraft was a killer job. The commute alone was an hour and a half each way, and it's not like I was passionate about cheese! I lived in a high-rise apartment building on Michigan Avenue, and every day I'd get up at 5:45 A.M. and go downstairs, sit on a marble bench outside my building, and wait for my ride to take me to the company's suburban offices. I'll never forget who sat on the bench with me, also waiting for a ride to her job: Oprah Winfrey, whose television show was just starting. There we sat,

*in the wee morning hours, two businesswomen so tired, we wouldn't even
talk to each other. [Laughs.]*

*For the next three years I spent my life on the sixth floor of the Kraft
building, surrounded by men. I became the public face of Kraft and
attended charitable and civic events on the CEO's behalf. Unfortunately,
Kraft was thrust into a food crisis after I joined the company and had to
recall ice-cream bars on the Fourth of July! Can you imagine? The
company would just spin from one crisis to another, and I quickly learned
that I did not enjoy crisis management.*

After three years Ella approached Kraft's chairman and conceded she
"just couldn't do it anymore." She left without another job lined up.
Kraft's chairman could not have been too upset, because he recommended her for a similar public relations position at Chicago-based ad
agency Leo Burnett. Ella took it, and there she stayed for ten years,
reaching her peak. "It was a love affair. Burnett was named the number-
one advertising agency and went through a golden period during which
the firm could do no wrong." Over the course of her tenure, Ella was the
public face for the agency. She was quoted regularly in the *Wall Street
Journal* and the *Chicago Tribune*. She also chaired the company's foundation and sat on several boards of local not-for-profit agencies. It was a
fun run.

"Still, you reach a point in your career when you're very good at what
you do, and I had finally reached that at Burnett. There just was no giant
challenge anymore." She officially retired in 1997 but was not long for a
life of leisure.

While she was chairing the board of a local hospital, one of Ella's fellow board members sprang a new career idea on her. Mike Keiser, cofounder and owner of Recycled Paper Greetings, turned to Ella one day
and said, "Why don't you start a greeting card company and go into partnership with me?" Ridiculous! Or was it?

*It was the funniest conversation I'd ever had. I did love greeting cards,
but I told Mike I had no experience. He replied that I would be very good
at it, that it was the sum total of everything I'd ever done: writing, editing,*

designing, packaging messages. I thought about it and realized that I'd always known women who had drawers full of greeting cards and who, like me, really loved cards. Even in down economic times, cards sell well.

So I started EllaQuent Designs and went into partnership with Mike as a contracted designer; his company tests and distributes the designs I come up with. I think women love color and charm, and my goal is to create a line of clever, colorful designs that speak with whimsy, eloquence, style, and joy. We're still struggling to achieve that 100 percent, but we're trying. One of our cards has been Recycled's top seller; all told we've had more than thirty different designs in more than 10,000 locations. I hire artists from all over the country who work as independent contractors. Sometimes they write the copy, sometimes I do, and sometimes I hire copywriters. I think I'm a better editor than writer, and I usually pick the best two copy options and send them to Recycled so the card can be tested in stores before it's mass produced. A good card can have a shelf life of ten years or more.

It's been a steep learning process, and I've probably learned more from cards that failed than from those that succeeded. And I've made some pretty big mistakes, like printing on the wrong paper stock, so the colors didn't come out well. But perhaps the biggest lesson I've learned is that there must be an exact match between a card's copy and its design—very much like corporate communications. Mike was right when he said this job is the sum total of everything I've done in advertising and public relations. A lot of my past jobs required I know how to appeal to target markets through design. But rarely have I actually produced a product, and now I especially love having the product in my hand. I walked into a drugstore the other day and saw a row of my cards in a big display, and I actually said "oooh" and "aahh" out loud! Everyone in the drugstore turned around and looked at me. [Laughs.]

A lot of women work all their life but don't have much to do when they reach my age. I think staying busy and active, keeping your mind engaged, is a very positive thing. I adore this business, and while I don't always enjoy the mistakes, it certainly keeps me on my toes.

Ella is a wonderful example of how to create a second career using trans-ferable skills. While it was not Ella who came up with the idea of a greeting card company—nor did she immediately recognize the similarities between packaging a sentiment and packaging a company—she remained open to the opportunity. How many times does someone hand you a company to start? The lesson here is this: Other people often see potential that we do not. And even if one volunteers such information, as Mike did for Ella, seek it out on your own. You just may find a second career you'll love as much as, or more than, the first.

There is life after being the life of the party. As After-Achievers prove, high-profile careers can be stepping-stones to more modest but just as fulfilling endeavors. Better yet, After-Achievers can transition without overhauling themselves. Indeed, none of the women in this chapter went back to school or had to start at the bottom of the corporate ladder (although, on a lark, Laura Pedersen volunteered as an intern on the set of a television show). That's because their new jobs tapped the very skills and expertise they used in their former professions; the job's purpose just shifted. Jan still reports and analyzes economic issues, albeit at a bank rather than at CNN. At eighty-two, editor Helen still tells writers and editors how to be true to *Cosmopolitan*'s mission, even though she no longer heads the franchise's signature U.S. publication. Chi's transition from volleyball player to coach, while not abrupt, took her out of the spotlight and onto the sidelines, where her knowledge and techniques are still valued. For millionaire Laura, life after investing on Wall Street is about investing time in children and her own writing. Finally, former public relations executive Ella is still crafting messages as a greeting card designer, although this time she does so in the name of emotion rather than corporate earnings.

Whether you are years from retirement or already pondering a major career shift, the After-Achievers' message is twofold: First, you don't have to reinvent yourself to reinvent your career. And second, working outside the spotlight can be just as fulfilling as when it shines down on you.

Chapter Eleven

The Hurdlers

Health care industry consultant, labor organizer,
janitorial company owner, corporate trainer, full-time
mother of four, flight attendant, hospital administrator,
community newspaper editor, and circuit court judge

Almost every woman has overcome obstacles in her working life, but this final group of Happy 100 women has faced hurdles so significant—the death of a spouse, depression, poverty—that surmounting them is reason enough to rejoice.

As a testament to their feats, I call them Hurdlers.

The women you are about to meet all love their jobs for reasons independent of their particular struggles, meaning they are not just Hurdlers but also Healers or Determinators, Counselors or Builders. But because their past pain is closely linked to their present peace of mind, the hurdle itself has become a defining element of their on-the-job happiness. For example, health care administrator Barbara Carlson had to overcome her husband's murder before she found life as a Builder. And for full-time mother Lara Mitchel, building a family and household was an overwhelming, depressive struggle before satisfaction set in. Determinators Pamela Washington and Maxine Aldridge White came back from bankruptcy and up from poverty, respectively. For former Enron secretary Debbie Perrotta, the demise of the Houston-based energy company—and with it her savings—ushered in a heroic line of work. As for Susan Murphy, when she lost the job of a lifetime at mid-life, she was forced to discover the Counselor within. Bad news seems to hunt down Joan Liman, while depression haunted Susan Holson for years.

In the aftermath of tragedy, each Hurdler bravely confronts darkness and eventually finds light. Life changes become work changes, and the pride these women feel in their newfound livelihoods is telling.

She chose to survive.

Barbara Carlson's husband never returned home one evening in April 1982. Jim had been out with a fellow detective from the Chicago police force, enjoying a "Polish sausage and a beer" while Barbara was home with their two-, five-, and six-year-olds. She fell asleep alone in bed that night, only to wake up alone and receive a phone call that changed her life.

Barbara's husband had been shot. He was dead.

"It was surreal," recalls the then-thirty-one-year-old. "I didn't know any widows." Barbara later learned that Jim and his friend were driving when they got into a drunken argument that turned physical. Instead of punching Jim, his colleague reached for a gun. Apparently Jim tried to get out of the car but was shot in the back five times. His colleague passed out in the backseat, according to Barbara. "It was tragic. They were just two young men who had both been stupid one night. Jim's was such a wasted life, and it certainly changed the course of my life."

Because her husband was off-duty at the time of his murder, Barbara and her three children were not eligible for on-duty death benefits and received only a minimal pension payment from the police department; it hardly made a dent when it came to helping the family of four survive on Barbara's nursing salary. The young mother, widow, and student—Barbara was in the midst of pursuing a master's degree—immediately faced several hurdles: She had to mourn her own loss, plan her family's financial future, and ensure her children were not emotionally scarred by their father's much-publicized death. The murder of one detective by another made headlines, and Jim was not always portrayed in the best light.

I had to get my mind straight fairly quickly. Thank God I had a health care background, because my kids asked a lot of questions and I was deliberate in my answers so they would not feel like victims. I focused on their mental health so they would not develop future problems. It took a while for me to gather my strength, and there were times I thought we would all be better off if we just ended it, if we were dead. I'm shocked now the thought even entered my mind, but choosing life or death became a very real decision for me. A year after Jim died, I was still not feeling any better and I went on a retreat called Joyful Again for divorced women and widows. Everyone was much older than me, and at an end-of-the-weekend Mass, as everyone said their prayers about "going forward," I recall thinking I could either choose to live like a survivor or die like a victim. It boiled down to choosing to live and having a new attitude. Practically, it came down to managing my time incrementally, and I put together a four-year, get-out-of-this-mess plan: Get the two-year-old to age six, remodel the house so I could sell it, relocate to the suburbs, finish my master's.

I did it. It was not fun, but I had to get on with my life.

Surviving was about not just attitude, but action. After Barbara decided in theory to move forward with her life, she articulated the very real steps she needed to take. Priority number one: finish graduate school. Nursing hours were much too unpredictable for a single mother, and an advanced degree in health care administration would not only give her more earning power but allow her to find a nine-to-five hospital management position that kept weekends and evenings free for family. Still, it was not an easy career transition, as Barbara was accustomed to the energy and physical work of critical care. It took some adjusting to sit at a desk all day.

Barbara's new line of work was, essentially, about restructuring how hospitals operate. Her first job was in the 1980s, when the hospital where she worked as a nurse changed owners and the new CEO put Barbara in charge of building a new outpatient wing.

In the years that followed, Barbara took on other projects, and today she plays a niche role in health care and hospital services modernization efforts, a fairly lucrative and in-demand specialty. Community hospitals hire Barbara as an on-staff consultant to assess, develop, and orchestrate multimillion-dollar, multiyear changes to their patient services. Barbara analyzes what's wrong or broken with the existing system, recommends ways to overhaul it, and manages the horde of consultants, hospital staff, boards of directors, community members, and vendors who execute her plan. Among her responsibilities, Barbara helps secure financing, get mandatory government approvals, construct new buildings, and change operational systems as needed. It's no wonder her projects take up to half a dozen years to complete. Most recently, Barbara oversaw a $300 million restructuring project for Central DuPage Health, which provides hospital services, a nursing home, independent living facilities, and primary care physicians.

It is quite a feat to remake a hospital from concept to implementation, and I compare my job to rafting: Everyone in the raft knows the destination, and the most important part of my job is to keep them focused on the goal despite distractions. Some people will fall out of the boat and never make it.

I am able to build teams of health disciplines all with the common goal of providing safe, effective, timely, patient-centered, and equitable care. I build prototypes from scratch, introducing new concepts in alternative health care delivery. Most of my work uses skills in building relationships, applying change management, conflict resolution, and stress and time management. I love my job because it allows me to be entrepreneurial, to create significant change that adds value to the community, and to hold myself and others accountable. I am able to integrate my personal and professional mission in life by putting people first for the good of all. I am also able to continue my first love, which is patient care.

Health care—and people—are very slow to change. For me, this job is often a study in human nature and behavior dynamics. There is nothing more satisfying than to work with a group to the point that you've actually made a contribution to the community and left a legacy.

Many months after Barbara and I first talked, she left Central DuPage Health after a new management team had taken over, as often happens on such projects. "I took the severance pay and am in the process of looking for my next project that supports what I believe is good patient care," she told me. "I'll absolutely stay in health care, but finding an organization that puts patients first is really important to me." The next project will, she says, require the same processes and philosophy that have defined Barbara's work for the past twenty years. "Meanwhile, my time off from work has afforded me wonderful opportunities to give back while experiencing new beginnings with new perspectives," says Barbara. Twenty-two years after losing Jim, she is volunteering as an advisory board member at Joyful Again, helping young widows reclaim their lives. She is also spending time with her first grandchild, named James, after the grandfather he'll never meet.

Barbara's career just may be her husband's most important legacy, as his tragic death led to her current line of work. And while Barbara is a Hurdler as a result of her extenuating circumstances, she is also, at present, a Builder and a Healer when it comes to why she loves what she does.

After Jim's death, Barbara rebuilt her own life in much the same way she rebuilds hospitals today: Analyze what needs to be fixed, identify short-term and long-term goals, and focus on incremental reconstruction. And, of course, adopt a positive attitude. Happiness can surface after tragedy, one step, one year, one challenge at a time.

She would not be a victim.

When energy company Enron infamously collapsed in 2001, Debbie Perrotta was a $50,000-a-year administrative assistant at Enron's Houston headquarters. She lost not only her job during Enron's demise, but $40,000 in retirement savings as well. Debbie was not alone: Enron's fall left thousands of workers jobless, and some 24,000 workers lost a total of $1 billion in retirement savings. The day thousands of employees were unceremoniously fired, Debbie was the primary breadwinner in her household because her husband had recently lost his job.

For Debbie—who had always worked hard and blindly trusted the system—Enron's fall was a wake-up call that forced her to adopt a new attitude and seek a new career.

An administrative assistant for twenty-five years, Debbie came to

Enron as a temp when she and her husband moved to Houston in 1997. Eventually hired full-time, she worked as an assistant to half a dozen engineering executives for Enron International and, later, for Enron India. She sorted mail, answered phones, arranged travel, coordinated the executives' massive expense reports, and even handled her bosses' personal affairs. Assistants at Enron were paid well and often rewarded with luncheons, days off, and spa visits. But it was hardly a cushy job. "Whatever rewards I got, I worked for," says Debbie, who arrived at the office every day at 8 A.M., left late, never left home without a cell phone or pager, and took calls from her bosses late at night and on weekends. Debbie's diligence was rewarded with "excellent" reviews. "Go to Debbie; she'll get it done," was a refrain she heard often. "I liked the responsibility and took it very seriously." And her pace never abated, even as Enron's stock tumbled and rumors of trouble percolated. Reassured her division was safe, Debbie was completely unprepared for what hit on Monday, December 3, 2001.

It was midmorning, and I was doing expense reports when the senior vice president of the division called everyone—assistants and executives— into a conference room at 11 o'clock. I took the elevator to the floor where the meeting was, and, no lie, as soon as we got off the elevator we could hardly walk, there were so many people. I felt like we were a herd of cattle. For about twenty minutes we waited, and finally a lawyer and someone else just told us we were all being laid off. They said nothing about money, severance, or benefits, just that we'd be paid up to Wednesday. They were not prepared to answer any questions. I was in shock and went back to my desk and just packed up my personal items.

To add insult to injury, Enron let throngs of employees loose at midday, when the local bus system was not running regularly. For hours, says Debbie, the bus stop outside Enron overflowed with angry, shocked workers with no way to get home.

As for Debbie, she was wiped out emotionally and financially. She had no more health insurance to pay for prescription medication, and about half her 401(k) was invested in Enron's sinking stock, which at the time of her layoff was worthless. She was shocked at first; her ire peaked when she got wind of the multimillion-dollar bonuses, loans, options packages, and cash paid to Enron senior executives. "I was so angry. I could just not believe that a corporation of this magnitude could do this to people and get away with it," says Debbie. In a fit of desperation to do something, she taped signs that declared WE GOT RAPED BY ENRON to the windows of her white Ford Expedition and parked it near Enron's headquarters. Debbie's daughter also called the media and told them about her mother's plight, and soon journalists were calling Debbie to hear her story.

Wary of the lawyers flocking to Houston to corral angry Enron employees into lawsuits, Debbie eventually became motivated toward activism by an unexpected source.

I am a Republican and was never a particular fan of Jesse Jackson. But when I heard he was coming to Houston and wanted to meet with Enron employees, I was impressed. Everyone else wanted to hook us up with lawyers, but he seemed to want to help us. After all, I was after justice. What right did Enron executives have to walk away with millions of dollars?

So I dragged a friend to the meeting with Jesse, and we were two of only ten or twelve employees who showed up! It didn't faze Jesse, who gathered us around a table and said the only way we'd get attention was to focus on the people who were hurt. Right now, he said, everyone is focusing on the executives. Jesse told us we had to go to Washington by bus and stop in every state capital on the way and make it known that we were coming. I figured I would go and see what would transpire. Understand that I was not a public speaker. I never got up and talked in front of people. But something had to be done. Some people said, "Be careful, Jesse will use you." But my statement was, "Fine. I'm going to use him." Who was it going to hurt? I'd already lost everything.

Three busloads of former Enron workers trekked to Washington, D.C., and Jesse Jackson pushed Debbie, a Caucasian, into the media spotlight so the public would understand that the issue at hand was not about race, but employee injustice. Once they reached Capitol Hill, Debbie and others met with several senators, including Edward Kennedy and

Joseph Lieberman, and she even attended President George W. Bush's State of the Union Address.

To her dismay, Bush refused to meet with Enron employees. Debbie's fire was lit, and in the months that followed she became a public spokesperson for Enron's displaced workers. She testified twice before Congress and traveled around the country telling her story as part of a group funded by the AFL-CIO, a national federation of unions. Debbie's goal: Get average workers more involved in their own fate.

I found that the majority of workers in this country were a lot like me: They did not get involved, and they trusted elected officials to do the best for them, and they trusted their companies. I tried to tell them I was one of them and never thought that this could happen to me. We all had to take care of ourselves because no one else was going to do so. But most people were afraid to speak out or question their companies for fear they'd lose their jobs.

All the while, Debbie looked for a new job back home in Houston— along with thousands of other laid-off Enron workers. Finally, someone from the AFL-CIO in Houston recommended Debbie for a job as a field organizer for the Texas Federation of Teachers, which recruited Texas teachers for its union and, in general, fought for teachers' rights through lobbying and education. The job was the most junior position at the union, and the pay was less than Debbie had made at Enron, but she still took it. "After Enron, I just couldn't go back to the corporate world. I had to do something to fight for people who were afraid to fight for themselves, and Texas is one of the worst states for teachers. They have very few rights and are often not eligible to receive Social Security."

As the result of Enron's fall, Debbie caught the activist bug and became a Heroine. Now fifty-five, she loves her work and says that, had she the money, she would happily travel around the world talking about corporate corruption. While she makes only $44,000 at the Texas teachers' union, Debbie is essentially living out her core desire to help the helpless in her small corner of the world. Every day she visits schools and talks to teachers about their individual grievances regarding overbearing administrators, students, and legislative issues.

"There's a lot I have to learn, but right now my belief in fighting for teachers is the most important thing. I don't know if I will ever make a difference, but at least I know one thing: I tried."

In her own words

Pamela Washington, 45
Founder and President, A-1 Janitorial Services
Las Vegas, Nevada

Pam owns a janitorial services company that cleans commercial spaces. Her most unique assignment is to clean the lion habitat attraction located in the MGM Grand Casino in Las Vegas. Every night, when the 400-pound felines are taken to an alternate facility, Pam's janitors mop and scrub the glass-enclosed cage. A-1's own three-room office space, much smaller than the lion cage, is located at the end of a small strip mall. In addition to being a Hurdler, Pam is an undeniable Determinator.

I've had every job in America except waitress. I've never been a waitress, although I did work in a McDonald's. I've been a file clerk, a stockbroker, a secretary, a bank teller, a caterer, an office manager, a maid, a day care worker. I've never, however, been a mother. In fact, one of the reasons my husband and I split was because he wanted a wife who worked but didn't have a "career." That was not me. I was motivated by money and freedom.

After my husband and I broke up I kept hearing about all the money you could make in financial services, so I entered a company's training program and became a stockbroker in Beverly Hills. I was a good salesperson, always motivated by contests that required measurable results. I'm African-American, and there were not a lot of black women stockbrokers in Beverly Hills. It was neat, and I felt a bit like a pioneer, although sometimes it bugged me. I did a lot of work on the phone, and when I would finally meet clients in person, I could always tell they were shocked when they saw me. They'd say, "You're so much younger and prettier than I imagined," but I knew what they really meant: I was so much blacker than they imagined. [Laughs.]

Slowly, I began to feel life as a stockbroker was slimy, dishonest work. I was really a glorified salesperson who got paid only if I made a transaction, and pay was slanted toward certain investments, which meant there was inherent conflict of interest. I began to be swayed by my own need to make money, and I remember thinking, One day I'm going to screw some little old lady out of her retirement so I get a commission. It was dishonest. There were other things I disliked, like getting all dressed up for work, wasting time putting on makeup and curling my hair and commuting downtown.

So I quit. I had about $10,000 in the bank, and no plan.

I always loved to cook, and someone suggested I do that for a living. I began to cater picnics and luncheons out of my house, and eventually I rented some commercial space and threw larger parties. I did it for three years and lost my shirt; I ended up filing for bankruptcy. I did so many things wrong. First, I didn't do much research, and I came up with the most ignorant name: The Imperial Group. I now know you should name your company something that people understand, and for a services company it's good to have a name that starts with a letter at the beginning of the alphabet, for when people flip through the Yellow Pages. I also did not manage money well and made the mistake of assuming that, just because banks were willing to lend me money, I should take it. I took out too many loans, and my overhead was too high. Then came the L.A. riots and my commercial kitchen was vandalized. I think I filed bankruptcy in 1991, and it stayed on my record for ten years, which was horrible. I'd also borrowed money from people and was unable to pay them back. I felt like such a failure.

Beat down and depressed—this was a very bad period of time for me.

A friend of mine from high school was a physician who moved to Las Vegas and knew I had some business sense—certainly more than most doctors—and she hired me to do some headhunting for her practice. We agreed to a temporary arrangement, and so I just left California, figuring that if Vegas didn't work out, I'd keep going east trying to find a place to settle down—hopefully before I hit the Atlantic Ocean. I moved, but my friend and I had a big falling-out and I had to hire a lawyer to get her to pay me. Meanwhile I took a job at a payroll processing service while I got settled in Vegas. Once again I was at loose ends, but this time in this strange, transient city.

I bought a little paperback book about the best home-based businesses for the 1990s, knowing I did not want anything with a lot of overhead and capital. Tired of scrambling for money every month, I also wanted steady income. The book listed several types of cleaning businesses, from windows to air ducts, and it appealed to me. By doing the work myself I could make $20,000 to $30,000 profit. I'd made $50,000 as a stock-broker, and here in Vegas the cost of living was even less. This time I did some research before I started the business: Most important, I got myself hired by another cleaning service to get a look at their operations.

I spent less than $1,000 on my supplies—a mop, a bucket, a vacuum, a broom, a dustpan, some Windex, and towels—put an ad in the classifieds, and hired a church group to hang my flyers around town. I took any job I could get and did it all myself. I could get houses done pretty quickly and was always honest with people if I messed up. One time I scratched up a lady's bathtub by scrubbing it with an SOS pad. I saw some disgusting apartments but also worked on beautiful houses in gated communities. I did beauty shops (you can never get all the hair off the floor) and even cleaned one guy's motor home—I just plugged a hose into a spigot and sprayed! I learned everything by trial and error. As I got more work than I could handle, I hired people to work for me. One gal knew which chemicals to use on different surfaces, and tricks like how to get hair spray off a mirror. She taught me a lot.

I liked doing windows but hated kitchens. I liked tile but not carpets. Overall I liked the immediate gratification of cleaning. You don't have to wait months to see the results of your efforts. I cleaned for five years, and the funny thing was, I made more money as a cleaning woman than as a stockbroker! And it was more ethical.

In the beginning I made the mistake of running the business out of my home but stopped after I had to fire a few people and they came by the house and threatened to beat me up. Let me tell you, finding good employees is still the hardest part of my job. I've been in this office space for about three and a half years, and I've been very careful with my money and not borrowed too much from the bank. I am also careful about my professional reputation, and I'll even risk losing money to make sure we get every job right the first time and clean up our mistakes.

I've also been lucky. In 2000, I met the director of purchasing for MGM Grand, who was motivated by diversity and hiring minorities and women. I asked if he needed a cleaning service and he said MGM had a special project: the lion habitat right in the middle of the casino. It just about scared me to death when I looked at it and saw the huge lions—this was not just vacuuming and taking out the trash!

In 2001 my company was named National Supplier of the Year by the National Minority Supplier and Development Council, and I was named a Woman of Distinction by the National Association of Women Business Owners and, in 2003, nominated as a Small Business of the Year by the Small Business Administration. In 2004, the Nevada Minority Business Council named A-1 the Minority Business Enterprise of the Year.

Last year I had $1.2 million in sales and sixty-seven employees, and I'm actually reining in growth because as A-1 grew, it got crazier and crazier to manage. Last year was a nightmare, and I didn't really have any fun. Now I cut my staff in half, got rid of some accounts that did not make us much money, and I'm not soliciting any new work, but I also don't turn anything down.

The money is about freedom to me. I have four cars, I have vacation property at a ski resort, a boat, and a snowmobile. I go into the office maybe three days a week and have had time to do things outside of work, like volunteer and get back into church. I really enjoy the flexibility, the casual dress, and the rush I get when I close a big sale. My company also has a very good local reputation, and that makes me feel proud. Plus, I hire a lot of immigrants, and feel I help them improve their lives by teaching them a skill.

I'm tickled about our ten-year anniversary. For me to have done something so consistently feels like an accomplishment. I was beginning to worry I was flighty!

Her reincarnation

Susan Murphy was devastated when she was laid off from her job at Club Med. As the company's director of travel industry marketing, Susan adored the position, which essentially required her to host travel agents and travel industry executives at resort destinations around the world.

Not a bad gig, and not easy to replicate.

"The layoff was so depressing, not only because I loved my job but because there are so few high-level jobs in the travel industry. No one wanted to hire a woman my age for much of anything," recalls Susan. Married and childless, Susan had no clue what to do with her work life. She had fallen into the travel business in her twenties and had never been forced to search for a career. Suddenly, Susan had no choice.

I was lucky to have found travel in my twenties, because growing up in St. Louis, all the girls I knew had four options: nurse, nun, teacher, wife. So I never thought much about having a career—until I was laid off in my forties. I did some interviews to try and switch into public relations, but everyone I met was rigid and inflexible. "What makes you think you can do PR?" Hello? I did PR for Club Med—we just called it marketing!

Finally, after six months I sat down and read the book What Color Is Your Parachute? *and realized that I loved to teach, but I'd taught high school for two years after college and the kids almost gave me a nervous breakdown. To double-check, I took a few personality tests with an outplacement firm. Sure enough, they said I should be teaching. It occurred to me that being a tour director was very much like being a teacher—you are essentially teaching people to enjoy themselves. As part of my job I also trained Club Med staffers and other tour directors.*

Epiphany: It hit Susan that a more adult form of teaching was corporate training: no kids, and it catered to her skills. She'd heard about a consulting company called Communispond, which taught businesspeople negotiation and presentation skills, and when she ran across a want ad for a part-time instructor, she brazenly wrote in, declaring, "My public speaking skills are legendary." It was unlike Susan to brag, but it caught Communispond's attention, and they invited her to try out to be a coach. Susan had to come up with speeches on the fly and present them to the company's executives. They also tested to see if she could take direction; anyone who bristled at the slightest criticism would not be hired. Susan, however, was accepted and worked for Communispond for four years. When the company's corporate politics wore her out, she became an independent consultant and started her own company: Murphy Motivation, which trains nonmarketing professionals, such as architects and engineers, in presentation and sales skills. That was fifteen years ago. Today Susan, now sixty, takes pride in how she brought her dead career back to life.

Architecture, engineering, and construction are about 90 percent of my business, and I love these industries because I find very little politics among the professionals. You either build something or you don't. You either get paid or you don't. You either carry your weight or you don't. You can be an orange woman with six heads and purple hair, but as long as you produce, they don't care. The people I train are also creative, ethical, and totally understand cause and effect.

I take arrogant architects and teach them skills to connect with the average guy or gal. I transform engineers into enthusiastic marketers and construction guys into polished public speakers. I teach them how to go into a room and make a sales presentation. I teach them how to handle their bodies. I teach them relationship-building skills, like subtle language techniques that let other people know they're cared about without getting too mushy. Instead of saying "the" project, say "your" project, which is the difference between saying, "I saw a movie you would love," versus "I saw a great movie last week." I teach clients how to listen and repeat what people tell them so others know they were heard.

Because I'm an outside consultant, I can be more in their face. I get to say to the men, "You are the most boring speaker I have ever heard in my life!" When I walk into a room, they understand they have to stand up straight and look me in the eye when I talk. When I leave, I make it seem as if the dominatrix will come back and yell at them if they don't do the skills I taught them. It's interesting that training is viewed as a woman's job. I do think that women are better at it than men, partly because in childhood, human beings are used to taking direction from women; it's Mom who usually says, "Do this" and "Do that." Men are not as good at instructing; they're better drill sergeants. I'm a drill sergeant with a mother's heart, and I try to entertain. They sense I care, and I also make fun of myself. "You know, Murph," one guy said to me, "you pretend to be tough, and we pretend to be scared."

To whip execs into shape, Susan charges $1,750 for half a day, and, working no more than three days a week, she brings in close to $150,000 a year. She gets new business via word of mouth and speaking at conventions and other events. "I love my job because I love my clients and I teach them skills that change their lives. Occasionally they call me and say, 'We just knocked an incumbent architect out of a project!' That's so exciting to me.

"My advice to other women is to find a job you would do for free. The women I know who love their jobs would still do it even if they won $80 million in the lottery." That's powerful advice coming from a woman who thought her life was over at age forty-five.

She never admitted it was hard.

For women without children, it is difficult to grasp the notion that motherhood is hard, time-consuming, and emotionally draining work. The hours never end, and neither do the repetitive chores. And just when a mom thinks she's mastered an age or a phase, the child is already on the next one. Lara Mitchel knows these challenges intimately, times four. As the mother of four boys in Sandy, Utah, Lara and her husband Nels's oldest son is five, their youngest is one. Do the math and it's obvious that Lara's been inordinately busy—and sleepless—these past few years as she's nursed, changed diapers, mixed baby food, carpooled, and played with and cleaned up after her brood. For Lara, thirty-four, the past few years have been not only hectic, but acutely painful as well.

A consummate giver and pleaser, having her own family pushed Lara to her limits. Yet the reason she loves being a full-time mom today is because Lara learned to prioritize and to be honest with her friends, her husband, and, most important, herself.

The daughter of a Greek-American army engineer and a doting, Philippine stay-at-home mother, Lara was not one of those girls who dreamed of being a mommy. She was an army brat and a tomboy, the old-est of three children and the only girl. Growing up, Lara never particu-larly loved children, and she was hardly a domestic diva, preferring after-school sports to baby-sitting and crafts to cleaning up around the house. Soccer was Lara's passion in high school and college, and she was extremely talented. Perennially friendly and sweet off the field, Lara was a tough competitor and held her own against boys in athletic settings. She met her husband, Nels, an engineer, on a ski trip, and the two soul mates were engaged within eight months, had a big wedding, and moved from Chicago to Utah to ski and start a family.

As for career, Lara never thought much about having one. Through-out her twenties she worked nine to five in accounting departments at various large companies, never particularly enjoying her work. With no regrets, Lara easily left the workforce to stay home full-time with her first child.

I love the place I am at right now, but I was not always the mother I am today. Our second child was born when the first was two, and it was very stressful. The toddler was energetic all day and the baby was up all night. I worried: Are my babies benefiting from my milk and from the food? What am I doing wrong? I never admitted it was hard, and neighbors and friends saw me as this mom who had it all together. I had play group and book group. I played soccer and hosted parties. I went to everything, and it started to wear on me. But I didn't tell anyone.

When I got pregnant with our third son, it was not planned, and communication between my husband and me started to break down. I was scared. After our son was born I had postpartum depression. I'd had the blues with my first two boys, but it was worse the third time. I'd be up at night and always tired. Nels got a new job and traveled a lot for work, and I was angry with him. He was angry with me for being angry. But I still kept my meetings and appointments and kept up appearances. I always had a smile on my face when I went out, but at home I'd cry and never told a soul. I loved my boys and would do anything for them, but I was not supposed to feel so sad, I was supposed to be happy that my babies were all healthy—right?

One day I was at the park and a lady sat down next to me and we realized our kids were all the same age. "It's hell, isn't it?" she said. I just started crying. It was eye-opening for me to finally admit that it was.

Lara finally went to a therapist, who immediately understood her plight. "You poor thing, you just want enough free time to take a shower!" the therapist said to Lara upon hearing the ages of her kids. Nels joined Lara at the next therapy appointment, and the two addressed a host of personal issues, agreeing things had to change. First, they started talking again and expressing how they felt. Second, Lara cleared her schedule and got honest with others. "When people called and asked how I was, I told them the day sucked, if it did." She quit the book group. She quit soccer temporarily but continued to go to the gym with her kids daily. And she reevaluated her friendships, deciding which were worthy of her time. She also turned down invitations, but when an opportunity to be a volunteer host at a nearby ski resort came up, she took it. All she had to do was ski the mountain and be friendly with skiers! It was a chance for Lara to get back in touch with a pre-mom part of herself and interact with people her own age. Meanwhile, Sundays became Nels's time to watch the three kids, not an easy marital transition at first.

In the beginning Nels just saw Sundays as baby-sitting. I'd come home from skiing and there would be no dinner or clean laundry. "We have no milk," he'd tell me. "Well, go get some," I'd say. Eventually he started to embrace Sundays as daddy's day, and he took the kids wall climbing, to the park, to play soccer—things he enjoyed, too. (And he'd buy milk!) We started to bond because he understood what it was like to watch three kids all day. A lot of wives do not have that experience with their husbands. I talk to so many women who do not let their husbands help with the baby. But if you don't let him help early, then he won't have the confidence or the willingness to help when the children are older and you need a break.

Indeed, not a lot of husbands will dedicate a Sunday to watch children so their wife can ski. But Nels was incredibly supportive, and he understood that Lara's time alone rebuilt not only her confidence and sense of self, but their relationship as well. On the slopes, Lara revived the athletic, fun-loving woman she was before parenthood, and she brought that part of herself home.

With her inner and outer life more balanced, Lara desired another child, a final chance to apply all she'd learned to a new baby so her memories of early motherhood would be positive. At first Nels didn't feel they could afford the financial strain (the three boys already shared a bedroom). But after Lara, who was flying to Salt Lake City from Chicago on September 11, 2001, was stranded in Iowa for several days, Nels acquiesced. "There were forty minutes when Nels had no idea where I was, and when I finally returned home, he said, 'If you want another baby, let's do it.' It was such an affirmation of his love for me."

Lara's fourth son was born September 9, 2002.

These days, as Lara sits in the park holding her youngest and listening to a new mom compare her own baby's milestones like first teeth and first steps, she is much more relaxed about the mothering process.

Most days I'm out and about, but I'm not high-maintenance, just high-activity. I take the kids to parks and museums and movies. I play soccer once a week, and Nels and the boys come to my games. We all ski together, which is why we moved to Utah in the first place. While I don't overschedule the boys—just like I learned not to overschedule myself—they all commit to one activity.

Finn, my oldest, is in school now, and I love to see him with his friends and learning. Alek is a little tiger on the mountain, who has no fear. Lars is my little introvert, who can just play by himself, and Elin the baby is a joy. Every day he learns something new. As for Nels, I take great pride in our relationship. He is a great dad, and an incredibly supportive and devoted husband. When things get crazy, we turn to each other and say, "We're doing the best we can."

So many women try to be the perfect mom, but there is no such thing. A mom can't take credit for everything her kids do well, or when they do something wrong or different she'll take it personally. I know my kids will get where they need to go, and I am no longer so stressed. I'm still a busy person. I still have bad days, but even then my kids look up at me with adoring eyes. I could be the worst mom or fall on my face, but my kids never demean me. That's the thing about kids: They just give constant praise. They are the hardest, most demanding bosses I've ever had, but they are also the best. The reward is their love.

Her fear of *not* flying

After years dreaming of being a flight attendant—but instead, working at uninspiring clerical health care jobs—Elizabeth Ehrmann finally got up the nerve to apply to Midwest Airlines in her late thirties. "A friend of mine said, 'You know, Midwest does not open up the phone book and call people looking for flight attendants.' So I finally dropped off my application in February 2000," recalls Elizabeth, a self-described "plain Jane." When she successfully landed a job as a Midwest flight attendant, she broke into tears of joy and reported to training in June 2000.

The fun and rewards at Midwest are without limits. I was so proud just to wear the uniform. It was such a joy to treat people like royalty. New passengers' jaws dropped when they saw our leather-seated planes and when we served champagne to everyone, not just to first class. Then they smelled dinner warming and just beamed when they got a whiff of the chocolate-chip cookies!

Elizabeth was in heaven even when her feet were on the ground. At least until September 11, 2001, when, for the second time in a year, Elizabeth shed tears because of her job. She was driving home from Milwaukee's airport terminal when news reached her that four commercial airplanes had crashed into the World Trade Center, the Pentagon, and a Pennsylvania field. Suddenly, flying was something to fear.

It took me so long to get a job I loved this much, and I refused to have my life turned upside down by terrorists. And after September 11, I never considered leaving Midwest. I said to my bosses, "You need me? I'm on the plane." Plus, I figured that the longer I stayed away from it, the more it might bother me. When airlines started flying again, Midwest had three of the first ten aircraft in the air. At first I felt helpless, but the minute I got back to work it was our turn, and as flight attendants we could do more to help fliers than anyone else. Passengers were scared out of their pants to get on airplanes, but for airline attendants, getting on planes was a way of life. We had to make passengers comfortable. That was our contribution to the rest of the country.

We never did resume the same level of service Midwest was known for, and for about a month after the attacks we served only chocolate-chip cookies and beverages. We used plastic forks for a while and went to half-sized food trays. The flight attendants had to literally rip apart the plane for security checks. We pulled off cushion seats, checked all the equipment. Also, there was a fine line between making passengers feel safe and being overly chipper. We even started serving champagne again, which seemed weird at first, but I think it helped all of us feel like things were getting back to normal.

Financially, the aftermath of September 11 hit the airline industry hard. Revenues dropped as people stopped flying, while additional security measures sent airline costs skyrocketing. Midwest Airlines was not immune, and in April 2003 it furloughed more than 100 flight attendants indefinitely, including Elizabeth. A forty-year-old single woman who supported herself, Elizabeth could not afford to treat the furlough as an unpaid vacation, like many of her colleagues who were married. Yet rather than give up and go back to the health care field, Elizabeth took a pay cut to work part-time cleaning airplanes at night with Midwest's regular cleaning crews.

The furlough was devastating, especially being away from everyone, and I went nuts being away from the airport. I could have taken another job or gone on unemployment, but I just wanted to be around the planes. I'm also a low-maintenance kind of gal and could live okay on the lower salary. Midwest was floored that a flight attendant wanted to clean planes, but I had a lot of loyalty to the company.

Five months later Elizabeth was recalled from furlough and returned to work, glowing. In 2002, she flew to New York City for the first September 11 memorial ceremony. "It still makes me so sad that people had to lose their lives, and this was a time to remember them. Most flight attendants love what they do, and I did not think it was possible to love this job any more than I already did. This is probably one of the worst times to be in the airline industry, but I would not trade my job for anything."

Indeed, the terrorist attacks prompted people all over the country to reflect on their own lives and livelihoods, and Elizabeth faced her own dilemma: The attacks and the furlough had the potential to derail her professional life. Yet Elizabeth hung in there, and today she's back where she happily belongs.

Her lemonade life

Sitting in a dark theater on a weekday afternoon watching a production of Langston Hughes's play *Little Ham,* Joan Liman, fifty-four, contemplated her future. She was just let go for the second time in two years, and sitting among strangers in the quiet New York City theater, Joan had no clue what to do next with her life.

Unfortunately, this was hardly Joan's darkest hour. Over the course of her health care career, Joan has been hit with so many setbacks that to call her resilient would be a gross understatement. Her story illustrates that just when you think your career—and indeed your life—is over, it may have only just begun.

My mom was a housewife, and my dad was a traveling salesman who sold wedding gowns. The proverbial jolly salesman, my father sold the fairy tale, every girl's dream! He schlepped the dresses up and down the Eastern Seaboard and just loved what he did. One night he came home dejected and told my mother he'd been fired. I was six years old and took it literally. All I could think of was that he had been thrown in a pot of boiling water, cannibal style, and literally fired! The image stayed with me for years.

My mom suffered depression all her life—which I later inherited—and so I grew up a nurturer and a helper. When she was depressed she got irritable and angry. I was the peacemaker, the healer, always restoring things to a healthy state. That probably affected my career aspirations. At the age of eight I had an affinity for medicine and wanted to be a doctor.

While I was never told I could not be a doctor, my parents' goal was for me to marry a nice Jewish boy, teach, and have summers off.

I also liked theater as a kid, and I usually helped write the scripts and song lyrics for high school productions. I loved hearing people applaud and laugh, but I never thought of doing it for real. It was 1965, and no guidance counselor would know what to do with me if I walked into her office and said I wanted to be a Broadway lyricist. I was just a little Jewish girl from Brooklyn! I was going to be a doctor.

Meanwhile, I loved school and was a wonderful student. Nobody had to motivate me to get all As. I shuffled off to college at the height of the Vietnam War and majored in psychology. I found it easy and enjoyed a great social life. I went to all the school mixers, recalling my mother's famous words: "If you don't meet 'im in college, you never will." I ended up meeting my husband on a plane in 1969. He was the gentleman sitting next to me reading the Wall Street Journal, *and he called me a week later. From the beginning we knew we were in love, and we married right after college.*

So that ended my childhood. I was twenty-one.

Joan and her husband, a jewelry manufacturer, bought a house in New Jersey and had a baby girl—"the highlight of my life"—but Joan was undeniably lonely as a full-time, isolated housewife. For a while she abandoned plans to be a doctor and took a job as a personnel interviewer for an insurance company, a job that, because it forced her to reject disabled applicants, inspired her to go to graduate school for vocational rehabilitation training. It was there that Joan's dormant interest in medicine rekindled, and in 1976, with a two-year-old daughter, a clinically depressed mother, and a husband all under her care, Joan began premed studies at Columbia University. She was thirty, the third-oldest student in her class, and the only mother.

I don't think my husband was thrilled when I went to medical school, and he wasn't as cooperative or supportive as I would have hoped. He probably would have preferred the life that he envisioned: dinner ready on the table; if it's raining I'd pick him up at the bus stop . . . but that was not me! He wanted to keep playing golf on the weekends and not be inconvenienced by my being in med school. Luckily, we could afford a baby-sitter and child care.

I loved medical school from day one and took to it like a fish to water. I planned to become a pathologist because I was fascinated by the causes of disease. Things went swimmingly until my second year, when we took our physical diagnosis course. One week they taught us about the head, neck, and lymph nodes, and we were trained to know what lymph nodes were supposed to feel like, and like a good student, I practiced on myself.

As I checked my face I found a pea-sized lump in front of my left ear.

My own doctor thought it might be my salivary glands, and I wound up getting X rays. My doctor said, "Let's take an X ray of your chest while you're here." It turned out that there was no problem with my glands, but the radiologist found a baseball-size mass between my lungs, behind the breastbone. It was serious. I had a biopsy and was diagnosed with stage-four non-Hodgkin's lymphoma, and it was spreading. I was given a two-year prognosis to live, and without chemotherapy, chances were such that I wouldn't even make it that long. I was thirty-two years old, in the middle of medical school, and busy studying for my boards.

Everyone thought I'd quit med school, but I was, like, "Quit? Hell no!" I wasn't giving up that easily, even if I had to get the degree posthumously. [Laughs.] My student affairs dean said, "No problem. If you want to stay, we'll figure it out." He was so nonchalant and supportive that I thought I could do it. In retrospect, I don't know how I did, but continuing with my third-year rotations helped keep my mind off of "me" and let me have a life while I was ill. It sounds a bit Kafkaesque: I'd gone from being a doctor to a patient in a matter of hours. There I was trying to put an IV into a kid during my pediatrics rotation, and a few hours later I'd walk five blocks to my own doctor, where I became a pincushion for him.

How did I have the energy? I had youth on my side, and I'd always been very determined, motivated, and goal oriented. I planned it so I had chemotherapy on a Friday. I'd puke for twenty-four hours straight, and by Sunday night my family would go to the local steakhouse, and I'd have steak and a baked potato and be ready for the school week.

As if medical school and cancer weren't enough, Joan's genetics caught up with her as she was interviewing for her residency. Depression had first interrupted her life when she was twenty-four, when it became so debilitating that Joan's doctor prescribed shock therapy. Like her mother she was unipolar, which, unlike bipolar disorder, has no manic phase. But this next depressive episode also hospitalized Joan, and she took a voluntary leave from medical school. Again, the school's sympathetic dean helped her rearrange her schedule and kindly waived her final elective requirement, and Joan graduated with honors and received a standing ovation from her classmates as she walked across the stage to receive her diploma.

Two years after being diagnosed with cancer, Joan was in remission and had her hard-won medical degree.

I graduated and started my pathology residency just as another lump showed up. It was benign, but depression kicked in again and my husband started to complain about my busy schedule. Personally, my marriage was in jeopardy and divorce was looming. Based on my medical and depressive history, I finally questioned whether I could handle the stresses plus the challenge of a medical career. Professionally, the medical field was also changing, and I could see the writing on the wall: Managed care insurance was undermining doctors' autonomy and patients' freedom.

Practicing medicine was no longer what I had envisioned.

So, six months after graduation, even though I was well enough from a physical and mental health standpoint to finish my residency, I didn't go on. I made a decision that, this time, my family was going to come first. Do I regret it? Only this: In order to be a licensed physician you have to have at least one year of residency, and I bailed after a month. Many times I considered going back to finish over the last decade, but as I got older I became too intimidated. I was hesitant to even go to my fifteen-year medical school reunion. But I did and discovered that while most of my classmates were practicing medicine, many were unhappy. One even closed her practice because she couldn't take the red tape of managed care. They were jealous of me!

What was Joan doing? After leaving medical school she embarked on a third career: medical administration. Between 1987 and 1993, Joan, ever the overachiever, went back to school (again) for a master's in public health, "another credential to be attractive to academia." It worked, and in 1993 she landed what would be perhaps the best job of her working life: dean of student affairs for New Jersey Medical School.

I liked the idea that I could help shepherd people through the medical triage that I had gone through. I planned orientation and graduation. I was a career counselor and helped students pick a specialty. Because I'd had a dean who had made such an impact on my life as a student, I felt I was continuing his legacy and paying him homage by helping other students who had problems as minor as a parking ticket to health problems as serious as my own. I used to joke that I had 700 children; my students were like my kids. I would have paid to do that job. I couldn't wait to go to work in the morning and I thought this would be the job I would retire from!

It was not to be.

In 1999, cancer caught up with Joan again, and after she had a mastectomy, she continued working, albeit from home. The return to work helped her focus on something outside of herself. Once again, work saved Joan's sanity during sickness. Then the familiar ache of depression crept up on her later that fall, but by this time, better antidepressive drugs were available, and by spring 2000, Joan was back to herself. But she had a new boss at the medical school where she worked.

P.S. I got a pink slip six weeks before my daughter's wedding and on the night of the annual student-faculty dinner. The new dean said he wanted to bring in his own people. I had no clue it was coming. Students loved me! They had given me the golden apple! I later found out, by reading a memo, that the dean replaced me with one of my own coworkers, who was also a friend. He couldn't even tell me to my face! My husband was livid. He said I should sue, but my daughter's wedding was coming up, and, since I had never once taken a summer off in my life, that's what I did.

P.P.S. It was a wonderful wedding.

Joan found another, less fulfilling, less prestigious job as dean of students at a podiatry school, and in her free time she volunteered at a not-for-profit theater company dedicated to racial harmony. She gave money, wrote lyrics for musicals, and became a staple presence in the theater donor community. The morning she was scheduled to see *Little Ham,* she was unceremoniously let go from her job at the podiatry school.

It was 9:30 A.M. when the dean called me into his office and said he was terminating me. We had different management styles, he said, and when I got back to my desk, my phone and computer had been cut off. I was shell-shocked but remembered I had a ticket to a play, so I went to sit in the dark and collect my thoughts.

I ended up sitting next to a woman who was thinking about investing in the theater. We stayed in touch, and eventually I agreed to invest about $9,000. I was losing money in the stock market, anyway, and thought, Hell, I might as well enjoy what I'm losing. [*Laughs.*] So I invested in Little Ham. *It was a blast, but the show closed about three months later and I lost my money. Still, it was a great entrée to the world of theater.* [*Laughs.*]

Around this time, a distant cousin of mine, Carole Hyatt, invited me to one of her career workshops for women in transition. It was September 2002, and as part of the workshop Carole makes everyone stand up and say, "I used to be a (fill in the blank with your current job) and now I am a (fill in the blank with your fantasy job)." I was not prepared to answer this, but I had just read the review of Little Ham *in* The New York Times *and when it was my turn, I said, "I used to be a dean of student affairs, and now I am a . . . producer."*

We had to stick with our fantasy job over the course of the two-day seminar, which helped us realize how to make it a reality. The idea of being a producer was not as farfetched as I'd thought. Carole helped me realize that I could combine medicine and theater. I could do this, and I came up with a little mantra to describe my future career: healing hearts through the performing arts.

For about a year Joan played unpaid producer—and hands-on investor—with an off-Broadway theater company. She joined the board, helped raise money, and even went back to school for a fourteen-week course to learn the "vocabulary" of the theater. She replaced some lost income by working as an assistant to her cousin Carole.

I'd been unemployed since June 2003, and even though the year was wonderful—I woke up at eight, leisurely read the paper, attended lectures in the afternoon—I had to get practical. The unemployment insurance was starting to run out, plus not having my own money and depending on my husband to fund my activities was something I was not used to. I was ready to return to work that felt meaningful. Not that theater didn't, but working in an inner-city hospital, providing quality care for patients who wouldn't otherwise get it resonated with my core values.

In hospital administration, I care for populations of patients as opposed to one-on-one as a doctor, providing benefits on a larger scale. Now I am assistant dean at New York Medical College, the same place where I did my pediatrics clerkship in 1981 as a medical student. (Some of the same secretaries are still here!) I wear two hats: As assistant dean for the medical school I get involved in educational activities, from planning orientation to scheduling residency rotations. As a hospital administrator I help prepare for upcoming accreditation visits, and I plan programs to educate our staff about the language and culture of our mostly Hispanic patients. My job is all administration, and it uses my skills in public health education. Plus, as a child of the sixties, it is very meaningful to work in an inner-city hospital.

This year I will turn fifty-five, and I'm throwing myself a party themed "Fifty-five and Still Alive: Better Living Through Chemistry (. . . and Radiation)." I often refer to my past as my "lemonade life." Not only is my last name Liman, but throughout it all—the sickness, the job losses—I've always taken the lemons and managed to find a life.

She was her own biggest obstacle.

Sometimes, life's hurdles are subtler than the slap in the face of death, the jolt of layoffs, or the dilapidation of disease. In this era of burgeoning professional choice, the working woman's greatest hurdle is often herself. Testifies Susan Holson, "I was my own biggest obstacle." In her twenties and thirties, Susan fought a tug-of-war in which she was on both ends of the rope, torn between female stereotypes and expectations when it came to her identity as a working woman and mother. It's tempting to assume that Susan—a smiling, married mother of two and co-owner of a whimsical community newspaper based in Burlington, Vermont—was one of those women blessed with a career compass. But her newspaper, *Kids VT: Vermont's Family Newspaper,* is the first of many jobs the forty-six-year-old Susan has actually liked, let alone loved. Although her road to owning and editing the 21,000-circulation paper was circuitous, at times as cold and lonely as Vermont winters, Susan's struggle was internal. To outsiders, she always looked incredibly focused. Says Susan, "Everyone else definitely thought I had it all together." Susan was the only one who knew that wasn't the case.

Caught between fantasies of a high-powered career and save-the-world idealism, Susan had a history of taking jobs only to realize within months that she hated them. The pattern of starting and stopping went on well into her thirties, when it was compounded by depression.

In college, Susan contemplated social work but was deterred by her mother's fears that she'd never "live comfortably" on a social worker's salary. She conveniently shifted her priorities to more practical ones, and a year short of graduating from college, eager to get on with a high-powered career, she left the University of Michigan and moved to New York City, where she worked by day and took courses by night, eventually finishing her degree. Although Susan dreamed of publishing, her sister was deemed "the writer in the family," so Susan focused on marketing and took an entry-level clerical job at a thriving advertising agency in Manhattan. "I took advertising very seriously and strived to be an account executive because they were the people I saw as having power and status." Susan worked hard and was given more responsibility, and when her boss won a huge airline account, Susan was made a member of the account team. For a while she basked in the professional life: the suits, the business travel, the title. Then, one day, while she was sitting in a crowded client meeting, something clicked. "As I sat and watched someone present market research for an airline ad campaign, I wondered, Why are we spending all this time and energy just to get a few more butts in the seats?

Why is this important? It was like an out-of-body experience." With her heart no longer engaged, Susan began to plot her escape from advertising.

Still caught between what she *should* do and what she *wanted* to do, Susan rationalized that she should go to business school to learn how to run a nonprofit agency, a practical job she'd feel good about. So without fully acknowledging her true feelings and goals, Susan returned to school in the 1980s only to separate herself from her classmates' so-called "Yuppie" aspirations. "The whole corporate structure was so ugly to me, I wanted no part of it. All my classmates were walking into jobs with a million ladders that had a million rungs to climb." Defiant, Susan showed up at on-campus interviews wearing bright suits and high-heeled purple cowboy boots.

She graduated without a job.

Ironically, Susan mocked corporate life but could not completely abandon her desire for the notions of safety and status it conjured. Rather than explore other options like working for a not-for-profit, Susan took a brand management job at Tetley Tea in Connecticut, a small outfit that struck her as having a slightly more humane business environment. After three years feeling stifled, she quit and joined a small ad agency in New York City, whose unethical owners overworked its account executives, and so she resigned to work for a family-owned ad agency.

Only a tragedy could jolt Susan out of her rut, and when her beloved uncle died of a heart attack, it threw the already aimless Susan for an emotional loop. It was also, perhaps, the beginning of her depression. Susan quit her job and, not interested in finding another, lived off savings and a small inheritance. For eighteen months she did odd jobs—sales clerk, ski instructor, freelance marketing—all the while reassessing her priorities. Says Susan, "My sister refers to this as my DUMPY stage: Downwardly Mobile Urban Professional. She was exactly right!" It was also during this period that Susan met a man from Vermont on a blind date, fell in love, and married eight months later. The New York City girl relocated to the mountains.

In New York, work was everything. I ate and breathed it. But in Vermont and in job limbo, I phased into the sort of 1950s babies-need-to-

*be-cared-for-by-their-mommies mentality, so I took very good care of my
kids on a full-time basis.*

*But I was really not happy and I felt something was missing. As the
kids grew up, I volunteered at their school, freelanced for a local
newspaper (hey, I could write!), and got involved in local politics. I was
also diagnosed with depression by a wonderful woman who really helped
me put myself back together. I did a little bit of this and a little bit of that:
I lost fifty pounds, went on medication, and refocused my life thanks to my
therapist and a women's group. The group helped me believe that my kids
would be better off if I was working, because I'd be happier and a stronger
role model. It took me a long time to buy into that, but once I did, I was
ready to go, and I had an epiphany: I ought to be a therapist. I went back
and forth about whether I should return to school—I actually took a few
classes—but figured out that not until I was sixty years old could I hang
out a shingle, and that did not work for me. I'm not saying late-in-life
career changes don't make sense, but I couldn't justify that much
preparation.*

*As I was making that decision, I got a call from an old friend who was
selling her half in a local newspaper written for Vermont families with
young children. "Are you interested?" she asked me.*

Susan was interested, visited the newspaper, talked it over with her family, and three months later became part owner and managing editor of *Kids VT*, a local monthly newspaper for families that ran stories
about summer camps and raising teens, dinner recipes and community
events. "My kids knew the paper because it had been around the house
since they were born." Susan easily fell into step on both the editorial
and business ends.

*Finally, I'd followed my passion! Insecurity early in my career led me to
make certain choices because I thought they were right, like pursuing an
MBA. I just bought in hook, line, and sinker to the idea of the superwoman and a job with a lot of recognition. I let the fires of my other
interests get reduced to embers, but they never totally disappeared, and I
flirted with them in different ways over the years. Still, I don't apologize to*

*myself for those other experiences. I gained a lot from each. Being as
fulfilled as I am now, I can point to different chapters in my life where I
learned lessons that range from practical to personal. One job helped me
learn how to get along with people I don't like, another helped me learn
about mailing lists, and my business background serves me well because at
the newspaper I am bookkeeper, accountant, purchasing agent, and sales
support. And as difficult as it was to come to Vermont from New York, the
move helped me refocus my values.*

*The veil of depression substantially prolonged my inability to combine
my education and skills in a meaningful, professional way.*

Deep down, Susan says, her passion is not so much for publishing but
for empowerment, both over her own life and over others whose lives
she can positively affect. It's a type of empowerment Susan imagined
she'd find in social work, and that she always failed to find in the corporate world. As co-owner, Susan can run to the dentist or attend her kids'
concerts without checking in with the boss. She also finally feels she's
doing worthwhile work by deciding what stories appear in the paper—
how to talk with your kids about war, for example, or how to help children handle schoolyard bullies. Susan influences a community of
80,000. "That's the other piece I've learned. You don't have to conquer
the world to feel the satisfaction of being involved."

She is worthy.

There is a scented candle and a desktop waterfall in the cavernous
courthouse chambers of the Honorable Maxine Aldridge White. The absence of wrinkles on her fifty-one-year-old face, as well as Maxine's
peaceful office, the glow of her red suit, and the pep in her step do not
immediately implicate her as a Hurdler. Yet Maxine has overcome
poverty, racism, and sexism to be where she is today: the first African-
American female judge to sit on the Wisconsin court of general jurisdic-
tion, and the only black woman judge in the state's trial court system.

Maxine, the eighth of eleven children, was born in 1951 to poor,
grade-school-educated sharecropper parents in Indianola, Mississippi.
The rural southern town was a white supremacist hub, and for years

Maxine's family earned a meager living farming cotton off land they leased from white owners. Except for their own labor, everything they had—their three-room house, their farming equipment—was leased. "The only thing we could control was how much cotton we produced," says Maxine. But even that did not guarantee enough money to support the family of thirteen. Families like the Whites bought cottonseed from their landowner, who in turn took a portion of the profits. The more money the sharecropper made, the more the landowner knew the sharecropper could afford to pay for seed. "The higher your profits, the more your cost of doing business increased," recalls Maxine. "There were various ways of ensuring that those who worked the land never profited from it. It was very difficult to win."

Eventually her father left farming and moved to Indianola's city limits, where he found work as a janitor while the children continued to pick cotton for low wages. Maxine attended a one-room schoolhouse and set her sights on college.

As a girl, Maxine was wise enough to her surroundings that she silently questioned why her parents did not aggressively fight the unfair system, but she would come to appreciate the immense pressure they were under. Blacks who asserted their right to receive more money for their labor were often beaten, even murdered. Maxine also came to appreciate other, more subtle ways in which her mother and father sacrificed on behalf of their children.

Two memories I have of my parents come to mind. The first was when my mother took me to a medical clinic to be treated for asthma. We had to ride part of the way in a neighbor's truck and walk the balance of the trip. When we got to the clinic, I waited on a swing outside while my mother walked in the back door and spoke to someone. She came back outside and sat with me for hours; she played games with me and watched while I cheerfully played hopscotch. It got later and later and I just assumed the doctor wasn't in. As the day drew to a close, it got darker, and, finally, we left. "We won't be able to see the doctor today," was all she said. Years later I overheard my mother tell someone that it was a white clinic and the doctor would see me only if he had time at the end of the day. I reflected on how happy I was in that yard and felt really sad to think that access to medical care could be cut off because of the color of skin. I felt anger at first, and then I resolved that my mother had walked a great distance to take her child to a doctor, entered through the back door in what was probably a humiliating experience, and waited all day in the backyard. She did everything she could to try and make it happen. So I thought, How dare I be angry at my mom, who did everything she could under the circumstances!

Years later, in high school, my father went with me to visit a local university because I was determined to go to college. I heard the college admissions person tell him the school had no money to offer his child and that I could not attend unless we could pay $600. My dad said he'd put up the house—the shack—we lived in and he offered to work overtime so he could pay whatever was needed to get me into college, but I refused to let him do it. I'd find another school.

There had been other times I watched my father be humiliated, and I was always very dismayed and angered by it. But he always used those days as lessons. For every problem, he always found a solution, whether it was building a relationship with another farmer or changing his lease so he could make more money. Through their hard work and good citizenship, my parents led us to believe they did not want us to stop pursuing our own dreams, they wanted us to become an educated generation. "You are worthy," they told us. I grew up believing I had a right to share in the American dream. It was mine. My parents also taught me that anger is cheap. It's easy to be angry and leave it at that, but it's also self-defeating. Anger must be processed appropriately, and mine became determination and persistence.

With a will to achieve and a work ethic to match, Maxine embarked on her path to adulthood. With the aid of a teacher, she found another college to attend—the all-black Alcorn State University—that gave her a small scholarship. For additional money for herself and her family, Maxine did laundry for a professor and was secretary for a dean; she also sold pecans that she picked off trees in campus orchards. After college, Maxine moved to Wisconsin to live with her sisters, who had moved to the Midwest in search of a better life, and she took a job as an "office girl" at a manufacturing plant. "You won't go anywhere here," an older, female coworker admonished the young Maxine. "This job is *okay* for us, but you go get yourself another one."

So Maxine spent her lunch hours answering want ads, and when she walked into the local Social Security office she was offered a job as a claims representative. Despite ongoing issues of gender and race, Maxine advanced from her entry-level position to management and took on special assignments in other cities, all the while saving money for law school. "I was on the path of having paychecks far better than my parents ever had," recalls Maxine. Toward the end of her tenure with the Social Security Administration, she competed for and won a chance to work for the federal Social Security office in Washington, D.C., where she simultaneously earned a master's degree in public administration. In 1982, at age thirty-one, Maxine returned to Wisconsin to attend Marquette Law School. During school she divorced her husband of twelve years and by graduation had a two-month-old baby to care for.

I saw law school as a confined three-year period where afterward I could make a pretty good living. At Marquette, I worked a job and studied hard; I was at the library when it opened and when it closed. I graduated and worked as a federal prosecutor for eight years and became a judge in August 1992.

I always saw the law as one of the systems in this country that allowed someone with my goals to do exactly what she wanted: serve people, but in a very specific way. As a judge I have a unique opportunity to make sure all people have access to the justice system. People come to court with all types of disputes, whether small claims or homicide. Court is the ultimate place where we can serve fellow citizens and help them solve some significant problems. Regardless of the crime or subject matter, I have the same responsibility in every case. I will research the law and make certain that I do everything possible to create a fair, impartial playing field where each side has a fair opportunity to present its case within the rules of the court. If I just wanted to defend a specific group, I would have remained a prosecutor. But as a judge, I'm an advocate of fairness for all groups, even though I grew up in a time when the law dictated unfairness for my group. My sense of what is fair and just comes from all the people I encountered in my life, especially my parents.

I am passionate about using every aspect of my being, my intellect, and my resources to make a difference in the lives of others. I feel compelled to do so not just because I too desire to live in a world with doors and not walls, but because of the huge price others paid to gain rights and access that have allowed me to experience such a wonderful life. I not only love my job, I love life itself.

When Maxine was named Judge of the Year in 2001 by the State Bar of Wisconsin, it was said that she practices "swift but compassionate justice." Of these and other honors, Maxine made it very clear that she does not want to receive sole credit for her accomplishments, because, says Maxine, she rode on the shoulders of men and women who came before her and paved the way. By this, Maxine is referring to her parents as well as teachers, coworkers, and "warriors of old," people she never knew but who fought for civil rights—men such as Martin Luther King, and women such as lawyer Patricia Harris, the first African-American woman to serve in a presidential cabinet, and Mabel Watson Raimey, the first African-American woman to attend law school in Wisconsin. "All these people were my rainmakers," says Maxine. "I always feel the coolness of their rain on my life." So, as the Honorable Maxine White wishes, I duly credit those who came before her and assisted with her journey. In turn, Maxine acknowledges her role as a rainmaker for women who travel in her own wake. Says Maxine, "My challenge is to do all I can to excel on and off the bench, while serving as an inspiration to others in search of their goals."

May Maxine and the ninety-nine other members of The Happy 100 serve as shoulders for you to stand on in your own pursuit of professional fulfillment, satisfaction, and joy. May Heroines, Healers, Sisters, Determinators, Surviving Artists, Builders, Counselors, Lovers, Thinkers, and the Faithful be *your* rainmakers, may their stories motivate and inform your quest. While women of The Happy 100 may not have explicitly set out to love their work, they all do.

We wish the same for you.

The Fourth P

You get what you settle for.

—Thelma and Louise, 1991

The women on these pages prove that happiness at work does not just happen. You must seek it out, foster it, fight for it. You need to believe that you deserve to be intellectually, emotionally, and socially engaged at work. Having a happy working life is not reserved for women with connections, education, chemical makeup, or money; it is reserved for women who act.

The Happy 100 find their various forms of happiness by being engaged in processes whose purposes they feel proud of and with people they respect. Process. Purpose. People. Yet there is another P that The Happy 100 women share, a trait instrumental to achieving that happiness at work: They are proactive. At some point, each took control of her career or job situation, and as a group their collective actions fall under seven guidelines to help you move your own job search and career reinvention forward.

Career Bliss closes on a practical note, with those seven proactive steps.

Know what you want.

Before going after what you want, you must first know what you want. And this is not always as easy as it sounds, especially for women who put wants and needs of others before their own. Take an internal inventory of the specific activities, values, and type of people that bring you satisfaction, as well as those that do not. Clearly identifying your own three Ps at work can mean the difference between finding a job you love as opposed to finding just another job. Remember Vermont newspaper editor Susan Holson? She based more than ten years of career choices on false assumptions about what was important to her, mainly power and impressive titles. Had Susan been more honest with herself earlier in life, she could have found a job that made her happy much sooner.

Self-examination is not a task you can accomplish alone. Recall that 55 percent of The Happy 100 have taken a personality test, and another 36 percent took tests that assessed their skills. A full 90 percent regularly consult friends, colleagues, or family about their careers. Serendipity did not land former CNN anchor Jan Hopkins at Citigroup. Jan not only met with a career counselor, she also recruited friends to interrogate her and unearth priorities she would not have recognized on her own. Jan also set up informational interviews with executives to learn how her journalism skills might transfer to other industries.

Another tactic to determine what you want: Examine how each of the three Ps is currently playing out in your present work life. First, observe yourself at work. For at least one week or a month, pay very close attention to your days, even keeping notes. Which activities most excite and interest you? What was the best part of your day? What was the worst part? Which days do you most look forward to getting out of bed, and why? In turn, what tasks do you dread? Where do you lack appropriate skills? Self-honesty about which activities you do not enjoy, or excel at, will steer you away from certain jobs and toward others. This worked for Lisa Lynn, who realized she was a talented problem solver but an ineffective manager, unable to motivate other workers. Her new career, as a personal financial planner, has her managing clients' portfolios but not managing people. Also, dig deep and isolate the core *processes* of each task that you really enjoy, or that put you in a state of flow. Consider banker Mary Erdoes, a Thinker who does not necessarily love investing, but rather synthesizing information.

Having isolated the activities that engage and stimulate you, confront how you feel about the effects of your work on others. If you feel ambivalent or negative about the end product of your labor, then it may be time to find an employer or an industry with a mission you can champion, or at least feel proud of. Magazine publisher Michela O'Connor Abrams loves sales, but she would not be happy selling just any product; Michela is happiest selling ideas that build reader and advertiser communities. Recall public relations practitioner Jacqueline Chen, who said, "Some people like selling Tide and SnackWells' because it fits their style. Me? I prefer writing earnings releases and dealing with complicated mergers, acquisitions, and IPOs." For Jacqueline, promoting consumer products, such as detergent, is not nearly as satisfying as promoting what she would describe as more intellectually challenging financial products, such as hedge funds. As for synchronized swimmer Ana Cukic, she loved swimming, but she did not like swimming for competitive purposes. In her new, happier life as a Cirque du Soleil performer, Ana swims to entertain, not to win.

Finally, if you enjoy most of the activities you do every day and feel good about why you do them but still feel something is missing, reflect on the people with whom you work. Do they appreciate you? How do their communication and leadership styles motivate or paralyze you, or detract from your enjoyment and productivity? Do they acknowledge your efforts and appropriately recognize your accomplishments, be it with more money, additional responsibilities, public praise, or a simple thank-you when raises and promotions aren't possible? Librarian Karrie Fisher-LaMay wanted to serve children, and she was thus unhappy working at a public library on weekdays, when kids were in school and her customers were all adults. Airline mechanic Mary Ann Eiff quit one job because she disagreed with her superiors' ethics. In turn, foundation president Karen Carlson has remained at her job for years because her colleagues encourage and respect her, and NASCAR's Keri Wright and South Pole chef Sally Ayotte both say the familial atmosphere of their work environments is a major reason they love their jobs.

Once you understand what's missing from your current work situation, you can focus on filling those gaps in your next job.

Ask for what you want.

After clarifying what you want, articulate it to others, as well as to yourself. Determinator Anne Janas says it well: Whatever you want, say it out loud. Do so, and desires start to become reality. No one can read your mind, and unless you speak up about your needs—be it a request for more responsibility, a new supervisor, a raise, a job at a specific company, a flexible schedule, or a full-on career switch—you'll definitely never get them. Remember: Ninety-one percent of Happy 100 women who asked for a raise received one.

Again, look to The Happy 100 for proof. Lynne Seus fought to receive royalties on behalf of her most popular animal actor, which helped sustain Lynne and Doug Seus's company. And recall how consultant Mary Ann Hastings, after hearing a job she wanted was already filled, boldly told the company it had made a terrible mistake and needed to interview her, or how *Dwell* publisher Michela O'Connor Abrams waltzed up to an advertising executive early in her career and announced, "I want to work for you." And lawyer Judy Harris asked to return to the same law firm after quitting three times. All three women—Mary Ann, Michela, and Judy—got the jobs they wanted by asking.

There are more examples of women who ask: At GE, former part-timer Jeanne Rosario sought out more responsibility from division managers instead of waiting for them to come to her, and at *Chemical Engineering* magazine, journalist Suzanne Shelley held her ground when her boss said a promotion meant she'd have to stop working from home. To diversify her retail experience earlier in her career, Hot Topic CEO Betsy McLaughlin requested a move from finance to merchandising, even though it was an untraditional transfer at the company. While recovering from cancer, pharmaceutical sales manager Donna Lindsay asked AstraZeneca to let her not only manage the sales force for one of the company's cancer drugs, but also work in another city and reduce her responsibilities for the same salary. The company said yes.

Of course, it's not always easy to ask for what you want, and women have a particularly difficult time, having been socialized to believe that asking for something, especially money, is simply impolite or unfeminine. But there are ways to get around these perceived obstacles. First, change your mindset. "Women tend to think about what they need rather than what they're worth," says Sara Laschever, coauthor of *Women Don't Ask: Negotiation and the Gender Divide.* Practice asking for what you want on a friend or a colleague, and enter a negotiation with specific reasons why you deserve (and how the company will benefit by) whatever you are asking for, such as examples of your past performance, or profit estimates a department or company will reap from your work. The manner in which you ask is also fundamental to getting what you want: Be straightforward, focusing on business rather than personal issues. And don't act as if the company is doing you a special favor by granting your request. You deserve it.

Reinvent the rules; recast stereotypes.

When it comes to finding happiness in the workplace, the only rules are to be proactive and creative. There is no right or wrong way to network or to learn about job openings.

The uninspired job hunter communicates only with a company's human resources department or checks want ads online or in the newspapers. The creative job seeker, however, knows that job leads can come from anywhere, at any time, and from anyone. Manufacturing engineer Lee Cromarty was on a routine business flight when a casual conversation about manufacturing trends with the man sitting next to her led him to recommend Lee for a job at his company. The bold job hunter also introduces herself to employees at a company where she wants to work *before* a position even becomes available. Then, when a position does come up, she is already on the short list and familiar with decision makers. That's how scientist Marina Ramirez-Alvarado landed at the Mayo Clinic. Marina had very few if any connections in Minnesota, where she and her husband wanted to live. Marina knew that Mayo was the best facility in the region, and so when she met a Mayo scientist at a conference, Marina asked to come visit. She made two informal trips, talking with people in different departments about their work. She was never told about any job openings, but when she read about an opening for an assistant professor in Mayo's biochemistry department, Marina called a clinician she had met and asked to interview for the job. Her skills got her hired, but Marina's self-made contacts helped her get noticed.

As for creativity, always think beyond industry stereotypes. Not all people who work in the entertainment business are entertained—or entertaining—every day. Not all artists are starving. And not all flight attendants are young and thin, as Anita Mucci learned after years convincing herself that Midwest Airlines would never hire a forty-year-old mother of two. But once Anita mustered the courage to apply, Midwest proved her wrong and invited her onboard. Be open minded: Industries and companies that do not initially excite you may have specific jobs that do. Every field, and every company, has innumerable positions that require unique combinations of skills. Susan Murphy, an extrovert who worked for Club Med until being laid off, never remotely considered working in construction and engineering. Too boring. But when a personality test highlighted her teaching ability, Susan found engineers and architects responded well to her training. For chef Sally Ayotte, the most obvious venues for her to work were restaurants, but they did not suit Sally, who needed to know her customers personally to feel fulfilled. Her innovative solution? Cook for institutions—places with a permanent and returning customer base—such as staff cafeterias at tourist destinations and, currently, the dining hall for scientists based at the South Pole.

When you shake stereotypes and look beyond the obvious, doors will open and opportunities develop.

Seek support.

Finding happiness at work is not a solo achievement. In addition to knowing and asking for what you want, you cannot be shy about asking for assistance along the way. Happy 100 women are not born superwomen that never need guidance. Indeed, most acknowledge that ongoing learning is critical to job satisfaction. Consider Ogilvy & Mather's chief executive officer, Shelly Lazarus, who found herself in over her head when she began her first job after business school. Rather than fret in silence and play superwoman, Shelly cut a deal with her supervisor: She would do her best as long as he made time to answer all her questions. He agreed, and Shelly succeeded. Going to school for a degree in social work at age fifty was not easy for Gloria Gaev, who compensated for her dyslexia and weak writing skills by seeing tutors and addressing her problems with professors. And at U.S. Genomics, Courtney Harris, a twenty-five-year-old marketing executive, could not possibly have as much knowledge as her more experienced scientist colleagues. If Courtney did not put ego aside and ask them to explain the complex chemistry behind the company's products, she could not excel. The same holds true for young engineer Laura Espinoza in Houston, who views coworkers as mentors. And remember Lois Padovani's early journalism struggles? Lois initiated meetings with her magazine's editors, insisting they tell her how to improve her reporting. Lois went on to flourish at the magazine.

Seeking guidance or advice—and accepting criticism—is not a sign of weakness, but of strength. It takes courage to acknowledge what you don't know. And the sooner you do, the sooner you will master, and enjoy, your career.

Explore—don't ignore—instinct and coincidence.

Many Happy 100 women recall the specific moment they intuitively knew what they should do with their careers. It hit them like lightning, and they trusted their gut. Actor Stockard Channing vividly remembers when the acting bug struck her: She was singing an emotionally wrought solo in a college production of *The Threepenny Opera* and describes it as a moment when her unconscious brain, emotions, creativity, and ego all combined. "It was extraordinary," she says. "Once I had that experience, I just couldn't give up acting." She didn't, and today she plays the First Lady on television's *The West Wing.* Karrie Fisher-LaMay forgot that she pretended to "play librarian" as a girl, but when the notion of becoming a librarian struck her out of the blue, Karrie did not ignore her instinct but shared her epiphany with her husband (she said it out loud) and then researched just how one embarks on a career in library science. A few months later, Karrie was back in school and on her way.

There are also times when unexpected events occur that lead to career answers. One way to take advantage of such situations is to live by some general rules. First, say yes to invitations. The more places you show up, the more opportunities you are likely to find. English professor Ann Stanford always says yes, so when someone suggested she take a writing class, she signed up, and the course jump-started her teaching career. Years later, when Ann was invited to speak to inmates about creative writing, she again agreed. After that, educating inmates became an integral part of her happy professional life.

The other guideline: When coincidental or seemingly unexplainable events happen, act accordingly. That means, essentially, take action in the face of happenstance. Remember when park ranger Jennifer Stowe mysteriously received an application from Unity College in the mail? Rather than throw it away, Jennifer read the catalogue only to learn that Unity offered unique conservation law enforcement programs that other schools did not. She applied to Unity and was accepted, and her education led to her current job. At nineteen, Kansas waitress and high school student Anna Pinto was certainly not in the market to buy a diner when her boss decided to sell his, but that did not stop Anna from evaluating the unexpected opportunity. The Happy 100 member, a Counselor, now owns two restaurants.

Fate does not deliver happiness. Your actions do.

Weigh the sacrifices.

To love your work does not mean everything is perfect, and women of The Happy 100 understand that happiness does not exist without sadness, anger, or disappointment. Indeed, many overcame hurdles, both large and small: Eighty-six percent of The Happy 100 still experience frustration at work; and 77 percent have cried in the workplace.

Because all workers get paid and can control only to a degree how much money they make, money often takes the biggest sacrificial hit.

About 21 percent of The Happy 100 do not think they are paid fairly (yet, they still love their work). Animal trainer Lynne Seus remembers lean years when she and her husband shopped at thrift shops for their children's clothes. While times are better for the Seuses, they still live frugally. Gloria Gaev jettisoned an already relatively moderate Manhattan lifestyle when she went from the fashion business to social work. Even seemingly small expenses had to go: Gloria cancelled her cable television subscription; replaced high-priced salon appointments with free stylings by student beauticians; and religiously took home half of all restaurant meals to eat as the next day's lunch.

Short-term sacrifices are especially common for women starting out in a career. In the 1980s, GE's Jeanne Rosario lost a degree of influence during years she worked part-time. And after college, Maria Peninger sacrificed location to work for Avon; although Maria had no desire to live in her hometown after graduation, she had enough vision to know that, if she excelled, she could eventually move to a larger city. As for *Cosmo-GIRL*'s editor Susan Schulz, she spent several years working for magazines whose content did not necessarily speak to her, but Susan knew that the editing experience would sharpen her skills for when the right magazine came along.

Exude confidence.

No doubt about it: It takes courage to be proactive and follow the above six suggestions. If you're not feeling quite up to the tasks, fear not. Confidence can be acquired, built up over time. Don't rush: Take time to assess what you want and evaluate your current work situation. And there's no need to ask for the world in one fell swoop. Start with small requests. Also, focus on tasks that you already feel comfortable with or are skilled at. Rather than initiate an informational interview with a CEO of a large company, take a friend to coffee and ask her about her own career. And before you take a huge salary cut to pursue a dream job—assuming that's an unavoidable circumstance—plan a budget for how you will accommodate the cut in pay.

When it comes time to make a truly dramatic life transformation, you'll have the requisite confidence to whip the rug out from under your life and embark on a new career, or start a new job.

It is not easy to take the seven proactive steps:

- Know what you want.
- Ask for what you want.
- Reinvent the rules and recast stereotypes.
- Seek support.
- Explore instinct and coincidence.
- Weigh sacrifices.
- Exude confidence.

I know it's difficult to be proactive, not only because I spoke with The Happy 100, but because I speak from experience.

At age twenty-seven I gave up a six-year career and $60,000 salary in marketing and public relations to pursue a lower-paying, riskier journalism career. I had pursued marketing after college because it was a practical way to engage in an activity that put me in a state of flow: writing. And while most of the marketing people I worked with were professional, supportive, smart, and lots of fun, marketing's purpose never captured my heart.

The impetus for my transition came unexpectedly and tragically, when one of my clients died of a heart attack. It happened so fast. One afternoon we said good-bye at the office, and the next morning he did not show up for work.

His secretary called me. "Dan's dead," was all she said.

I was in shock. For more than a year I'd watched this talented man work frenetically to please his own clients and deliver results. For all his dedication to the job, I was never convinced he loved it. He often half-joked that he had no life outside work and felt unappreciated. At his emotionally charged funeral, his family was not only in mourning, they were angry. I believe they felt it was the stress of work that ultimately killed their brother, husband, son, and father.

A few weeks after Dan's death, I was accepted into Northwestern University's School of Journalism. I had applied for the same reason Anita Mucci applied to be a flight attendant: She did not want to look back and regret never pursuing her dream. Still, I was not sure I had the courage to abandon a stable, familiar career and lifestyle. But with my colleague's death fresh on my mind, my decision was suddenly easy. Life was too short to work hard at a job that did not make me happy. So I left a prestigious employer, the income, and a comfortable apartment, and lived off student loans for a year: $11 a day. The sacrifice was worth it. Graduate school was a rebirth for me. Never before had I felt so proud of my career ambitions, and it was a year dedicated to learning.

I was challenged. I was fulfilled. And I was surrounded by talented people.

After graduate school, my plan was to write about business; its complexity and characters had always intrigued me. My first job in New York City was as an associate editor of a retail trade magazine covering a topic that did not inherently interest me: shopping centers. I was not particularly fond of malls, but I dove in because it was a chance to hone the skills of my newfound profession. Because my long-term goal was to work at a national business publication, I eventually called the woman in charge of hiring at *Forbes,* a name given to me by a friend of a friend of a friend, and went in for an informational interview. Two weeks later, when a job for a fact-checker opened, I was invited back for an official interview, and I went on to work at *Forbes* as a reporter and then a writer from 1998 to 2003. It was the best job I had ever had.

Although it was during those years that I came up with the concept of The Happy 100, the project's roots extend back to my childhood, to my parents' influence, to books I read, and, no doubt, to my former client, whose untimely death changed my working life.

Other people have the power to stir us, their influence to move our hearts and minds, but they cannot act for us. And while it behooves companies to facilitate their employees' quest for a happy working life because satisfied workers are more productive and loyal, it is not incumbent on employers to do so.

The onus falls on the individual, it falls on *you,* to be happy at work.

What Type of
Happy Working Woman Are
You Destined to Be?

In *Career Bliss,* I identify ten categories of happy working women. Which one are you? Determine your category and narrow down the type of job that best suits your nature.

Read through the following descriptions, honestly assessing to what degree they apply to you. Chose A if the statement truly reflects your personality and primary motivations; B if the description only somewhat applies to you; and C if it reflects only a small part of who you are or does not apply at all. Then, read on to discover your type(s) and the work opportunities that are most likely to fulfill you.

1. You have an intense hobby or an innate, almost irresistible passion for one *thing,* such as animals, fashion, or cooking.

    A. Truly reflects me.
    B. Somewhat reflects me.
    C. Not me at all.

2. You have an artistic bent and gravitate toward activities like writing, painting, or performance. While you have an undeniable talent, most do not deem your talent a practical career option.

    A. Truly reflects me.
    B. Somewhat reflects me.
    C. Not me at all.

3. Either you, a friend, or family member has spent significant time and energy trying to overcome a personal or professional obstacle in life, be it sickness, discrimination, or financial woes. As a result, you seek out others who have also struggled in the same way.

A. Truly reflects me.
B. Somewhat reflects me.
C. Not me at all.

4. You regularly seek out opportunities to learn new things, and it is common for you to get lost in thought whether you are tackling complex issues, reading, or conversing with others.

A. Truly reflects me.
B. Somewhat reflects me.
C. Not me at all.

5. You are ambitious, determined to succeed at whatever you put your mind to, and you routinely set new goals for yourself. Some might call you a type A personality or a high achiever.

A. Truly reflects me.
B. Somewhat reflects me.
C. Not me at all.

6. You are social, patient, and jump at opportunities to assist others no matter how minor their problem. Just knowing that you improved someone else's circumstances is extremely fulfilling to you.

A. Truly reflects me.
B. Somewhat reflects me.
C. Not me at all.

7. You are comfortable with risk and can easily envision something that does not yet exist—be it a company or a new and better product. Overseeing a project from idea to conception is intensely fulfilling.

> **A.** Truly reflects me.
> **B.** Somewhat reflects me.
> **C.** Not me at all.

8. You consider yourself quite spiritual and/or religious, and tend to make decisions from your heart rather than your head, often trusting gut feeling over fact.

> **A.** Truly reflects me.
> **B.** Somewhat reflects me.
> **C.** Not me at all.

9. You are a good listener who is empathetic and nonjudgmental. Others feel comfortable asking for your guidance, and advisor is a role you pursue.

> **A.** Truly reflects me.
> **B.** Somewhat reflects me.
> **C.** Not me at all.

If you answered A to #1, you may be a Lover.

What to do: Consider starting your own business selling whatever it is you adore. If entrepreneurship is not for you, identify positions—from administrative to management—at a company that is associated with your passion. Surrounding yourself with people who share your interests is more important than a job's day-to-day tasks. To learn more, read about Mary Ann Eiff and Keri Wright in chapter 1.

If you answered A to #2, you may be a Surviving Artist.

What to do: With a little creativity and compromise, you can incorporate your art into your work. Isolate the specific activity that you truly enjoy and find ways to replicate it in a commercial endeavor. For example, do you love to draw? The *act* of drawing, in and of itself, may contribute to your happiness more than the subject you are drawing (i.e., you could be just as happy drawing a tube of toothpaste or a flower.) To learn how other artists make a living, read about Tracy Lee Stum and Sam Racine in chapter 5.

If you answered A to #3, you may be a Heroine or a Sister.

What to do: Work for a cause to which you have a personal connection. Consider starting or joining an organization—not for profit, university, small business, government—that is dedicated to helping others overcome obstacles similar to the ones you, or others, experienced. While you must be skilled at the job's day-to-day tasks, your daily activities are less important to your happiness than the mission at hand. To be inspired, read about Catherine Simpson, Neva Walker, and Julie Ratner in chapter 4.

If you answered A to #4, you may be a Thinker.

What to do: Look for jobs where the majority of your time is spent in some form of critical thought, such as writing or analyzing, or where the goal is to solve a problem, be it how to market a new product or invest other people's money. Consider science, engineering, or finance as well as management positions that require strategic planning and high-level decision-making. To see the variety of jobs for Thinkers, read about Shelly Lazarus, Lesley Stahl, and Richele Scuro in chapter 2.

If you answered A to #5, you may be a Determinator.

What to do: Look for positions with unlimited potential for promotion, feedback, and where you are a visible player. You will enjoy jobs where your work touches many people, and where your ideas and actions have the potential to affect change. Don't limit your job to senior titles, but do surround yourself with other high achievers. Apply to companies that are leaders in their industry, and strive to work with people who are smarter than you. To see what jobs made other Determinators happy, read about Christine Jacobs and Margaret Peterson in chapter 3.

If you answered A to #6, you may be a Healer.

What to do: You'll find true fulfillment in a job that lets you interact one-on-one with others in a caretaking role. Health care and social sciences are obvious areas to investigate, but also consider management positions that require you to assist people with business and on-the-job problems. To learn about unconventional ways you can make people feel better, read about Sally Ayotte and Anita Mucci in chapter 4.

If you answered A to #7, you may be a Builder.

What to do: Not surprisingly, many engineers are builders. But if engineering is not your cup of tea, consider any position that requires you to influence, organize, and motivate others, and to create camaraderie and a sense of community, and to share and present ideas. To learn about how Builders find happiness at work, read about the careers of Michela O'Connor Abrams and Jennifer Todd in chapter 7.

If you answered A to #8, you may be among the Faithful.

What to do: It is very important for you to work for an organization whose product or service you truly believe in and whose values coincide with your own. When you go on interviews, look for workplaces that boast strong cultures, a sense of community, and where making money is valued but not over doing meaningful work. To understand how faith and happiness mix at work, read about Kim Simon and Lori Rodney in chapter 6.

If you answered A to #9, You may be a Counselor.

What to do: You have the potential to be a successful manager regardless of the organization you work for. The key: Don't limit your job search to specific industries. Do consider the social sciences, but also focus on jobs that allow you to lead a team of people and assist customers and colleagues, jobs that position you as an expert and require one-on-one interaction. Anna Pinto and Donna Lindsay hold some of the surprising jobs for Counselors in chapter 8.

I wish happiness and success!

Joanne Gordon

PHOTO: © JULIE BRIMBERG

JOANNE GORDON is a contributing editor for *Forbes,* where she was a reporter and writer for five years. She has also written about management, career, and workplace issues for *Boston* magazine, *Working Mother, CosmoGIRL,* and the *Chicago Tribune.* Before following her dream to become a writer, she spent six years in marketing and public relations. She has a master's degree in journalism from Northwestern University, and is the co-author, with Mike Marriner and Nathan Gebhard, of *Roadtrip Nation.* She lives in New York City with her husband and son.

About the Type

This book was set in Fairfield, the first typeface from the hand of the distinguished American artist and engraver Rudolph Ruzicka (1883–1978). In its structure Fairfield displays the sober and sane qualities of the master craftsman whose talent has long been dedicated to clarity. It is this trait that accounts for the trim grace and vigor, the spirited design and sensitive balance, of this original typeface. Ruzicka was born in Bohemia and came to America in 1894. He set up his own shop, devoted to wood engraving and printing, in New York in 1913 after a varied career working as a wood engraver, in photoengraving and banknote printing plants, and as an art director and freelance artist. He designed and illustrated many books and was the creator of a considerable list of individual prints—wood engravings, line engravings on copper, and aquatints.